Orbiting Ray
Bradbury's Mars

CRITICAL EXPLORATIONS IN SCIENCE FICTION AND FANTASY
(a series edited by Donald E. Palumbo and C.W. Sullivan III)

Orbiting Ray Bradbury's Mars

Biographical, Anthropological, Literary, Scientific and Other Perspectives

Edited by GLORIA MCMILLAN

Foreword by Peter Smith

CRITICAL EXPLORATIONS IN SCIENCE FICTION AND FANTASY, 41
Donald E. Palumbo *and* C.W. Sullivan III, series editors

McFarland & Company, Inc., Publishers
Jefferson, North Carolina, and London

LIBRARY OF CONGRESS CATALOGUING-IN-PUBLICATION DATA

Orbiting Ray Bradbury's Mars : biographical, anthropological, literary, scientific and other perspectives / edited by Gloria McMillan ; foreword by Peter Smith.
      p.   cm. — (Critical explorations in science fiction and fantasy ; 41)
    [Donald E. Palumbo and C.W. Sullivan III, series editors]
    Includes bibliographical references and index.

    ISBN 978-0-7864-7576-6
    softcover : acid free paper ∞

    1. Bradbury, Ray, 1920–2012—Criticism and interpretation.
I. McMillan, Gloria (Professor) editor of compilation.
II. Title.
PS3503.R167Z79 2013
813'.54—dc23   2013031526

BRITISH LIBRARY CATALOGUING DATA ARE AVAILABLE

On the cover: (foreground) Ink drawing of Ray Bradbury by John Tibbetts (www.johnctibbetts.com); (background) Painting of a canal-lined Mars by William K. Hartmann of the Planetary Science Institute

Manufactured in the United States of America

McFarland & Company, Inc., Publishers
  Box 611, Jefferson, North Carolina 28640
  www.mcfarlandpub.com

Table of Contents

Part Three: Literary Lens

Part Four: Scientific Lens

Part Five: Media Lens

Part Six: Educational Lens

Acknowledgments

Many people have aided in the completion of this book. First, I would like to thank our editor Donald E. Palumbo for his timely interventions and useful tips. I would also like to thank Jim Corrick for sharing his expertise in editing a collection of essays. Marleen Barr provided moral support on days when it seemed a daunting task, as did Carol Nowotny-Young, Chris Cokinos, Tish Haymer, Shirley Curson, Curt Stubbs, Bjo and John Trimble, Karen Anderson, Carol and Warren DePriest, LAFAS member Karl Lembke, and others too numerous to get their just mentions. John Tibbetts put in a heroic effort to give us an artist's view of Ray Bradbury the man, as did photographer and filmmaker Terry Sanders. And all of our contributors wish to thank BASFA (Baja Arizona Science Fiction Association), the local Tucson science fiction club, which jumped on board and made immediate plans to highlight this book and the local participants at a forthcoming TusCon. The TusCon programmers Scott Glener and Joe Palmer gave real thought to making this project grow legs. The Kuiper Circle, the Educational and Public Outreach Advisory Board of the University of Arizona's Lunar and Planetary Lab has also given valuable guidance and support. The chair of the Kuiper Circle EPO subcommittee David Acklam even wrote an essay!

Last but not least, my family helped in the production of this text by making many practical adjustments to their lives so that I could have the time to work. My mother Gloria Ptacek and mother-in-law Mary McMillan gave moral support. My sister Holly provided good laughs. My husband Bob put up with the usual stresses of collecting widely diverse essays and wrangling them into a somewhat consistent form. And thanks to our son Chris, who was extraordinarily kind and patient to a distracted mother.

Many thanks to all. I could never have done this without you.

Foreword

PETER SMITH

Recently, I opened my copy of *The Illustrated Man* and quickly entered the world of Ray Bradbury, which I had visited many times as a youngster. The story begins on a back road in Wisconsin where the author meets a singular man who is covered not in tattoos, but in illustrations. These are vignettes that, when stared at for a time, begin to tell a story, their movements evoking strange tales that become alien and scary. But worse, if you are not careful, the illustrations begin to tell the tale of your own life and, be especially careful, your future.

Bradbury is the Illustrated Man and, as a child, I could feel his arm around my shoulder leading me into alien landscapes never imagined. There the future was as real as the past. These journeys became an obsession and allowed me to explore unknowable worlds from my armchair. The greatest adventures were those where the trail of fantasy crossed the highway of reality. I have lived my life on this crossroads.

In the late fifties, when I was engrossed in science fiction and fantasy, the planets were fuzzy images with structures all but invisible when seen through Earth's shimmery atmosphere. My scout troop gave a stage play about the planets; I was Jupiter. Each of us recited the facts about our planet painted on cardboard and held up for all to see. I remember being amazed that we knew so little about our neighbors. However, the fuzzy images became clear when I read *The Martian Chronicles* and on long journeys with Ray I could find the underlying Martian communities.

Later in life Bradbury was with me on that crossroads as I produced the first map of the surface of Titan with my colleague Mark Lemmon. He must have smiled as the first images of the outwash plains of Are Valles were imaged by my Pathfinder camera in 1997. We realized the depths of mystery surrounding Mars at the Opportunity landing site in 2004 and the icy polar regions brought to life by the Phoenix Mars Lander. Yes, Ray's arm was around my shoulder throughout all these adventures because there are still those blurry regions at the edge of our ability to measure where fantasy and reality are on equal footing.

So, as we prepare another mission (OSIRIS-REx) to explore our origins by sending a robotic mission to a nearby asteroid and returning a sample to Earth, we are already imagining what might be hidden in some small crater ready to be brought to light. Is it possible that organic material seeded the early Earth with the raw materials of the first cells? Does this material predate our solar system and come from some ancient galactic source that, in fact, suffuses the universe with the precursors of life? Are the hundreds of new planets that are rapidly being discovered also receiving these molecules? Will the molecules eventually encounter a watery world to blossom and evolve into an ecosystem of life, filled with new stories and myths? These possibilities emerge from the stories that thrilled me as a youth and, once again, I long to visit Ray in reality's basement where he lives today.

Peter Smith is a senior research scientist at the Lunar and Planetary Laboratory of the University of Arizona, principal investigator for the $420 million robotic explorer Phoenix, which landed at the north pole of Mars on May 25, 2008, and lead scientist on the NASA mission set for 2017 to sample and return material from an asteroid.

Preface

GLORIA MCMILLAN

Ray Bradbury's poetic and metaphor-rich style has been the subject of many essays scattered among journals over the years, but the new essays in *Orbiting Ray Bradbury's Mars* probe deeper into the cultural milieu (biographical, anthropological, literary, scientific and so on) that stimulated Bradbury's remarkable imagination and unique prose style.

Considering the number of published essays, there have been surprisingly few essay *collections* on Ray Bradbury. The 2001 *Ray Bradbury* (*Bloom's Modern Critical Views*), also available in a new 2010 edition (containing a different line-up of essays), is the most recent; both editions were edited by Harold Bloom, and feature essays that examine a narrow range of literary and dramatic qualities in Bradbury's work. *Ray Bradbury* (1980), co-edited by Martin Harry Greenberg and Joseph D. Olander, offers a wider range of older essays that come closer to the broad scope of our own collection. These essays offer a closer examination of Bradbury as a genre writer, taking into account his relation to the gothic and science fiction conventions. It also explores Bradbury's themes of the Cosmos, symbolism (religious and dystopic), and the ways in which his image-based style advances perhaps all of these themes. While Greenberg and Olander assemble a credible selection of literary scholars who explore a variety of themes in Bradbury's work, they remain within the humanities.

One major difference between Greenberg and Olander's collection and ours is that we cross disciplinary boundaries to add the voices of scientists who have read and been influenced by Bradbury's texts, especially *The Martian Chronicles*. The focus of their collection is fairly tightly woven around a literary assessment of Bradbury's authorial themes and world view. It also focuses on his role in the history of science fiction and fantasy. The contexts are defining ones: Is he anti-scientific? Is he really a science fiction writer at all? Does he take on social issues (at least) as powerfully as mainstream novelists? Our collection's scope, then, is broader, with a wide range of interdisciplinary contributors. The Greenberg and Olander collection, ground-breaking in its day, focused on finding Bradbury's internal world; our collection is as much about his impact on America as it is about America's impact on him.

We imagine our readers coming from a variety of backgrounds, so this collection should give a novel view of Bradbury, no matter whether a reader is first encountering Bradbury and wants to know more or is a serious devotee of Bradbury's fiction. We see value in viewing Bradbury through our series of lenses that scan many fields. Thus, our collection fills a void in the critical literature that asks for a bridge in the case of the unique Renaissance Man who was Ray Bradbury. Certainly that subject-hopping reader Bradbury would have asked why there is not more academic boundary-crossing. The answer is commonplace: because institutions compartmentalize. The dangers of stepping between fields of study are many. Bradbury escaped a college teaching career so he only knew of the pressures to stay in one field as an outside observer. Of course, there are jokes. The often-quoted saying goes that getting scholars in science and the humanities all into one bag is like herding cats. But despite the differences of style and interests, the effort is well worth the struggle, both for our contributors and for our readers. We hope that our readers will find new insights in the earnest efforts of many specialists to look clearly at Ray Bradbury from their own field's perspectives. Seeing one person from as many angles as we view Ray Bradbury in this collection should help our readers to get to know a beloved author much better.

Introduction

Landing on Bradbury's Western Mars

Gloria McMillan

There is a depth and breadth to Ray Bradbury's fiction. His Martian landscapes recall the dusty, windswept streets and washes of Tucson, Arizona, and the home he longed for and remembered in his Martian stories often resembled "Green Town," Illinois. By uniting regional fiction's strengths and a working knowledge of astronomy, Bradbury created a literary metaphor of a believable human society on Mars, different from ours, yet strangely evocative and familiar. His world view hearkened back to the 1920s Midwest and his broad imagination anticipated events now occurring on the planet Mars in all their philosophical and ethical complexity. This book intends not to show this or that side of Bradbury but to unite some of these disparate threads together as Bradbury does so seemingly effortlessly in his fiction. The scope of Ray Bradbury's work has been scattered in a number of locations and is only recently coming into focus due to the exhaustive work of biographers like Jonathan Eller and Sam Weller. Because Bradbury was a man of many aspects, we hope here to unite some of these in one collection of essays taking a look at Ray Bradbury through a number of lenses. Our contributors have come from the diverse fields of literature, planetary science, media studies, and rhetoric and composition. These different lenses offer a kaleidoscopic picture of Bradbury's time spent in the Southwest and of how his work was influenced by the landscape and people from the West.

While we will not have a final say about the "true" Ray Bradbury and what he means to our literature, there are two reasons for this book. First, a biographical thread of Bradbury's life in the Southwest has been little known even to his personal friends and yet this period was formative in his evolving mental landscape of Mars. Secondly, Bradbury is not what has been called a "hard science" science fiction writer in that he was far more concerned with the human meaning of space travel and technology than the intricacies of rocket propulsion or bio- and mechanical engineering. In this role, Bradbury, perhaps more than any other science fiction or mainstream American writer, has bridged the gulf between art and science, those two squabbling domains of academics.

Why are these two aspects of Ray Bradbury important to bring forth now that the man has passed away? Bradbury was constantly searching for metaphors to live by in his stories and a sense of wholeness in life. By filling in some missing pieces of his life and art, we may help readers to meet Bradbury's major dimensions while going beyond the biographical to the issues that were dear to his heart. Bradbury's "almost a year" spent in the Sonoran Desert shaped him in ways that he never could have foreseen. He plugged along on his little toy typewriter (which actually worked) as a twelve-year-old boy in Tucson, writing continuations of John Carter on Mars. How these early thoughts echoed as he created the stories that became *The Martian Chronicles* is a matter for speculation.

Some readers may be surprised that Bradbury educated himself at his local public library because it was the Depression and his parents had no money for college. The benefit of his self-education is that, at the public library after high school, he escaped some of the mental boxes that circumscribe and limit the imaginations of those more formally trained. He had taken a class in astronomy in high school and picked up the major concepts of planetary science as were known in the 1930s. He also knew the powerful regional fiction that spoke to the American reading public during the Depression. Bradbury was able to translate Sherwood Anderson's *Winesburg, Ohio*'s saturated prairie loneliness into nostalgia for Earth as home from the perspective of Mars. Anderson's story collection depicts characters whose lives had frozen inward, leaving them emotionally miles apart in this rural Ohio town. Bradbury's literary quality of real life and the interior needs and monologues of his characters made them stand apart from most science fiction of the 1930s and 1940s, which focused mainly on the events and inventions of space travel, technology, and future speculations.

The essayists in the present work view Bradbury's literary metaphors through a number of lenses: biographical; anthropological; literary; scientific; media; and education. The anthropological is important because Bradbury wrote of Martians who were reminiscent of Tucson's centuries-old, vanished American Indians, the Hohokam, and also the living urban members of the two local Native American nations most in evidence: the O'odham and Yaqui.

One of our collection's contributors, Grace L. Dillon, looks back at Bradbury from the other end of the lens, the Native American's view. How did Ray Bradbury view Peter Smith and his team's choice of the digital copies of *The Martian Chronicles* to land on Mars with NASA's University of Arizona–based Phoenix Mars Lander? Did he rejoice at starting the first public library on Mars or did he think our earthly landing gear polluted Mars, similar to *The Martian Chronicles'* astronaut character Biggs who throws empty bottles into a Martian canal? This is an unprecedented question because no other writer has had cause to decide how he feels about his works being planted on another world. Although other writers were represented in digitized form on the Phoenix Mars Mission's CD, most of these others were dead while Bradbury lived to know his book had made it to Mars. Few, if any, other writers have investigated the ethics of space travel as minutely as Bradbury has, so he has a powerful connection to real life astronomy and the world of aerospace that is represented in this collection. Some of our contributors are planetary scientists, aerospace engineers, or work in other capacities on Mars-based NASA projects. These scientists have felt changed by reading Bradbury and will have surprising things to say about our border-crossing writer's ability of move between the worlds of art and science.

Summaries of the five different "lenses" and of the essays are provided here.

Biographical Lens: The collection opens with a look on Bradbury's life and "Miracles of Rare Device: Bradbury and the American Southwest" by Jonathan R. Eller, director of the Ray Bradbury Research Center at Indiana University, opens a window to the formative time that Bradbury spent in the Southwest. All the essays that follow will in some way hearken back to this one. In order to trace the evolution of Bradbury's style from its Midwestern roots, Wolf Forrest's "The Sorcerer's Apprentices: How the Lives of Three Regional 'Weird Fiction' Writers Became Creatively Entangled" compares Bradbury to two Midwestern writers, August Derleth and Robert Bloch. Bradbury met and became friendly with Robert Bloch (author of *Psycho*) after he moved west to Hollywood, but he may never have met Derleth. Forrest also compares the two "weird tale" writers with Western and Southern regional writers.

Anthropological Lens: Marleen S. Barr's "Prescient Border Crossing: 'I See You Never' and the Undocumented Mexicans Americans Prefer Not to See" confronts today's society with Bradbury's pioneering writing about human minority cultures in one of his mainstream (non-science fiction) stories. Barr questions whether or not Bradbury's story "I See You Never" is, after all, science fiction. Next, Grace L. Dillon's "Bradbury's Survivance Stories" follows Dillon's process of reading Bradbury's allegory of settlers meeting Martians, *The Martian Chronicles,* as a Native American growing up on and off the reservation. Adam Lawrence's "A 'Night Meeting' in the Southwest: Hospitality in *The Martian Chronicles*" analyzes the radical shift of Bradbury's fictional earth missions to Mars over several stories into a search for community, friendship, communion, and an embrace of otherness. And, finally, Francisco Laguna-Correa's "Illustrating Otherness: Crossing Frontiers in *The Illustrated Man*" takes on the accuracy of Bradbury's vision of Mexico, using his collection of stories (or "novel") *The Illustrated Man* as the textual source.

Literary Lens: Bradbury was noted throughout his life as perhaps the most poetic science fiction writer, so language was more to him than a mere vehicle to carry ideas. Bradbury talked often of guiding metaphors and poetic imagery. Aaron Barlow assesses the impact of Tucson on Bradbury's poetic vocabulary and also his images and loss of myths to live by in "Loss in the Language of Tomorrow: The 'New West' as Model for 'Usher II.'" Rather than loss, Kimberly Fain explores how Bradbury found the new alien surroundings to be rich in metaphor as well as healing in "Bradbury's Mars: Pathway to Reinvention and Redemption." Christopher Cokinos' "The Desert Is Earth and Mars: An Ecocritical, Bachelardian Exploration of 'And the Moon Be Still as Bright' and *It Came from Outer Space*" self-reflects on his own relocation to Tucson's desert to teach in the University of Arizona's English Department at the same time he was rediscovering ecological science fiction. He blends critical scholarship with the poetic and personal, including a narrative of his visit to Bradbury's Tucson haunts and a Bachelardian critique of the film *It Came from Outer Space*— screen treatment by Bradbury.

Scientific Lens: In "Why Does Mars Beckon Us?" Ari Espinoza of the HiRISE Mars High Resolution Camera Project identifies an answer to the common question "Where do you get those crazy ideas?" Bradbury got his not-so-crazy ideas about Mars from astronomy authorities of past generations. Espinoza also compares Bradbury's depiction of Mars with current images and reflects on the two visions. Aerospace engineer David M. Acklam investigates his own past readings of Bradbury and the ethical and philosophical challenges of space travel in "The Exploration of Mars: An Unintentional Invasion?" Chuck L. Dugan, Jr.'s "A Martian Chronicle" specifically connects Bradbury's fiction to his own youthful reading. It also connects Bradbury to the Mars Science Laboratory mission, explaining how, when grappling with the real, scientists often fall back on Bradbury's images of awe. NASA scientists Christopher P. McKay and Carol Stoker's "The Naming of Names" takes up the issue of humans giving names to Martian topography. Bradbury detailed his very mixed emotions about the names humans apply to Mars throughout *The Martian Chronicles*, so this contribution from planetary scientists should open a new window on the important issue of names.

Media Lens: Paul Cote's "De-Alienating the Alien: The Limits of Empathy in NBC's *The Martian Chronicles* miniseries" examines the costs and benefits of translating the novel *The Martian Chronicles* into a televised miniseries in 1980. Filmmaker Howard Allen explores the Southwestern desert byways of the illustrated man's camp in "*The Illustrated Man* Illustrates Our Future" touching on mirage and the dangers of virtual worlds. Finally, film scholar Martin R. Hall's "Silver Locusts on the Silver Screen: Bradbury's Western Mars Confronts 1960s British Art-Cinema" examines how Bradbury's western Mars and his frontier metaphors confront and fit into the world of British new wave films of the 1960s in a comparison of the TV miniseries *The Martian Chronicles* and the Truffaut film *Fahrenheit 451*.

Educational Lens: In "Teaching Martians in Tucson," I reflect on my years teaching *The Martian Chronicles* at Pima College and how students respond to this writer who is local, internationally famous, and interplanetary. They relate to the Mars colonizers' pain of the new, the challenge of contacts with cultural difference, and the pangs of loss of home. In addition, the essay teases out the way that Bradbury's *Martian Chronicles* allows students, tired of familiar arguments on both sides, to approach the controversial issue of border crossers and cultural boundaries in an oblique and fruitful way.

In June 2012, the world mourned Bradbury's loss, which, at the age of 91, cannot be called "untimely." Yet he had more to say. He wanted to "live forever," as the carnival magician "Mr. Electrico" told him to do one night in Waukegan when he was a small boy. To that end, he worked at a feverish pace over seven decades enlarging his base of knowledge and polishing his craft. We hope this kaleidoscopic view of a fascinating writer will help others to use their potential and know that it is all right to be a person who likes libraries, likes to read, and most importantly, likes to write.

Miracles of Rare Device
Bradbury and
the American Southwest

JONATHAN R. ELLER

During November 1926, six-year-old Ray Bradbury accompanied his parents and his older brother Skip on a five-month adventure, traveling from northern Illinois deep into the American Southwest. After two weeks in Roswell, New Mexico, the family moved on to Tucson, where the boy resumed his first grade school year in a new environment. In an historical sense, names and places still meant very little to him; he couldn't know the notoriety that would come to Roswell two decades later, as it became the center of America's first major flying saucer controversy. And at first, he didn't know the legacy that was already implicit in the name of the very street where he now lived in Tucson. Years later, he would come to understand the magic of that name:

"When I was six years old I moved to Tucson, Arizona and lived on Lowell Avenue, little realizing I was on an avenue that somehow led to Mars because it was named for Percival Lowell, who took fantastic photographs of the planet and promised a future to children like myself, if we would just look through a telescope." These words open an unpublished essay from his middle years titled "Lowell Avenue to the Stars," in which Bradbury reflected on how Lowell Avenue eventually became, symbolically, his road to imagining Mankind's first steps out to the Red Planet, and beyond.

These notions were, of course, still far in the future of the young boy's life. At the time, the 1926 Tucson venture represented Leo Bradbury's first attempt to transplant his family from their familiar Midwestern roots in Waukegan, Illinois, to the open lands of the Southwest that he had come to know as a wanderer and occasional prospector in the years before his marriage.

11

A new child, Elizabeth Jane Bradbury, was born that winter in Tucson, but the lack of steady employment led Leo to take his wife and three children back to Waukegan in March 1927. Ray Bradbury returned to the wider family circle and familiar surroundings of northern Illinois, unaware that a longer 1932–33 sojourn in Tucson would fill much of his seventh-grade year and pave the way for a third and final Westering adventure in 1934, when the family moved permanently to Southern California. Over the next three decades, his ever-widening encounters with the American West would play into some of his best fantasy and science fiction.

Ray Bradbury's second stay in Tucson would prove pivotal to his creative development. The earlier journey of 1926–27 had been accomplished largely by rail, but Leo Bradbury's second attempt to start a new life for his family out West began differently — and far more urgently. It was now late in the third year of the Great Depression, and Leo had lost his job as a power company lineman in Waukegan. In the fall of 1932, with very little money in hand, the Bradburys headed out in an overloaded '26 Buick, navigating over the perilous and sometimes unpaved Route 66 all the way into Arizona before looping south on state highways to Tucson.[1]

Young Ray Bradbury still had memories of his family's first stay in Tucson, highlighted by his sometimes unsupervised wanderings through the museums of the University of Arizona campus and the birth of his tragically short-lived sister Elizabeth, who died shortly after their 1927 return to Waukegan (Weller 36–41). Now, back in Tucson at the age of twelve, he encountered cultural influences that were at once both familiar and new. This time, the contrast between the brick-paved streets of Waukegan and the wild beauty of Tucson struck an even deeper emotional chord; as the family settled into a house on the outskirts of the city, Bradbury felt a distinct sense of rebirth every time he walked out into the new world around him. There were, for example, large spiders in the woodpile, amazing spiders of a kind and size he had never seen back East. Even in the 1930s Tucson had the feel of a frontier town, and Bradbury soon discovered that many of the streets still had hitching posts for horses. Privately, he would remember such discoveries across more than six decades of time as essential to his evolving sense of newness and creative optimism:

> The thing is, if you're in a climate of birth, if you arrive in a town that's birthing itself, then you are part of the birth process, and you are optimistic. It gets in your flesh, it gets in your mind. You grow differently in a town that's still not born yet. Waukegan was already born, it wasn't going anywhere for a long time, and when it grew somewhat bigger, it wasn't that exhilarating. It was an old town by the time I was born. But Tucson was very new, and everything was

fresh, and nothing had been touched yet. The age of the car hadn't ruined it, and the age of space and jets hadn't touched it. So I felt like a desert rat. I loved going to school every day, and walking across through the cacti and seeing the spiders and occasionally a snake or all kinds of lizards. That was wonderful stuff. So I felt new ... that's the thing I came away with. I was re-birthed along with the town [Bradbury interview, 2004].

His first significant experience with acting came just before Christmas 1932 at Amphitheater Junior High, where he had transferred into the seventh grade. The school's music teacher cast and directed a seasonal operetta, *A Wooden Shoe Christmas,* and Bradbury was thrilled to win the lead role. Eight years later, in the slim writer's journal he kept briefly after leaving high school, he recalled this experience as a memorable "first" in his young creative life: "The first time I had a lead in an operetta. The way I swaggered, the bloated conceit and tingling elation that was mine. The thrill of wearing makeup, except lipstick, because my lips have always been redder than red." This was the final "first" recorded in a long chronological list that included Waukegan memories as well: his first Christmas memories, his first drink of dandelion wine, and, eventually, his first awareness of sexuality.

> The toy dial-a-letter typewriter that he received from his parents for Christmas in Tucson is one of the most significant treasures surviving from these years, for it provided the means to form the habits of a professional writer. He could now begin to write every day, as he had pledged just two months earlier, after receiving Mr. Electrico's small-town carnival admonition to "live forever!" His encounter with the hair-raising static charge that climaxed Mr. Electrico's carnival sideshow act had happened in October 1932, just before leaving Waukegan for Arizona, and the new toy machine given to him in Tucson provided his first adolescent chance to reach for the potential immortality of a writer [Weller 56–58].

A few typewritten exemplars from this machine survive today, including letters home to his cousins, but his first and most ambitious toy typing project remains unlocated — the opening pages of his own juvenile "John Carter of Mars" novel (Eller 14). In his non-sequential reading of Burroughs's popular Martian series back in Waukegan, Bradbury had somehow missed volume three, *The Warlord of Mars,* which took up the saga of Earth's master swordsman John Carter and his exquisite Martian princess, Deja Thoris, after their heart-wrenching separation at the end of volume two, *The Gods of Mars.*

For a boy of twelve, especially a boy with the passion for Burroughs that Bradbury had developed, the temptation to carry on the adventure in his own words was irresistible. At the end of *The Gods of Mars,* John Carter finds that he must wait a full Martian year for the Temple of the Sun to turn one full rotation on its axis and free his princess; as the portal to her prison cell rotates shut, he sees one final image of the ruthless Phaidor, proud daughter of the evil High Priest Mattai Shang, launch a knife stroke at Deja Thoris — but did the blow strike home, or was it deflected by the noble Princess Thuvia, who also shares his beloved wife's prison cell? Burroughs had left his readers with this agonizing line: "The last crevice had closed, and for a long year that hideous chamber would retain its secret from the eyes of men" (Burroughs 347–48).

Bradbury's adolescent sequel was sparked by those thrilling words, no doubt prompting him to forgive Burroughs's grammatical flaw ("retain ... from") and focus on the power of the visual image itself. "She's trapped, and it ends with us wondering, at the end of a year, if John Carter would meet his wife when the sun prison came around. And I sat down when I was twelve and I wrote the sequel to that book. When I was twelve years old. It began my career" (Bradbury interviews, 2005, 2007). The act of typing a novel, letter by letter, turning the toy dial by hand before each keystroke, was an exhausting proposition. The original was probably only story-length, if he finished it at all, and the details are long gone from Bradbury's mind. But there's little doubt that he continued the same general story line set up in the final pages of *The Gods of Mars,* and that he would later read in *The Warlord of Mars* — Carter must rescue his princess, and track down the cruel Mattai Shang. "I'd like to remember how I did it. If I could find it [today], that would be wonderful."

In Tucson, over the span of a few short weeks at the age of twelve, he had touched both the writer's and actor's crafts first-hand. Later, in Los Angeles, he would become an excellent touch typist, composing stories for his 11th grade fiction class during lunchtime stints in the typing classroom before finally buying his own used machine on installments during his senior year. A manuscript page written in Bradbury's hand is a rare find indeed, for he has always preferred that his magic be transferred to paper through all ten fingertips. The machine became a master metaphor all its own for Bradbury, and this metaphor still resonated three quarters of a century later: "That's the process, that's why people like me, because my fingertips are releasing life into my stories, and that's why I'm popular. Not for my intellect — my intelligence is in the background, and stands there and watches, but it watches the fingertips, and all the stuff comes out in the typewriter" (Bradbury interview, 2006).

By the early 1940s he had fully disciplined himself to write in such bursts of emotional energy, letting each story reveal itself, re-typing it each day for a week, permitting his intellect to come in only for the final revisions. A writer never completely represses conscious sequential thought, but Bradbury's unusual level of self-control provided an effective safe haven for his creativity. Unconditional belief in this metaphor of the subconscious allowed him to avoid self-conscious artificiality and writer's block throughout his life. "That's a real gift, and I thank God for that. I was made this way, and I can't stop my fingertips."

During the three months they lived on the edge of the desert, one of his only connections to popular culture was local radio station KGAR, which offered many of the programs he had become attached to back home. After Christmas, the Bradburys rented part of a house in the center of Tucson, almost next door to a junkyard and only a few blocks from a rail yard with eight or ten retired locomotives — a paradise full of imaginative adventures.[2] In fact, the large brick-and-stone structure had been built to house railroad crews and yard hands in more prosperous times. From this new location he soon discovered that he now lived within walking distance of KGAR, a combined affiliate of CBS and the West Coast regional Don Lee Network broadcasting (at that time) from the Tucson Motor Service Company downtown. He soon became acquainted with two boys who read juvenile roles for the station's evening broadcasts of comic strips, and they brought him over to the station. After a few weeks of helping out the staff with menial chores, he was rewarded with the on-air role of creating aviation sound effects for "Tailspin Tommy" and Tommy's home-made monoplane. Thanks to his emerging talent for accents and character voices, he was given an actual reading part when a new character was introduced into the comic strip's story line.

The real test of his moxy, if not his talent, came when a boy didn't show up one night for the 8:30 broadcast of pilot scripts for one of the first radio police drama shows, "Calling All Cars." It premiered as a West Coast CBS regional network series in the fall of 1933 with a rotating cast of real Los Angeles police officers, but in the winter and spring of 1933 Bradbury recalled getting a chance to broadcast from pilot scripts at KGAR. He was asked to fill in with only a few minutes to rehearse; it was terrifying, but to his great surprise his performance was nearly flawless. The single slip was nonetheless aggravating, however. In rehearsal he had trouble pronouncing "Halstead Street." It should have been easy, for this was also the name of a major Chicago thoroughfare he knew well, but even with coaching he flubbed it on the air; to make matters worse, the rest of the cast ad-libbed around it to correct him without breaking the flow of the dialog (Bradbury interview, 2008).

But he had helped the station through a tough situation, and, if we can believe his high school essay on this adventure, he was rewarded with a permanent part on the show. During his four months with the station, he also continued to voice his part for "Tailspin Tommy" and picked up other roles in "The Katzenjammer Kids" and "Bringing Up Father" (Bradbury interview 2008).[3] A final on-air farewell from the station staff capped his first insider experience with radio broadcasting. Overall, the KGAR experience provided Bradbury with a naïve confidence that exceeded any sense of reality, and set the stage for his sometimes overly-exuberant attempts to connect with prime-time radio personalities in Los Angeles throughout his high school years.

The station staff paid him in movie tickets for first-run films, and this good fortune could not have had better timing. The family's financial woes meant that the boy often had to settle for cheap revival movie bills, and in fact second-run double features would prove to be the way he saw hundreds of films over the next two decades. But here in Tucson, for a brief time, he had free tickets to first-run films, and he was able to see a film that had a monumental impact on his heart as well as his developing appreciation for the value of sustained suspense in storytelling: Merian C. Cooper's production of *King Kong*.[4] KGAR's tickets also took him to see Boris Karloff as the title character in *The Mummy*. It was a film where the unremarkable acting was eclipsed by a suggestion of fantasy and the kind of dream-like atmosphere that would later attract Bradbury to a number of noir and dark fantasy films of the 1940s. He also saw *Mystery of the Wax Museum,* a film nicely enhanced by the two-color Technicolor process that Bradbury was growing to appreciate (Bradbury interview 2008). In spite of the film's stock horror ingredients, Lionel Atwill's excellent portrayal of a disfigured wax sculptor resonated with Bradbury's vivid memories of Lon Chaney's Phantom.

There were also moments of heartbreak in Tucson, and not surprisingly one of the greatest of these involved his growing love for the imaginative adventure shows that came to him through the radio. From the moment he arrived in Tucson, Bradbury had been captivated by KGAR's broadcasts of *Chandu the Magician*. It was a new show originating from KHJ in Los Angeles, one of Don Lee's earliest network acquisitions. The story lines combined supernatural adventures with Eastern mysticism as Frank Chandler, trained by an Indian Yogi, takes on the identity of a crime-fighting magician. This was still only a West Coast program, but the network affiliation permitted KGAR to broadcast from recordings shipped in from Los Angeles. Shortly after beginning his broadcast routines, Bradbury discovered that a staff member routinely destroyed the 20-inch shellac transcriptions of *Chandu the Magician* as soon as the broadcasts were over. Proprietary restrictions no doubt required the destruction of the duplicates sent out to affiliate stations, but one night Bradbury urged the man to let him take the precious disk home. He quickly found out that not everyone at KGAR respected youthful naiveté:

[He] fixed me with a cold eye, smiled, and cracked the transcription over his knee. While doing this, he watched my face for the horror that grew there. The transcription fell in a dozen pieces as the owner spun about and marched off. Struck numb, I finally bent and plucked up the two-dozen pieces of Chandu, Roxor the Villain, the Psychic Summons, the gong, the incredibly moving music, and carried the sad fragments home.

What did I do with the broken bits? Played them with my fingernail.... If you run your fingernail in the grooves of any record, you can summon the ghost voices, two syllables or sometimes two words at a scrape. I ran my fingernail through all the grooves on the bigger fragments so Chandu whispered, Roxor laughed, and the gong struck, just for me. Tears ran down my face [Bradbury, "Infinite Riches"].[5]

He kept the fragments for years, and even began writing out *Chandu* scripts from memory. This real-life pathos would echo from time to time in such memorable Bradbury characters as the pitiful old Tarot Witch of *Dandelion Wine*, who young Douglas Spaulding tries to bring back to life after the arcade owner casts the broken-down mechanical doll into the Green Town ravine. Of course, Bradbury couldn't have played the twenty-inch transcriptions even if his family had brought a phonograph to Tucson, but the loss of Chandu hurt like the loss of his first Buck Rogers strips two years earlier — he had torn them up when his classmates ridiculed his collecting habits, but that very act had nearly broken his heart.

He was beginning to learn that his love of magic and space travel were treasures that should be stored away, not cast away as one grows older. In similar ways, the fantastic world of *King Kong*, perhaps the highlight of his eight months in Arizona, also had an abiding impact on his life; the fabulous beasts of Skull Island renewed the wonder he felt in seeing *The Lost World*, and the great ape's final tragedy brought back the sense of unrequited love he had first seen in Lon Chaney's Hunchback and Phantom. Like Emerson, Bradbury would come to believe that the child is father to the man, and he would never shy away from presenting universal themes of loss from a child's point of view.

Good memories at KGAR outweighed the bad, however, and his radio days helped him work through the challenge of fitting in at yet another new school. He had just gained some measure of security at Amphitheater School before Christmas, when he starred in the *Wooden Shoe* play, but after the New Year's move downtown he had to transfer to Roskruge School. The only class-mate who stuck with him from Amphitheater was John Huff, who became his best friend through the winter and spring of 1933; more than two decades later, he would earn a lasting place in Bradbury's fiction as the protagonist of "Statues," one of the most nostalgic *Dandelion Wine* tales. Huff's companionship was not the only compensation, however; Bradbury soon found that downtown Tucson offered the adventures of the rail yard and the radio station, and more — there was also the University of Arizona campus, where he occasionally explored the halls and exhibits of the Natural Science building.

As he settled in at Roskruge School, he wrote his own comics and created pulp illustrations for his art class. In fact, his reading of the science fiction pulps became a full-blown habit in Tucson, for he found a way to read them at a time when his family still could not afford to buy them. One of his new friends, Bob Tucker (no relation to the fanzine editor and author Wilson "Bob" Tucker), had nearly complete collections of *Wonder* and *Amazing Stories* that Bradbury could borrow freely. In this way he was able to fill in many gaps in his early genre reading, and began to develop a preference for certain writers as he had already done with illustrators. On weekends, he would draw Western "movies," frame-by-frame, on long "reels" of paper with John Huff.[6] This activity was clearly an extension of his fifth-grade production of "Aladdin and His Lamp" two years earlier, another half-cousin to both cinema and comic strip storytelling.

But this phase of his life was soon over; his father's business venture with chili bricks did not succeed, and the family returned to Waukegan yet again in the late spring of 1933. Leo Bradbury was able, for a time, to return to work with the power company, but as the Depression continued it was clear that he could be laid off again at any time. Life was also stressful for his younger son — the twelve-year-old boy entered or re-entered four seventh-grade classrooms that year, starting and ending at Waukegan's Central School. Yet as the years passed, Bradbury's powerful creativity proved over and over again that his time in Tucson had provided vast resources for his maturing imagination.

Not surprisingly, landscape figured prominently in his memories of those days. He had witnessed one of the recurring mirages that appear from time to time at various points in the Southwest, and he eventually used this experience as a frame for one of his most famous stories, "A Miracle of Rare Device" (1962), the tale of two itinerant travelers who discover a permanent mirage of an amazing cityscape and manage to keep another drifter from commercializing the site.[7] Bradbury's most vivid desert memories also informed award-winning stories. The declining Arizona boom towns, and the terrifying beauty of sudden desert rain-bursts, combined to shape "The Day It Rained Forever" (1957), a *Harper's* magazine story that won Bradbury his fourth appearance in the *Best American Short Stories* anthology series.

"Powerhouse," a 1948 *Charm* magazine story that earned Bradbury his second appearance in the annual *O. Henry Prize Stories* anthologies, is a beautiful tale of a rancher's wife who spends a stormy night in an isolated Arizona desert powerhouse, grieving for her dying mother until the magic displayed by the far-traveling electric power grid offers a way to accept the ambiguities of life and death: "Her grief was but one part of a vast grief, her fear only one of countless others. And this grief was only a half thing. There was the other half; of things born, of comfort in the shape of a new child, of food in the warmed body, of colors for the eye and sounds in the awakened ear, and spring with flowers for the smelling. Whenever a light blinked out, life threw another switch; rooms were illumined afresh" (Bradbury, *Golden Apples*, 176).

The Arizona desert of Bradbury's Tucson days also came to symbolize urban and cultural decline in some of Bradbury's great mid-century works of fiction. These works offer cities — on Mars and on Earth — that are metaphors for the decline or fragmentation of art and imagination in the modern world, warning of even more barren vistas to come. Bradbury's most vivid urban metaphors are those of "The Pedestrian" and *Fahrenheit 451*, where the city reflects the solitude and desolation of a desert landscape. For Bradbury's city-dwellers, locked away from the buckling sidewalks and abandoned plazas, reality is merely an illusion, simulated on large-screen televisions or narrated through tiny seashell earphones.

In the broadest biographical and creative sense, Tucson proved to be the perfect prelude for things to come. In the late spring of 1934, barely a year after the family's return to Waukegan, Leo Bradbury was laid off for the second time by the municipal power company. Once again the family headed west in the '26 Buick, this time journeying all the way to a new beginning in Los Angeles. This time the family made a go of it — just barely — until 1942, when Leo found the relative security of a long-term power company position in nearby Venice Beach. During the war years, Bradbury kept a day office in a tenement owned by friends in the multi-racial neighborhoods around Temple and Figueroa Streets in downtown Los Angeles. This environment, and the occasional journeys he made across the border into Mexico, opened up the Hispanic and Indian cultures that he had only glimpsed during his Tucson years. The desert Southwest had now opened out into the diversity of the California coastal cities, the beauty of the California high desert, and the vast complexities of Mexico, where he traveled extensively in the fall of 1945 (Eller 119–125; Weller 125–130).

These experiences produced Los Angeles–centered stories of the immigrants who fled the unsettled aftermath of the 1911 Mexican revolution, as well as their American-born children. These include "I See You Never" (1948), a poignant *New Yorker* tale of illegal immigration that became the second of Bradbury's four appearances in the *Best American Short Stories* anthology series.

"Bradbury with Powerhouse." Still from *Story of a Writer* by Terry Sanders (courtesy Terry Sanders, http://www.americanfilmfoundation.com/order/ray_brad bury.shtml).

Perhaps the most impressive consequence of his permanent relocation to the American West surfaced through the stories that he wrote about Americans in Mexico and Central America, most notably the masterful variations on death in Mexico provided by "The Next in Line" (1947), "El Dia de Muerte" (1947), "The Candy Skull" (1948), and "The Life Work of Juan Diaz" (1963).

Many of these stories were inspired by his own terrifying encounters with the subterranean mummies of Guanajuato during his fall 1945 travels through Mexico. Others, like his short-short story "The Highway" (1950) and his lengthy masterpiece "And the Rock Cried Out" (1953), turned to a new question facing the post-colonial world — if the northern hemispheres were destroyed by nuclear war, would American survivors marooned in the southern hemispheres be able to adjust to a new world order? The title allusion (a well-known spiritual lyric) is apt: "I went to the Rock to hide my face | And the Rock cried out, 'No Hiding Place, | There's no Hiding Place down here" (Bradbury, "Rock," 121).

These were among the best stories of his early career, but it would be the American West's overarching sense of newness and the excitement of exploration that proved to be the most enduring stimulant for Bradbury's imagination. As his career progressed, his gradual and often interrupted Westering journey finally arrived at the true terminus of Percival Lowell's Avenue of the Stars. In the 1950s he made his first journey out into the high desert to see the great 200-inch mirror of the Hale telescope on Mount Palomar, and soon began a long and fruitful association with Caltech and the Jet Propulsion Laboratory. Many of the scientists and engineers involved with the space program had been inspired by *The Martian Chronicles*, and over time Bradbury's writing about Mars turned from fiction to fact, relating how these men and women allowed him to witness the successive orbital photographic missions and surface rover explorations of the Red Planet.

The Martian landscapes of Ray Bradbury's imagination, brought into sharper focus by each successive NASA orbiter and lander mission, were a natural extension of his own Westering experience; during his lifetime, the lands he traveled — from Southern Arizona to Southern California — became home to some of the most far-reaching Earth-based telescopes of our age. In 1973, he concluded Caltech's collaborative volume *Mars and the Mind of Man* with this wish: "I would love to be around when we make landfall there ... the sooner the dream, the sooner the foundation beneath the dream and the sooner men will seed themselves to Martians before our astonished gaze" (143).

Notes

1. The seven months of adventures in Tucson, comprising all but the beginning and the end of Bradbury's 1932–33 seventh grade year, are summarized in Weller, Bradbury Chronicles, 63–66. My own essay on these events was eventually cut from *Becoming Ray Bradbury* because of space limitations; this unpublished account forms the basis for a significant portion of the present article.

2. Bradbury's enduring tale "The Rocket" (originally "Outcasts of the Stars," 1950) grew out of these discarded relics: "Right next door, the very next lot was a junk yard where people had just thrown things. I don't know who did it — old cars you could sit in and 'drive,' you know, open-top cars, jalopies, and all kinds of tubes and metal, old batteries, bric-a-brac. You could put together a rocket ship.... It was a combination of those locomotives and the junk yard next door that made it natural for me to write that story" (Bradbury interview, 2004). Details about the multi-family house in downtown Tucson where the family relocated comes from an October 2007 interview by the author with Los Angeles publisher and bookseller Craig Graham, who researched and visited the house to gather information for the 2005 Weller biography.

3. Bradbury recalls spending twenty weeks working for the station, but given the family's late spring return to Waukegan, it was more likely closer to sixteen weeks. An early account of his "Calling All Cars" debut is preserved in a tenth-grade L.A. high school essay dated September 30, 1935 and titled "Mike-fright" (4 pp. holograph), for which he received a

content grade of "B-minus." His line flub is ironic if in fact these were pilot scripts for "Calling All Cars," for the show's trademark use of real police officers led to constant misreadings and mispronunciations throughout the 1933–1939 run of this popular West Coast program.

4. Weller notes that Bradbury's appreciation for suspense, more fully influenced later by Hitchcock's films, probably begins when Bradbury saw *King Kong* in 1933 (66).

5. In this unpublished essay Bradbury indicated that the station owner was the culprit, but in a subsequent interview he recalled that an assistant, not the station owner, actually broke the transcription disk (Bradbury interview, 2008). He also maintains that his habit of writing out Chandu broadcasts from memory served as a way to improve his own storytelling (Bradbury interview 1969). An undated inventory of his keepsake trunk from the 1940s lists a "File of Chandu radio scripts, written in green ink from memory" ("Misc. 1944–1949," Albright Collection).

6. Bradbury, interview with the author, October 20, 2007, documents Bradbury's school transitions during the 1932–33 academic year. John Huff's late-life recollection of the Western "movie" strips is found in Weller, 63.

7. "I have long since forgotten the name of the mirage — probably something like Mirage View or Mirage Point — but I have not forgotten the fabulous town that lay buried in the shimmering silver depths of the strange warm water lake that was the center of the mirage. I have carried that memory from my twelfth year.... The way to write a story about anything is to bring on several characters who have need, one way or another, for the thing you wish to write about. So I finally sat down and put two needful characters into an old car and ran them over the desert and onto the scene and then sat back and typed and let the characters speak and live and write the story for me. The result was 'A Miracle of Rare Device'" (Bradbury, "Miracle" headnote).

Works Cited

Bradbury, Ray. "Afterthoughts." In *Mars and the Mind of Man.* New York: Harper, 1973. Print.

_____. "And the Rock Cried Out." In *The Vintage Bradbury.* New York: Random House, 1965. Print. Originally published in *Manhunt* magazine (Sept. 1953) and in early editions of *Fahrenheit 451.* New York: Ballantine, 1953. Print.

_____. Author's headnote to "A Miracle of Rare Device." In *The Worlds of Science Fiction.* London: Gollancz, 1964. Print.

_____. "I Have All the Answers." Unpublished interview with his agent, Don Congdon. New York, 1969. Transcript.

_____. "Infinite Riches in a Little Room: Radio from Crystal to Seti to Gridlock." Unpublished essay, c.1990. The Albright Collection, Muncie, IN; from a photocopy, Center for Ray Bradbury Studies, Indiana University School of Liberal Arts (IUPUI). Typescript.

_____. Interview with Donn Albright (for the author). 8 Mar. 2004. Transcript.

_____. "Lowell Avenue to the Stars." Unpublished typed essay, c. 1970. The Albright Collection; from a photocopy, Center for Ray Bradbury Studies. Typescript.

_____. "Mike-fright." Unpublished holograph high school essay, 30 Sept. 1935. Manuscript.

_____. Personal interviews with the author. 6 Oct. 2004, 9 Oct. 2005, 13 Oct. 2006, 23 Oct. 2007, 20 Oct. 2008. Transcripts.

_____. "Powerhouse." In *The Golden Apples of the Sun.* Garden City, New York: Doubleday, 1953. Revised from *Charm* (Mar. 1948). Print.

_____. Unpublished and untitled fragmentary typed writer's journal, 1939–41. The Albright Collection; from a photocopy, Center for Ray Bradbury Studies. Typescript.

Burroughs, Edgar Rice. *The Gods of Mars*. Chicago: A. C. McClurg, 1918. Print.

Eller, Jonathan R. *Becoming Ray Bradbury*. Urbana: University of Illinois Press, 2011. Print.

Weller, Sam. *The Bradbury Chronicles*. New York: Morrow, 2005. Print.

The Sorcerer's Apprentices

How the Lives of Three Regional
"Weird Fiction" Writers
Became Creatively Entangled

WOLF FORREST

Genre writing is heavily influenced by its predecessors, more so than other types of writing. In the case of science fiction, fantasy, and horror, it begs the question as to which came first — The Chicken Heart That Ate Philadelphia, or The Egg from Outer Space? Science fiction as literature can be traced back to Lucian of Samosata's energetic description of a trip to the moon in his "True History." Horror as an outgrowth of campfire ghost stories is undoubtedly even older. Fantasy emerged from the myths of pagan cultures, and civilizations like those of ancient Egypt and Greece refined this mythic storytelling to an art. Regional writing has a more personal component to it. It should be noted that those who write with a regional flair, whether they are practitioners of chronicling fiction or fact, are also inexorably siphoning the imaginations of their predecessors, mentors, and family members who carry the torch of culture and local mythology forward. The differences are subtle, and there is often great overlap. The temptation to exclude, by design, elements that are characteristic to each type of writing when selecting the other as a format, would seem to be a conscious decision by the writer as an exercise in streamlining the piece without relying on the conventional props of physical circumstance, or oral or written history. More often than not, the effectiveness of a text is bolstered by these same conventions. By selecting the careers of three men, we can observe this process intimately.

When Ray Douglas Bradbury was born in Waukegan, Illinois, on August 22, 1920, little did he know that a three-year-old Robert Bloch, born only

40 miles away in Chicago, was also destined to make his mark in the annals of weird fiction. Someday both would be working for the master of suspense, and 150 miles away in the neighboring state of Wisconsin (Bloch would subsequently move to Milwaukee in 1929) an 11-year-old named August Derleth would one day enable Ray and Robert Bloch to see their first hardbound collection of short stories. As youths, each showed marginal interest in writing, though Bradbury was probably most aware at the earliest age of his future as a man of letters.

Ray Bradbury's seminal influences came from five major sources — movies, carnivals, magic, books, and his Aunt Neva. Just ten years older, she was more a sister than aunt, taking him to experience the world of fantasy in a progressive succession of horrors and intellectually liberating pursuits. She gave him his first book of fantasy, a collection of fairy tales, when he was five, and introduced him to Baum's *Oz* series. She also read from Poe's *Tales of Mystery and Imagination* (Weller 42). Her resources and abilities no doubt gave Bradbury the confidence to explore the world and all its incredible offerings. His mother aided and abetted this work-in-progress by taking him to the movies. Such influences provide a core of support that is extremely useful to a child's absorptive mind. H.P. Lovecraft, another writer of weird fiction, also had a doting mother and aunts, who, in the absence of a father doomed by psychosis, gave the boy freedom to stretch his curiosity in the world of science and history (deCamp 37). In Bradbury's case, Neva was the progressive sibling that his older brother Skip was not.

Bradbury saw the *Hunchback of Notre Dame* at three, and *The Phantom of the Opera* at five. In a way, his mantra throughout his life — "Live forever," as proclaimed by Mr. Electrico, the carnival performer he became enthralled with, was a reflection of the star of those two films — later on, the pronouncement of one of his future close friends — Forrest Ackerman, who exclaimed, "Lon Chaney shall never die!" after the silent film star succumbed to throat cancer at 47 ("Hooray"). This cry was an affirmation of theme that Bradbury put to ultimate use in *Something Wicked This Way Comes*. These films were to be major influences in his life. Robert Bloch also saw *The Phantom*, in Chicago, gazing upon that "naked face of horror," and was it probably the catalyst for his own writing career (Pfefferkorn). His move to Milwaukee in 1929, and his friendship with the editor of the high school literary magazine resulted in Bloch's first fiction contribution. A few years later Bradbury also saw *King Kong*, whose iconic depiction of a noble beast exploited at the hands of greedy entrepreneurs galvanized his sympathetic understanding of the world, and the film would also figure strongly in the careers of Forry Ackerman and another man, Ray Harryhausen — someone who would one day count Bradbury as a kindred spirit and change the face of fantastic cinema.

When Bradbury was seven, he saw a poster plastered on the Genesee Theater in Waukegan, advertising the craft of Blackstone the magician (Weller 41). After Harry Houdini died in 1926, a sea change was afoot for stage magic — within two years, the genteel pace of producing illusions had been replaced by a more frenetic performance emphasizing sleight of hand, and Harry Blackstone was the new face of this change (41). It captivated America, and Bradbury's acquaintance with the magician came years after he had bought tickets to every show and studiously examined all the tricks in Blackstone's repertoire. So another die had been cast. At this point the young Bradbury was creating his own mythology as a wellspring from which to draw the elixir of imagination later on.

August Derleth, born in Sauk City, Wisconsin, in 1909, also came to an avid love of books as a child, and like Bradbury, considered the public library to be his sanctuary. It took him three years and forty rejections, but, in 1925, at the age of 16, he sold his first story to *Weird Tales*, guided by a love of the bizarre and arcane. By the mid–1930s he was lecturing in American regional literature at the University of Wisconsin, and, as a recipient of a Guggenheim Fellowship, chose to use the money to augment and bind his comic book collection rather than travel abroad, a move that the young Bradbury would have surely appreciated (Kirchstein). His most important contribution to regional writing was his Sac Prairie saga, which covers the area of Wisconsin around Sauk City from the 19th century forward, and was admired by Sinclair Lewis. Novelettes like *The Place of Hawks* and *The House of Moonlight* echo the spirit of Walden, Thoreau, and Whitman in their outlook and approach. As a regional writer, his biggest influences were also Emerson and Mencken. The saga is less remembered than Edgar Lee Masters' *Spoon River Anthology*, or the *Winesburg, Ohio*, of Sherwood Anderson, although Anderson was also one of Derleth's fiercest critics (Kirchstein). The Sac Prairie saga also covered journals and poetry, and he returned to add to the series through the 1960s. Followers of the series will notice a shift in tone from the early travelogues which developed the idea of a homogeneous society and its struggle in the elements. *Wisconsin in Their Bones*, published in 1961, was a compilation of some of the better tales, and it began with a Christmas story.

Derleth exemplifies the perfect fusion of a genre and regional writer — able to communicate the mundane aspects of geography as well as the more salient characteristics of a pioneering people. His contributions to the genre of horror are well-documented, and he etched his name into the genre of mystery with the creation of the detective Solar Pons, who appeared in some 70 stories. Not content to limit himself, he branched out into children's literature as well. Arguably, his most important contribution to publishing was the creation of Arkham House, after other publishers balked at his attempts, along with co-founder Donald Wandrei, to find an outlet for the collection of H. P. Lovecraft's stories.

Derleth's effort eventually led to the publication of story collections of other writers of weird fiction. If Bradbury had ever intended to become a regional writer or poet like Whitman or fellow Midwesterner James Whitcomb Riley, devoid of supernatural influences (although Riley's "Little Orphant Annie" recounts children beset by a number of horrors), his choice of literature as a formative element distracts us from that conclusion. Of all the types of writing that he has cited as helping to mold his career, there is little to indicate that regional writing played a major part. But the very essence of all types of writing suggests that Bradbury was just tapping into a vein shared by those whose craft has been honed to a sharp edge by invoking the spirit of visualization.

Regional writing seems to more often than not, contain the underpinnings of Gothic romance. Exceptions like travelogues or discourse on the natural and historical singularities of an area serve to highlight the careers of authors who take pride in establishing themselves as fiction writers — as if the relevancy of the area was dependent on, and embedded with, supernatural content. Regional writing often uncovers the horrors found in local accounts of crime, or stories perpetuated by the families of writers. Science fiction, fantasy, and horror writing frequently use descriptions of actual places and people, and circumstances to give their stories validity and familiarity. Certain archetypes also reappear in genre and regional writing. H. P. Lovecraft is an excellent example of a horror writer using regionality as a setting for his stories. Although a recluse who never moved away from his beloved Providence (except for a brief stay in New York City), he loved traveling and writing extensively in reams of correspondence to colleagues, and explored his antiquarian desires and Anglophilia in a myriad of notes and essays.

Bradbury's fiction can be understood within the broader frame of three other regions. The regional writing of the Midwest, the Northeast, and the South contain a variety of styles that complement each other and serve to illuminate Bradbury's Southwest–inspired fiction. For instance, Midwestern horror differs from the New England horror of Hawthorne. Entrenched in residue from Colonial times and a connection to England, Hawthorne's output can be compared to that of Algernon Blackwood, and his ghostly tales like "The Egyptian Hornet," or Arthur Machen, who created a world of the supernatural culminating in such fantasies as "The Great God Pan." In his survey *Supernatural Horror in Literature*, Lovecraft considered Machen to be one of the finest practitioners of the weird tale. Washington Irving and Nathaniel

Hawthorne wrote as contemporaries and with a singularity of voice. Although he was technically not a New Englander, Irving's stories of the Catskills and Hudson River Valley would be most at home in Salem, Massachusetts. His writing is also reflected in the literary style of M.R. James, a practitioner of ghost stories *par excellence*, as in "Casting the Runes."

Southern regional writing often draws from the social turmoil based on the culture of slavery and its ramifications. Missouri, as a compromise state, and home to its most visible regional writer Mark Twain, produces writing that shares historical and geographical elements with the Midwest and the South. The writings of Faulkner, Welty, Williams, McCullers, and even Capote display a conflict of genteel versus downtrodden, a clash of cultures that Bradbury displayed in *The Martian Chronicles*. Carson McCullers' *The Heart Is a Lonely Hunter* also deals with outcasts, including the point of view narrator who is deaf.

A character in the Southern writer Eudora Welty's "A Worn Path" reminds us of Bradbury's Jim Nightshade. "A Worn Path" also shows grim reminders of passages in *The Illustrated Man*. The opening of the latter is particularly reminiscent of Welty. The protagonist, in the manner of *Moby Dick's* Ishmael, begins his soliloquy: "It was a warm afternoon in early September when I first met the Illustrated Man. Walking along an asphalt road, I was on the final leg of a two weeks' walking tour of Wisconsin." His peripatetic journey, which mentions the hills of Wisconsin, is also a nod to Derleth's *Sac Prairie*. Bradbury surely would have appreciated Welty's protagonist, Phoenix Jackson — an elderly black woman who struggles to procure medicine for her grandson. She begins her trek and encounters many obstacles in her path, including threats from wildlife. Like Odysseus, Jason, and countless others whose quest is marred by impediments, her determination triumphs. By making comparisons to the process of writing itself, Welty and Bradbury share an intimate desire to strip away the illusion of the writer as unbiased and dispassionate. (In another curious parallel, Welty published a collection of stories called *The Golden Apples* in 1949. Bradbury published his own collection of stories four year later called *The Golden Apples of the Sun*.) Another Mississippian, Tennessee Williams' greatest inspiration came from his time spent in New Orleans. What he shares with the reader is a determination to highlights the quirks of human nature, using his own family as a template for his characters. Similarly, Bradbury's nuclear self-referencing is much muted, although his story "Uncle Einar," about a "loving vampire with a vast span of green wings" is an obvious tribute to his own Inar, a "loud, boisterous, drinking Swedish uncle who burst into our home with a great cry and left with a shout" (Weller 24).

Certain aspects of Twain's character Injun Joe resemble Bradbury's Mr. Dark. Injun Joe, after having been beaten by a peace officer, turns his hatred into striking feat in the hearts of children by using murder and blackmail. Mr. Dark's *raison d'etre* is more sinister — by appealing to the secret fantasies of all who come to his carnival via tattoos on his body, it is the logical extension of the Illustrated Man's capabilities.

Southwestern writers are a different lot. As the area has become a melting pot of sorts, there is not the hoary infrastructure found in New England or the South beyond the influence of Mexico and Native American cultures. Byrd Baylor, a children's author, who covers many topics unique to Arizona in her books like *Yes Is Better Than No* and *Coyote Cry*, and Joe Lansdale, a native Texan who writes on fantasy and horror topics from Bubba Ho-Tep to mystery novels and Batman, combine genre writing with regional writing. (Baylor also shares a bit of technophobia with Bradbury — both eschewed computers for typewriters — indeed Baylor lives in a house without electricity but with three manual machines.) Southwestern, as well as other regional writers employ cross-cultural topics like baseball or religion, each with their own set of histories or values, to administer metaphors of continuity and convenience — the vagaries of isolating them in shadow nearly neutralize their effectiveness.

Bradbury's archetypes are even more shadowy. Does Montag in *Fahrenheit 451* share more than a few traits with Captain Ahab, or is he more like Henry Fleming, Stephen Crane's protagonist in *The Red Badge of Courage*? Was Verne a regional writer? Bradbury certainly fell under his spell. Verne's philosophy was far ahead of his countrymen's, and little love for his native country, save for the boats that sailed on the Loire River which fueled his imagination, crops up in his stories. The hybrid writing that Bradbury employs closely follows Verne's ability to extrapolate wildly from contemporary scientific and social progress, which is the blueprint for most science fiction writing, although the technologies of Bradbury's stories are more backdrop for his social conscience.

Regional writing by design encompasses aspects of local history, tradition, contemporary politics, and social concerns, and it's certainly not limited to American writers. Charles Dickens, a favorite writer of Bradbury's, is a prime example of an author who exploited his times for commentary on the social justice system of England, particularly as it related to the working class. And he was not averse to employing fantasy and horror to make his points. One only has to think of *A Christmas Carol*, and his graphic account of spontaneous combustion in *Bleak House* is worthy of production in any *Grand Guignol* offering. Ultimately, Dickens would figure in one of Bradbury's more nostalgic efforts, the charming "Any Friend of Nicholas Nickleby's Is a Friend of Mine."

Some of the best known regional writers employ a mode of storytelling that is personal and resonant. Melville is a hard writer to classify. His regionality was expressed in the detailed description of men in whaling boats, and his first novel *Typee*, recounts some of the life he lived among cannibals in the Marquesas Islands, after deserting the whaling ship *Acushnet*. Melville acutely emphasized regionality with Moby Dick which also draws from classical literature as the hero (or anti-hero in Ahab's case) fights against the ultimate dispassionate god. As Bradbury worked on the screenplay for *Moby Dick*, he experienced his own clash of aesthetics with bigger-than-life director John Huston.

Another commonality of genre writing is the creation of a fictional setting for a number of stories or novels, often based on the writer's own experiences and stories told to them by elders and community members. Faulkner had Yoknapatawpha County, Lovecraft had Arkham, Massachusetts, and Bradbury had Green Town, based on the Waukegan he knew and loved and extrapolated from (not unlike Derleth's Sac Prairie) — a vestibule to harbor the undercurrent of mystery, and serving up a *frisson* of delights in *Dandelion Wine*, and, in the case of *Something Wicked This Way Comes*, evil. The essence of Midwest horror comes from the horror of flatness. In Melville's Moby Dick, Ishmael refers to the "horror of whiteness" as embodied by Moby Dick himself. Lovecraft referenced this dread in his novel *At the Mountains of Madness*, itself an extension of Poe's *The Narrative of Arthur Gordon Pym of Nantucket*. (It is interesting that Poe somehow escaped the stamp of regionality, after living in Richmond, Philadelphia, and New York.) When Bradbury was contacted by John Huston to write the screenplay for Melville's classic, based on the success of *The Beast from 20,000 Fathoms*, he knew that this was another tale of the sea swimming in metaphors, which would show his skill at adapting another's work.

Midwestern horror can be captured in film too. Philip Ridley's *The Reflecting Skin*, although the location is Idaho and the film Canadian, has the look of the rural Midwest. Capote's *In Cold Blood* recalls brutal murders in Holcomb, Kansas, and the isolation felt in the novel is palpable. The antithesis of claustrophobia, it differs from southern Gothic and the writings of Faulkner, Lee, Welty, Williams, and McCullers. In the visual arts, there have been some striking examples of lonely tableaus — Grant Wood's "American Gothic" with its frame house in the background, looming over the dour-stone-faced farming family the heartbreaking "Christina's World" by Andrew Wyeth, with its solitary frame house and barn in the distance, and the house in "Psycho" with its dimly lit windows perched hawk-like on a southern California hill.

Prairie novels exhibit a certain indelible and ineluctable dread engendered by open spaces. In Bradbury's poetry, a body of work considered palliative by his critics, has more of this essence in work s like "If Only We Had Taller Been" and "The Beast Atop the Building, the Tiger on the Stairs." "The Beast" is divided into two parts, both cinematic tributes to two of his favorite films: *King Kong* and *Sunset Boulevard*. The tenth line, "To rave in clouds, and send the airships down in fire," and the last line, "Gone mad in final dark, we weep," underscores the maddening sense of aloneness felt in the poem, especially after the lights come up and the story is over (Bradbury *ll.* 10, 66). You are in a crowded theater, yet utterly vulnerable to the strangers with whom you hopefully have felt a connection. "If Only We Had Taller Been" highlights the yearning of two boys who want to touch the sky (maybe Nightshade and Halloway again?). The lines, "If we could reach and touch, we said/'Twould teach us somehow never to be dead," reinforce their belief in the future of mankind's place among the stars, tempered by their naïveté of the perils lurking in space — the ultimate horizonless environment (Bradbury *ll.* 8–9). Another poem, "Too Much," speaks of the bounty of too much sky and land, and the sensory overload it produces. In Bradbury's fiction, his gift is the disarming sense of ease with which he lulls you into a story. It is the sweet nectar of a Venus flytrap that leads you to your doom. The poetry is much more imitative, although his refusal to abandon the form indicates that there was more embryonic prose floating in his subconscious than ever was committed to paper.

Bradbury made two stops in Tucson, Arizona, six years apart. His first stint led him to explore the wonders of the desert for the first time, and the collection of antiquities and dinosaur bones in the University's museums, fueling a major interest in prehistoric reptiles that would influence much of his writing. The beginning of Bradbury's second stint in Tucson in late 1932 saw his parents give him a toy typewriter for Christmas — the beginning of his legitimate foray into becoming a writer, as he instilled in himself the discipline of writing a story a week. Oddly enough, the second home Bradbury lived in while in Tucson was more reminiscent of a Midwestern house, or a New England frame house, a composite of American Gothic and Nathaniel Hawthorne, with its gables and sprawling porch, than a typical southwestern adobe or stucco house. In the spring of 1933, his interest in radio crystallized, and his viewing of *King Kong*, probably at the Fox Theater, sent him into the stratosphere. He also became involved with a local radio station, first acting as a gofer, and then reading Sunday comic strips on the air. But by late spring his time in Tucson ended, and it was back to Illinois for a brief stay, and Bradbury's exposure to the 1933 Chicago World's Fair fueled his unquenchable optimism in the world of tomorrow. His uncle Inar moved to Los Angeles in early 1934, and after glowing reviews of the almost Oz-like environment,

Bradbury and his family followed when his father was laid off from a utility company (Weller 68).

It is unclear when Bradbury's interest in Mexican culture started. We do know his first trip to Mexico was with his friend Grant Beach late in 1945, after a massive sale allowed him that extravagance. Ultimately he wound up in Guanajuato, and its famous mummies, generating at least three stories from the experience: "The Candy Skull," "The Next in Line," and the Hitchcock teleplay, "The Life Work of Juan Diaz." Ultimately "The Next in Line" would be reproduced in its entirety in the 1978 coffee table book *The Mummies of Guanajuato*, along with photographs by Archie Lieberman. But Bradbury may have walked the short distance from his Tucson home to visit the wishing shrine downtown, known as *El Tiradito*, and its accompanying tale of murder and revenge, and been captivated by tales from Tucson's past, and its roots in Mexican and Native American culture. Examining his body of work, it's a compelling assumption.

When Bradbury moved to L.A., the land of illusion and magic, he made that fateful transition to a writer of fantasy. His roots would always nourish his writing, and whatever magic dust he swept up from the desert floor of Tucson he carried with him the rest of his life. His association with the Los Angeles Science Fantasy Society brought him into contact with the likes of Henry Kuttner, C. L. Moore, and Leigh Brackett, all who contributed to *Weird Tales*, one of many pulp magazines that flourished from the 1920s through the 1950s, and the greatest outlet for writers of weird fiction — cheaply-produced monthly or quarterly magazines that often only paid a fraction of a cent per word to their contributors, but helped many young writers break into print. Bradbury made his first sale to *Weird Tales* in 1941 with "The Candle" (Weller 110).

Brackett was to become a mentor to Bradbury by helping him to polish his writing, and she became one of the first Weird Tales contributors to write for Hollywood, writing screenplays over a long career that included *The Big Sleep, Rio Bravo, Hatari!*, and *The Empire Strikes Back*. The Society also gave Bradbury two lifelong friends — Forry Ackerman and Ray Harryhausen, who made their own indelible marks in the field of popular culture.

Robert Bloch had taken a similar writing path as Bradbury. Both men wrote and performed extensively for radio, and both wrote for *Weird Tales* — Bloch had made his first sale to the magazine with his short story "Feast in the Abbey" in 1934. Bloch also wrote for the radio program *Stay Tuned for Terror* in the 1940s, contributing 39 episodes. Bloch's correspondence with Lovecraft resulted in several offerings in the *Cthulhu Mythos*, a collection of interrelated tales penned by many authors, contributing to Lovecraft's pantheon of a race of beings that once inhabited Earth. Bradbury never wrote *Mythos* stories and was less inclined to borrow from other writers' style and theme than his contemporaries. But in November of 1939, he wrote a letter to August Derleth and Donald Wandrei, who had just published their first entry in the newly minted Arkham House imprint, H.P. Lovecraft's *The Outsider and Others*, praising their efforts (Weller 101).

Bloch's *The Opener of the Way*, his first collection of short stories, was purchased by August Derleth and Donald Wandrei, and published by Arkham House in 1945, which contained his oft-anthologized "Yours Truly, Jack the Ripper." When Arkham House published Bradbury's story collection *Dark Carnival* in 1947, Frank Capra's *It's a Wonderful Life* premiered. Bradbury's "Green Town" reminiscences could have come from that plot, and Jimmy Stewart's line to Donna Reed — after promising to lasso the moon for her, and suggesting she swallow it, his remark that "the moonbeams would shoot out of your fingers and your toes and the ends of your hair" is as Bradburyesque a quip as you'll find in cinema. Ironically, some of Bradbury's later books were published by Capra Press, although there is no connection to the filmmaker.

Bradbury's association with Alfred Hitchcock began in 1955 when Hitchcock asked him to write the first draft of an adaptation of Daphne du Maurier's *The Birds*, but his commitment to Hitch's television show prevented him from accepting the assignment. Bloch moved to L.A. around in late 1959, after winning a Hugo Award for his story "That Hell Bound Train," and at the behest of a colleague to submit a script for the TV detective drama *Lock-Up*. The gamble paid off, because he wrote four more episodes and ensconced himself in Hollywood. Bradbury did five teleplays for *Alfred Hitchcock Presents*. On the heels of *Psycho*, Bloch did ten scripts — the last being "The Sorcerer's Apprentice," which was denied broadcast because of its ghoulish elements, although it was later syndicated (McCarty 239). When the show morphed into *The Alfred Hitchcock Hour*, both men continued to produce scripts. Bloch contributed seven teleplays, and Bradbury produced two of the show's most memorable episodes: "The Jar" and "The Life Work of Juan Diaz" (the latter airing just a week after Bloch's "Water's Edge"). Neither Bloch nor Bradbury wrote for *The Outer Limits*, though Bloch has a tenuous connection to the show. One of its co-creators, Joes Stefano, wrote the screenplay for Hitchcock's *Psycho*, based on Bloch's book. Bloch also wrote for *Thriller*, Boris Karloff's TV anthology series, as did August Derleth, and *Star Trek*, contributing three episodes, but Bradbury had no connection to any of these shows. Bloch never contributed a script for *The Twilight Zone* either, although he did contribute a script for Rod Serling's follow-up, *Night Gallery*, also working with Derleth by adapting one of his stories.

In retrospect, it is disappointing that the works of Joe Mugnaini, the illustrator most closely associated with Bradbury, were not featured pieces in the *Night Gallery* openings. Not having one of Bradbury's stories appear as an episode preceded by one of his friend's nightmarish paintings is probably one of the great losses in the history of televised fantasy series. If Bradbury had found a life-partner in Mugnaini, whose style resembled the etchings of Gustave Dore, this partnership also reinforced his strength as a visual writer, invoking a luminous desire to touch, to feel, and to be a part of that textural universe. Bradbury's purchase of Joe Mugnaini's gothic haunted house painting, a veritable incarnation of Hawthorne's House of the Seven Gables, became an inside joke as the image resurfaced time and time again in Bradbury's career. The gothic house showed up with slight variations on the cover of the Ballantine edition of *The October Country*. Not missing an opportunity to exploit the larger art world, a Bantam edition of *Dandelion Wine* borrows heavily from Wyeth's "Christina's World."

In between stints as a story writer, scenarist, and poet, Bradbury found time to do some uncredited narration for Nicholas Ray's *King of Kings*, a recapitulation of voice work during his youthful radio days. Bradbury contributed one episode to *The Twilight Zone*—"I Sing the Body Electric" (two other stories were considered, but not produced because of budgetary considerations). His association with Rod Serling, the creative force behind the series, was rocky from the start. Too many episodes bore a strong resemblance to Bradbury stories without giving the writer credit.

Bloch had successfully weaned himself off the influence of Lovecraft and away from the Lovecraftian Mythos. But were there any direct influences on each other's lives? In Sam Weller's biography of Bradbury, there is not a single reference to Bloch, and it remains a mystery as to how well they knew each other. Professionally, they surely crossed paths at science fiction and fantasy conventions as well as book signings and awards banquets. Both men considered themselves close friends with husband-and-wife writers C.L. Moore and Henry Kuttner. They lived only seven miles apart, as the crow flies — Bloch in the Hollywood Hills, Bradbury near Culver City — a stone's throw by Los Angelean standards, even closer to each other than in their childhoods.[1] Yet their connection survived. Bradbury's teenage friend from the Los Angeles Science Fantasy Society, Forry Ackerman, tabbed Bloch for an article in his juvenile publication *Famous Monsters of Filmland*, and the latter two shared a love of bad puns and wordplay. Forry's monikers included Dr. Acula and the Ackermonster, as well as 4SJ (a play on his first name and middle initial, and was fond of advertising the fact that he lived in Horrorwood, Karloffornia). Bloch's standard retort, when asked about his philosophy in life, was to say, "I have the heart of a small boy — I keep it in a jar on my desk." Maybe that quotation was extant when Bradbury wrote "The Jar," his chilling and seemingly regional short story about a country bumpkin who buys a sideshow attraction from a dwarf.

In 1972 a small imprint called Peacock Press put out a soft cover issue devoted to Bloch and Bradbury with that title, and subtitled "Whispers from Beyond," reprinting a number of their most popular stories, and a few rarities, with additional articles by Noël Coward, Houdini, and Mark Twain. Bloch and Bradbury also appeared together in a 1984 anthology called *Masques*. Bloch's contribution was "Everybody Needs a Little Love," and Bradbury's story entry was "Long After Ecclesiastes."

And Bradbury certainly made the connection between the loneliness wrought by the expansive treeless prairies of the Midwest that is echoed in the deserts and broad vistas of the American Southwest. Mars is the ultimate expansive setting. When Viking I landed on Mars in 1976, its first pictures of the Red Planet's surface were immediately compared to the Arizona desert (Bradbury wrote a poem called "Why Viking Lander, Why the Planet Mars?" as a tribute). As Bradbury played in the dry washes of Tucson, and then watched them fill up during a thunderstorm, he may have recalled Lowell and Schiaparelli's interpretation of the dark lines on Mars as canals distributing water from the polar caps to nourish thirsty Martians, and perhaps the seed was planted then to write about the old Mars, and the coming of the new Martians. Bradbury's association with Mars would run deep. In a *Twilight Zone* episode entitled "Will the Real Martian Please Stand Up?" a busload of passengers is holed up in a rural New England diner on a snowy night, waiting for a bridge to be repaired. At the same time, a UFO has crashed nearby, and the occupant has entered the diner with the bus riders. When state troopers try to determine who got off the bus, and who followed them in, one of the riders, a knotty old coot played by veteran character actor Jack Elam exclaims, "She's like a science fiction, that's what she is! A regular Ray Bradbury! Six humans and one monster from outer space!" Then he turns to another passenger and exclaims, "You wouldn't happen to have an eye in the back of your head, would you?" The episode, written by Serling, may have been an acknowledgment of Bradbury's inspiration, if not his voluminous contribution, to the show. If Bradbury's *magnum opus* bears more resemblance to Willa Cather's *O Pioneers!* than it does to Steinbeck's *Grapes of Wrath*, it isn't accidental. The optimism that lurks even in Bradbury's darkest tales explodes in stories like "The Rocket," "Here There Be Tygers," or "The Wonderful Ice Cream Suit." Yet the Martians are passive to the point of letting the Earthmen take over their planet.

By contrast, Bloch's contribution to regional writing lay in his exploitation of crime when he recounted the life of Ed Gein — an urban myth that was all too real. It was a natural progression after he had used Jack the Ripper as subject matter. The notorious serial killer that morphed into Norman Bates later spearheaded a movement of copycats in that same region — most notably John Wayne Gacy and Richard Speck in Chicago, and Jeffrey Dahmer in Milwaukee. Had Bradbury stayed in Tucson, or Waukegan, his romanticism would have likely been funneled into a more prosaic view of the world, although influences of the dark and fantastic still would have crept into his writing. While Bradbury was obliged to move to Los Angeles with his family, Bloch made the move as a professional choice, suggesting that Bradbury's formation as a writer was far from complete.

In an online edition of *Wired Science* dated November 26, 2012, it was reported that SpaceX founder and CEO Elon Musk wants to establish an 80,000-person colony on Mars. It is regrettable that Bradbury did not live to read that article, as his joy might've reached a point similar to his feelings on July 20, 1969, and later, as he sat with interviewer Mike Wallace discussing the first moon landing. Of the three, Derleth was the most effective regional writer, primarily because he never strayed far beyond his beloved Sauk City. Because Derleth also wrote about nature and issues of conservation, he thoroughly encompassed the spirit of an auteur. The critical argument of the fantasy/horror/science fiction genre versus regional writing may never persuasively tip the balance in terms of influence on a particular practitioner of the craft. But men like Bradbury, Bloch, and Derleth, who always knew they would mine the blank pages of their precious ore, occupy a tidy space in the chronicles of weird fiction, and at least displayed a working knowledge of their environment. Bradbury's time in the Southwest was limited — but his formation as a writer was solidified there, and the germ of future tales firmly planted.

Despite Burroughs' exotic Martian novels' influence on the young Bradbury while he lived in Tucson, characters in *The Martian Chronicles* did not give exotic place names to their new homes. The real Mars includes places with Latinate names such as Chryse Planitia, Valles Marineris, and Olympus Mons. Bradbury might have rejected the re-naming of Olympus Mons for a lack of metaphor, preferring the original, and more poetic designation Nix Olympica. He may also have taken the opportunity to rework the book into a more cohesive structure, substituting Latinized, or even Native American or Spanish clues for his own Martian "Green Town." Had Bradbury stayed in Arizona and not continued the move westward, he might have absorbed more of Tucson's and Mexico's historical and archaeological heritage. With greater exposure, his collection of Martian tales could have spawned the unearthing of mummies, or assumed an avenging spirit closer to the kind often seen in the stories and novels of Sherman Alexie, such in *Reservation Blues* where the indigenous cultures rise up against the new invaders.

Notes

1. Ironically, in death the two men became even closer, physically speaking. Both are buried in the postage-stamp sized Westwood Village Memorial Park Cemetery, less than 100 yards from each other — and home to a bevy of Hollywood luminaries, including Marilyn Monroe, Don Knotts, Jack Lemmon, Dean Martin, Billy Wilder, Frank Zappa, and Jack Arnold, who directed *It Came from Outer Space*, based on Bradbury's 90-page treatment (using the working titles "Meteor" and "Atomic Monster") he developed for screenwriter Harry Essex.

Works Cited

Abrahams, William. *American Gothic Tales*. New York: Plume, 1996. Print.
Bloch, Robert, and Ray Bradbury. *Whispers from Beyond*. Garland, TX: Peacock Press, 1972. Print.
Bradbury, Ray. *The Complete Poems of Ray Bradbury*. New York: Del Rey, 1982. Print.
Carter, Lin. *H.P. Lovecraft: A Look Behind the Cthulhu Mythos*. New York: Ballantine, 1971. Print.
deCamp, L. Sprague. *Lovecraft: A Biography*. Garden City, NY: Doubleday, 1975. Print.
Derleth, August. *An August Derleth Reader*. Ed. Jim Stephens. Boulder, CO: Prairie Oak Press, 1992. Print.
_____. *The Four Lost Sac Prairie Novels*. Oakdale, NY: Hawk & Whippoorwill, 1961. Print.
_____. *Thirty Years of Arkham House*. Sauk City, WI: Arkham House, 1969. Print.
Hooray for Horrorwood. Dir. Ray Ferry. Perf. Forrest Ackerman. Dynacomm, 1991. VHS.
Kirchstein, Jim. "Autobiography of August Derleth." *The August Derleth Society Webpage*. 2010. 1 Dec. 2012. Web.
Lovecraft, H. P. *Supernatural Horror in Literature*. New York: Dover, 1973. Print.
McCarty, John. *Alfred Hitchcock Presents: An Illustrated Guide*. New York: St. Martin's Press, 1985. Print.
Pfefferkorn, Michael G. "The Unofficial Robert Bloch Website." 2007. 27 Nov. 2012. Web.
Weist, Jerry. *Bradbury: An Illustrated Life*. New York: William Morrow, 2002. Print.
Weller, Sam. *The Bradbury Chronicles*. New York: William Morrow, 2005. Print.

Prescient Border Crossing

"I See You Never" and the Undocumented Mexicans Americans Prefer Not to See

MARLEEN S. BARR

Embedded in the memory of Mexican Americans ... is always the continual need to prove our humanity. In the eyes of the law, we have never been human enough. Not American enough. Not loyal enough. Not pure enough. Not legal enough. Not legitimate enough. Even in the realm of language, neither our English or Spanish have ever been good enough.... So when you enact laws that require us to prove our citizenship, when you enact laws that forbid us from learning our thousands-of-year cultures from this very continent [HB 2281, Arizona's anti-ethnic studies law], then you give us but one clear message: the need to once again prove our humanity. You also send out another message: not welcome.—Roberto Rodriguez, "Arizona: Indian Removal or Modern-Day Reducciones?" An Open Letter to Arizona's [Attorney General] Tom Horne, [Superintendent of Public Instruction] John Huppenthal, [State Senator] Russell Pearce, [Sheriff of Maricopa County] Joe Arpaio and [Governor] Jan Brewer: An Appeal to Your Conscience and Your Humanity [*Dissident Voice*]

On numerous occasions, the white majority has relocated or exterminated nonwhite populations that stood in the way of its quest for wealth, energy, or a more congenial environment. Each time we used religion, legal doctrine, and myth to rationalize our actions. When the white settlers arrived, they found a continent rich in land, water, game, and minerals. They set out to make it their own. When some of the Indian tribes resisted, they were quickly and ruthlessly put down. One of the largest and most advanced tribes was relocated more than a thousand miles from its homeland in a "Trail of Tears" which saw many die and nearly destroyed its culture. — Richard Delgado and Jean Stefancic, "Derrick Bell's Chronicle of the Space Traders: Would the U.S. Sacrifice People of Color If the Price Were Right?" [*University of Colorado Law Review*]

Science fiction's future forecasts are, of course, usually associated with technology. Arthur C. Clarke's relationship to communication satellites and William Gibson's term "cyberspace" come to mind. In contrast, Ray Bradbury's "I See You Never" is about social, legal, and generic prediction. His 1947 story anticipates twenty-first century attention to America's undocumented Mexican workers to the extent that it can be read as a companion piece in relation to University of Arizona Mexican–American Studies Department professor Roberto Rodriguez's open letter to Arizona officials. I will discuss Bradbury's story with specific attention to its science fictional and real world affinity to the social invisibility James Tiptree discussed in "The Women Men Don't See." I will emphasize that Bradbury's protagonist Mr. Ramirez, an undocumented Mexican residing in Los Angeles, is positioned in accordance with the content of Rodriguez's letter. In terms of Rodriguez's words, Bradbury seems to emphasize that "[i]n the eyes of the law ... [Ramirez has] never been human enough. Not American enough. Not loyal enough. Not pure enough. Not legal enough. Not legitimate enough" (Rodriguez). In addition, Bradbury's grammatically incorrect title, "I See You Never," exemplifies that "[e]ven in the realm of language, neither our English or Spanish have ever been good enough" (Rodriguez). When "the continual need to prove our [Mexican American] humanity" (Rodriguez) is applied to the story, it is clear that Ramirez's categorization as subhuman and alien makes him analogous to a person kidnapped by extraterrestrials. This dehumanization positions Ramirez as a walker on the Trail of Tears Richard Delgado and Jean Stefancic equate with Derrick Bell's science fiction story "Chronicle of the Space Traders."

Section one of this essay, "Subtle Science Fiction or How the West Was Lost to Mr. Ramirez," focuses on the social implications of the racism Rodriguez describes in terms of its applicability to Ramirez; he is forced to reside outside of American borders. Section two, "The Trail of Tears Is 'The American Way': Alien Abduction Stories," coheres with Delgado's and Stefancic's description of the white majority's actions; the section equates "Never" with two science fiction alien abduction stories — *Cocoon* and "Space Traders." My reading leads to an understanding of how these stories function in accordance with "legal storytelling," an emerging form of legal scholarship which crosses the usual borders separating the law and literature. The conclusion, "Ramirez

Is Science Fiction," explains that Ramirez allegorically represents science fiction's exclusion from the canon as well as Bradbury's status as a generic border crosser par excellence.

Subtle Science Fiction or How the West
Was Lost to Mr. Ramirez

The science fiction tropes in "Never" are subtle, difficult to see. In fact, as the following *New Yorker Magazine blog* description of the story shows, they are commonly rendered as invisible as Tiptree's women men don't see: "As opposed to most of Bradbury's work, the story ["Never"] is not science fiction or fantasy but rather a vignette about a Mexican immigrant named Mr. Ramirez who is forced to leave the United States after he overstays his visa" (Michaud). Not so; as the following sentence shows, science fiction inconspicuously permeates the story: "Mrs. O'Brian [Ramirez's landlady], for the first time, noticed a suitcase standing behind him [Ramirez] on the porch" (Bradbury 108). Is this seemingly mundane language in fact "the language of science fiction" (Samuel Delany's term)? Or, in other words, is the suitcase a sentient being who is literally "standing" on its feet? In addition, the Mexican border town which Ramirez will be returning to has landscape like "the iron mountains and the dusty valleys and the ocean beaches that spread hundreds of miles with no sound but the waves — no cars, no buildings, nothing" (Bradbury 109). This "nothing" is what humans will encounter when they first land on another planet.

In addition to his suitcase and his native terrain, Ramirez's job also subtly connects him to science fiction. Readers are told that "[d]uring the war, he had worked at the airplane factory and made parts for the planes that flew off somewhere" (Bradbury 108). Do the planes fly off to an alternative reality? Forty-four years separates the story's 1947 publication date from the pre–December 17, 1903, Wright Brothers' airplanes as a science fictional notion first flight era. When Ramirez works at the airplane factory, he makes a formerly science fictional technology real. The year 1947 is also relatively close to the 1932 debut of Superman, Ramirez's fellow Americanized immigrant. Despite the fact that Ramirez "had made big money" (Bradbury 108) in Los Angeles and is financially strong, the American government's anti-immigration laws serve as Kryptonite which nullifies his economic security.

The police officer protagonists could have taken orders from a time traveling soon-to-be-forgotten Arizona sheriff Joe Arpaio who lands in 1947. Ramirez is treated in the same way as Darth Vader figure Arpaio deals with his Latino victims. This is a description of the United States Department of Justice's complaint filed against Arpaio: "On May 10 [2012], the Department of Justice filed a formal legal complaint against Sheriff Joe Arpaio and the Maricopa County Sheriff's Office (MCSO) alleging widespread constitutional violations and lawless mistreatment of Latinos. According to the complaint, Arpaio and his staff engaged in widespread, violent and demeaning mistreatment of Latino residents of Maricopa County, often targeting individuals solely because of their race" (Milhiser). "Never" predicts Arpaio and his racist governmental ilk with the exactitude that Jules Verne foresaw the submarine. The story interweaves past and future real American racist reality with subtle science fiction tropes.

In a *New York Magazine* piece called "Mayberry R.I.P," which points to the death of Andy Griffith to discuss the "declinist panic" characterizing 2012 America, Frank Rich provides a means to make the unseen science fiction tropes in "Never" glaring visible. In the wake of Griffith's death, liberal media commentators felt that "Sheriff Andy Taylor of Mayberry, North Carolina, was 'one of the last links to another, simpler time' (the *Miami Herald*).... In reality, *The Andy Griffith Show* didn't transcend the deep divides of its time. It merely ignored them" (Rich 18, 20). A simpler time and place, the utopian halcyon past American small town ideal Mayberry epitomizes, is a fiction. Sheriff Andy Taylor of Mayberry never existed; Sheriff Joe Arpaio is alive and well and living in Arizona. Sheriff Arpaio is rooted in the racist reality of small town America *The Andy Griffith Show* ignored. An understanding of the science fictional aspects of the Los Angeles Bradbury creates clearly reveals this racist reality. The Los Angeles Bradbury's rooming house owner Mrs. O'Brian and her best tenant Mr. Ramirez inhabit is no large scale Mayberry. It is, instead, more akin to the setting of an episode of *The Twilight Zone*.

Rich's comments about a particular *Twilight Zone* script magnify the, at first, subtle science fiction characterizing "Never." He explains that "seven months before *The Andy Griffith Show's* 1960 debut on CBS, the same network broadcast an episode of *The Twilight Zone*, 'The Monsters Are Due on Maple Street,' in which the placid all–American denizens of an (all-white) suburban enclave turn into a blood-thirsty mob hunting down any aliens in human camouflage that might have infiltrated the neighborhood.... Rod Serling, makes clear in his parable's concluding homily ('Prejudices can kill...'), [that] the hovering aliens who threatened to drive Americans to civil unrest and self-destruction ... were not necessarily from outer space. The wave of nostalgia for Andy Griffith's Mayberry and for the vanished halcyon America it supposedly enshrined says more about the frazzled state of America in 2012 and our congenital historical amnesia than it does about the reality of America in

1960" (Rich 20). "Never" science fictionally portrays racist 1947 American reality and inadvertently indicates that 2012 Arizona is rooted in that decidedly non-halcyon twentieth century era. "Never," no completely reality-infused vision, functions as a *Twilight Zone*–esque alien encounter story between reader and text.

In order best to understand Bradbury's story, readers need to recognize that in the Los Angeles Bradbury conjures, the monsters in fact exist on a Maple Street equivalent. The police are monsters who categorize a benign and well-meaning Mexican human as a monster. The initial normally human police and Mexican man act as "aliens in human camouflage." The police function as invading alien infiltrators who turn Ramirez into something Other than American humanity, an alien in relation to the America he calls home. The police, who might be from outer space, could send Ramirez there. As I will explain, the Los Angeles Ramirez inhabits is a reality based (not all white) urban version of Mayberry relocated from North Carolina to the West. It is constructed from mid–twentieth century racial and racist reality; science fiction accoutrements illuminate this reality. Bradbury's Los Angeles could have been invaded by extraterrestrials (Martians?) in human camouflage police guise. "Never" is an alien abduction horror story in which the American government defines Ramirez as an alien subhuman, captures him, and removes him. In contrast, Mrs. O'Brian, whose last name identifies her with white Irish immigration to America, is viewed as normal.

Bradbury's 1947 story anticipates Rodriguez's 2010 appeal to the "conscious[ness] and humanity" of the Arizona officials whom he says define Mexican Americans as nonhuman. Bradbury responds to categorizing Mexican Americans as not human enough and as literally not welcome; he turns to science fiction to express the outrage he and Rodriguez share. Because the American government defines Ramirez as subhuman, it has the power to turn him into an invisible man whom O'Brian cannot see. The story is silent on the subject of where Ramirez is removed to. Is he sent to the realm of fantasy, the supernatural? Is he imprisoned within something as unreal as the Superman milieu Phantom Zone? Readers will never know. What is clear, however, is that Ramirez is relegated to existing on a different plane from Americans who are not designated as subhuman. The police remove him from O'Brian's rooming house and deposit him in some unknown version of a roach motel. They check him in and he can't check out. He is removed from the United States; he can never go home again.

Ramirez is re-located to an end of narrative space place readers cannot know. Ibsen's Nora — and Thelma and Louise, respectively, slam a door and careen over a cliff; they inhabit a place which includes imaginative geography, terra incognito, and the over the edge of the flat world map "here be dragons" location. Acting according to an alien abduction scenario, the police transform Ramirez into an alien and force him to leave America against his will. They turn a normal human being into a monstrous stranger in a strange land.

Applying the term "illegal alien" to real human beings is itself monstrous. It is illogical and unreal — and science fictional — to define a human as being alien in relation to other humans. In reality, only Native Americans are not illegal aliens in relation to America. But white Americans have applied no such logic to their dealings with American Indians. For example, this is what happened to the Indians who lived in proximity to Sedona, Arizona: "The Yavapai and Apache tribes were forcibly removed from the Verde Valley in 1876, to the San Carlos Indian Reservation, 180 miles southeast. One thousand five hundred people were marched, in midwinter, to San Carlos. Several hundred lost their lives. The survivors were interned for 25 years" ("Sedona"). Ramirez becomes analogous to these Indians in that he shares their fate: government sanctioned removal. The forced removal of the American Indians illustrates why it is illogical to turn human beings into science fictional alien abduction victims. All Arizonan Indians have the logical right to become immigration officers; they can logically demand that Sheriff Arpaio and his ilk go back to Europe, fade into the sunset.

Sedona, "Arizona's Little Hollywood" (McNeill) which played host to more than sixty Hollywood productions from the 1920s to the 1970s, is particularly relevant to discussing the merged science fiction and reality in "Never." The town's red rocks, which have an affinity to the unreal, represented Texas, California, Nevada, and Canadian border territory. During the 1930s, many grade-B westerns, including some that featured cowboy star George O'Brien, were filmed there. O'Brien might be pertinent to "Never" for the following reasons: his name evokes Bradbury's protagonist O'Brian, his father was the Director of Penology in California, and he served in President Eisenhower's "People to People" program. O'Brien, then, incarnates the story's main themes: the interplay between immigration, the penal system, and the need for improving "people to people" relationships. And, in addition to resembling various western locations, Sedona's red rocks could star as Bradbury's Mars.

The film *Der Kaiser von Kalifornien* (1936) is the most pertinent connection between Arizona and "Never." *Kaiser*, shot in Sedona, the first Nazi western, is an anti-capitalist propaganda diatribe about the rise and fall of German immigrant Johann Augustus Suter. *Kaiser* portrays a slightly modified swastika located on an Indian tent. This symbol is emblematic of "Never": the 1947 story appropriately links Ramirez to World War II–era removed Jews as well as to removed Indians. He can be seen as an Everyman in relation to minorities who are forcibly removed from their homes.

Since Ramirez has done nothing wrong, it is reasonable to ask why he is subject to involuntary removal. When formulating an answer, it is also reasonable to emphasize the story's 1947 publication date. Perhaps "Never" relates to "never again." Perhaps "Never" is an alternative history story in which American Nazis commit genocide against Mexican aliens. Perhaps Ramirez's arbitrarily applied alien status means that he could be sent to an American continent version of Auschwitz; upon arrival, he could be exterminated due to his arbitrarily applied subhuman classification. This potential horror story becomes even more depraved in that Ramirez's removal occurs against the background of extremely normal mundane behavior. When the police order Ramirez to vacate O'Brian's boarding house, her son worries that his dinner will "be cold" (Bradbury 110). He responds as if it is normal to turn a minority group member into an alien subhuman. He remains calm as he watches the police act like the firemen in *Fahrenheit 451*; Ramirez might be fated to become literally analogous to the books they burn.

The appearance of the word "oven" (Bradbury 108) in the story, of course, relates to burning. Bradbury's "oven," however, refers to American discrimination against brown skinned people, not the final solution to the Jewish question. Ramirez's complexion is compared to the color of O'Brian's pies: "Inside Mrs. O'Brian's kitchen, pies were baking in the oven. Soon the pies would come out with complexions like Mr. Ramirez's, brown and shiny and crisp.... The policemen leaned forward, lured by the odor" (Bradbury 108). Discriminating against people whose skin is as brown as O'Brian's pie crust is as American as apple pie. This normalcy is an American horror story. Real horror mingles with science fiction when Ramirez's skin color causes him to become a deported alien. Reading Bradbury's pie baking scene in terms of the cake eating revenge scene depicted in *The Help* imbues the story with a pie in the face response to racism. Hopefully, the policemen eventually do eat Bradbury's pie—along with the filling I imagine it contains—under circumstances exactly analogous to the culinary revenge the protagonist of *The Help* exacts. As the film stresses, racists who treat brown people like feces deserve to swallow real versions of their metaphorical intentions.

Even if Ramirez is not destined to become a North American Final Solution victim, he still faces a living death horror story scenario. If he is merely deported to a concentration camp free Mexico, he will endure science fiction alien hell on Earth: he will always differ from Mexicans who have not acculturated to America. He will be an alien who is in a worse situation than Steven Spielberg's E.T. landing in Los Angeles. E.T., who is rescued by his own kind and who can go home again. Ramirez, in contrast, can never go home again. Mexico is no longer his home. Immigrants, to a lesser degree than the metamorphosis Kafka describes, change into something different. A Mexican American cannot change back into an unhyphenated Mexican any more than a butterfly can regain its caterpillar status. Upon return to Mexico, Ramirez will become a stranger who is powerless ever again to live in the American world he calls his own.

Ramirez becomes an exile because the American government, represented by the police, is unable to see his humanity. The police transform him into an invisible man; the word "man" suddenly no longer applies to him. He becomes an invisible man both in H. G. Wells' science fictional sense and Ralph Ellison's racial sense. Ellison's unnamed protagonist's assertion "nor am I one of your Hollywood-movie ectoplasm" (Ellison 1) applies to Ramirez. Bradbury, Ellison — and Tiptree — allude to science fictional invisibility to rail against discrimination.

Rodriguez states that Mexican Americans, in regard to language, are labeled as not being good enough. Combining Bradbury's use of language with science fiction's invisibility trope reveals how the genre functions in "Never." "I See You Never" could mean that Ramirez is blind. When the phrase is read in terms of the language of science fiction, however, it becomes clear that "'I" refers to the American government which will never see Ramirez's humanity. This blindness results in the government having the illocutionary force to make O'Brian's following grammatically correct statement become a chilling true blunt finality: "I'll never see Mr. Ramirez again" (Bradbury 110). The police, who blithely dehumanize Ramirez, do not see the white O'Brian, whose family originated in Ireland, as being connected to immigration. They arrest Ramirez while they are "tipping their caps to Mrs. O'Brian" (Bradbury 109). Their intermingled respect and disrespect is as illogical as displacing Indians. O'Brian and Ramirez are both linked to immigration. Discrimination, then, is a cultural code which must be learned to be seen. This point — the subject of the *South Pacific* song "You've Got to Be Carefully Taught"— is exemplified by the *Star Trek* episode called "Let That Be Your Last Battlefield" (which is about aliens who have half white and half black bodies). Viewers have to learn that discrimination depends upon which half of the individual alien's body is black and which half is white. The arbitrary nature of learning to see racism pervades human cultures. While, for example, Americans valorize French Canadians for being French, British Canadians have discriminated against them. Americans have not learned to see white French people as subhuman. The point is that, in relation to Ramirez, it is grammatically correct for the government to say "I See You Never." "I See

You Never" is an edict. Ramirez is the person the government might never see as a human. The dehumanization he experiences in 1947 remains a normal occurrence in early twenty-first century America.

Rich explains why early twenty-first century America is not devoid of improvement in terms of how it treats the nonwhite racial Other. He emphasizes that a nonwhite racial Other is the President of the United States: "The election of an African American president is in itself an instance of American exceptionalism — an unexpected triumph for a country that has struggled for its entire history with the stain of slavery. 'Only in America is my *story* [italics mine] even possible,' Obama is understandably fond of saying, knowing full well that as recently as the year of his birth, 1961, he would not have been welcome in Mayberry, let alone the White House" (Rich 24). From our present perspective, we can see that American exceptionalism has made possible a less unhappy ending to Bradbury's story. Bradbury enables readers to see and correct past racist truth with an eye toward writing a better present and future. Obama calls his life a "story" — and Bradbury's story is pertinent to it. The president's story would have been impossible both in 1961 and in 1947 because, during these years, it would have been categorized as science fiction about a Midwestern white woman who marries a Kenyan and gives birth to the biracial president of the United States. Even in 2008, many people could not at first believe that a black American president was real. The Arizona racists Rodriquez addresses wish to erase Obama's story — send America back to the future. They wish to invent a time machine to send America back to the 1947 pre–Obama racism Bradbury depicts.

The following phrase is an appropriate response to the Arizona racists' desired science fiction assault: I see you never. Those who, like Rodriquez, oppose the Arizona racists never want to see America go back to the future to embrace past discrimination. Racists' going back to the future agenda must never happen; racism must become the reality Americans will no longer see, not the objective racists want to achieve. Hence, the title of Bradbury's subtle science fiction story, "I See You Never," when read in the context of President Obama's only recently no longer science fictional "story," shows that Bradbury uses words in a manner which linguistically involves seeing the future. He rewrites Rodriquez's following comment: "[e]ven in the realm of language, our English or Spanish have ever been good enough." Ramirez's English finally does become good enough. Bradbury's story and Obama's story "send out another message" (Rodriquez): welcome. Welcome to Mayberry, young Mr. Obama. Welcome to the White House, President Obama.

Obama has literally laid out a partial welcome mat to young illegal immigrants. According to the *New York Times*, "the federal government will grant a two-year reprieve from deportation to the illegal immigrants who are under age 31, have been in this country since they were children and meet other requirements. President Obama initiated the [Dream Act] program on June 15 [2012] using his executive authority.... He made broad use of his presidential powers, with as many as 1.7 million immigrants estimated to be eligible for deferrals" (Preston A14). Obama authors a story about these young illegal immigrants which is about how they will not live Ramirez's story. Arizona governor Jan Brewer writes in a manner which edits the positive story Obama intended the young immigrants to experience. She "issued an executive order on Wednesday [August 15, 2012] barring immigrants who are granted a reprieve from getting public benefits or obtaining drivers' licenses" (Preston A24). Obama is a higher powered executive than Brewer. Perhaps Obama's executive order will stand as a precursor to making real a story about immigration based upon the science fiction trope which describes Earth as one national entity, the egalitarian home of all humans.

This unification story has been made real in part: residents of all fifty states can travel freely throughout the United States and residents of many European countries can travel freely throughout the European Union. "I See You Never" suggests a stronger version of this existing border fluidity: all national boundaries should be eradicated. Earth is the home of all humans and all humans should be able freely to travel and live on Earth as they see fit. Making this science fiction scenario real nullifies the term "illegal alien"; the term becomes linguistically impossible—i.e., science fictional. Brewer requires help in regard to comprehending that, from the broad view science fiction provides, all humans are Earthlings; Earth, not a capriciously demarcated "United States" or "Mexico," is humanity's home. Now that humans have seen their planet from the perspective of outer space, it is clear that this view does not include the national boundary lines we arbitrarily put on maps.

What to do about Brewer's resistance to this universalist vision? Extraterrestrials could abduct her and force her to attend a University of Arizona science fiction course. This imagined alien abduction scenario can be expressed by using Bradbury's words: "The soft knock came at the ... [Arizona governor's mansion] door.... [Governor Brewer] just stood there, walled in and small.... [S]he did not seem to have words to explain" (Bradbury 108). If Brewer fails the imagined science fiction course's final on *The Martian Chronicles* and *Fahrenheit 451,* her resistance will be futile in relation to being forever deported to a science fiction classroom where she will be forced to learn the science fiction words which clearly explain that Earth is a unified whole.

The Trail of Tears Is "The American Way": Alien Abduction Stories

Equating Brewer with science fiction is not farfetched. In January 2012, when Brewer stood on the tarmac with Obama at Phoenix–Mesa Gateway Airport, she famously pointed her finger at his face — and became associated with science fiction language. A *Politico* article describing the event was called "Obama's Tarmac Tiff with Jan Brewer: The President Fights Back" (Brown). In addition to being the more powerful governmental executive, in terms of the *Star Wars* terminology the article's title evokes, Obama *is* the empire. Brewer called the situation an "uncomfortable encounter" (Brown). The "encounter," in terms of science fiction language, is a close encounter in which Brewer gives Obama her finger imbued with phallic power. She treats the President of the United States with the same audacious power entitlement with which the police treat Ramirez. Brewer does not touch Obama; "The police did not touch him [Ramirez]" (Bradbury 108). In both instances, extreme nonviolence is juxtaposed with extreme horror.

A CBN online article about Obama's chances of winning Arizona in the 2012 presidential election also uses science fiction language to describe Brewer. The article's title calls her a "conservative 'superhero'" (Brody). Bradbury would not concur with this "superhero's" particular version of "truth Justice and the American way." When responding to the possibility of Obama winning Arizona, Brewer says, "Not on my watch. Arizona is a red state, and we're going to keep it red" (Brody). Her diatribe shows that it would be natural for her to echo a racist edict such as the following one which the police issue to Ramirez: "That's six months too long" (Bradbury 108). Her vehemence can be countered by Bradbury's particular understanding of Arizona as a red state. According to Bradbury, literal redness causes Mars to be equated with the West. He turns to Arizona's Sonoran Desert red rock terrain when imagining his *Martian Chronicles* vision of Mars. Arizona is as red as Bradbury's red planet which, like Arizona, has an immigration problem. His science fiction novel's text chronicles the conflict between human colonizers and aboriginal Martians. This conflict underscores the fact that, like its real Mayberry counterpart, the supposed idyllic small town America *The Martian Chronicles* portrays is far from being so. Bradbury's Martians of course represent his concern for the racism American Indians and Mexicans such as Ramirez experience in America. What is black and white and red all over? Answer: Bradbury's science fiction texts which — counter to Brewer's racist red state assertions — assert that black/brown people and white people should be treated (or read) equally.

When Governor Brewer closely encounters Obama and vociferously insists upon her version of "the American Way" (a mythological unity), she resembles a parodic Mel Brooks movie protagonist. More specifically, when she "turns up the Arizona heat" (Brody), she acts analogously to plot elements in Brooks' *Blazing Saddles*. By showcasing a hero black sheriff who presides over an all-white town, the film satirizes the racism Hollywood myths about the West obscure. When Brewer points her finger at Obama on the tarmac located in a western state, she evokes Brooks' hilariously portrayed close encounter between Madeline Kahn playing Lili von Shtupp and Cleavon Little playing black Sheriff Bart. Brooks' West and Bradbury's West both satirize the "American Way" of the West. This "Way" involves social border crossings between groups who are culturally alien and experience unequal power in relation to each other. Like the Indians of the Southeast, the Arizona Indians and Ramirez are removed from their homes and forced to journey on a Trail of Tears.

Rich points out that the "American Way" Bradbury and Brooks satirize was a mid–twentieth century American social tenet: "In her revisionist 2008 excavation of that period, *Inventing the 'American Way,'* the historian Wendy Wall shows how America's mid-century political and business Establishments were sufficiently frightened about the prospect of disunity that together they manufactured an American consensus and sold it as a brand, the 'American Way.' The 'American Way' was promoted in every medium available, from billboards to Superman comics" (Rich 22). An example of this pervasive initiative shares the 1947 publication date of "Never." Rich explains: "One representative stunt in 1947 was the Freedom Train, a red-white-and-blue locomotive christened the *Spirit of 1776* and charged with barnstorming the nation to exhibit a bounty of historic and patriotic documents.... The mission was to demonstrate to one and all that America 'was unified, consensual and inclusive'—or, in other words, a nation adhering to 'the vital center,' a term that would be coined by Arthur Schlesinger, Jr. in 1949.... Attempts to permit white and black viewers in the South to mix freely were met with resistance, with the consequence that at a few stops, the Emancipation Proclamation was exhibited to segregated audiences" (Rich 22). Hence, the "American Way" is alternative history science fiction. Bradbury and Brooks de-mythologize the "American Way" in relation to the American West, pull back the curtain on American propaganda wizardry to reveal the true horror of racism and forced removal. The Freedom Train tracks are laid along the Trail of Tears.

Alien abduction is science fiction's version of the Trail of Tears. "Never" is written in a less fantastic (according to Eric S. Rabkin's use of the term) vein than two other science fiction alien abduction narratives: *Cocoon* (directed by Ron Howard in his future in relation to playing Opie Taylor of Mayberry on *The Andy Griffith Show*) and Bell's "The Chronicle of the Space Traders." The depiction of removal in these works differs, though. Like the Parsons women in "The Women Men Don't See," the elderly Floridians portrayed in *Cocoon* elect to be abducted by extraterrestrials. They conclude that embracing an alien unknown is a fate better than the ageism and death they will face if they remain on Earth. In contrast, "The Space Traders" depicts the racial Trail of Tears forced removal Ramirez experiences.

Even though *Cocoon* portrays a benign non-racialized version of alien abduction, the film is still applicable to "Never." When Wilfred Brimley playing Ben Luckett indicates to his grandson David that he will very soon be gone forever in outer space, David says, "And I'll never see you again." This statement, approached from Luckett's perspective, is a positive version of both O'Brian's sentence "I'll never see Mr. Ramirez again" (Bradbury 110) and Bradbury's title "I See You Never." David's comment connotes democratic choice, a true instance of the "American Way." Bernie Lefkowitz, Luckett's elderly friend, describes his reason for not choosing to cast his lot with the aliens: "This [Florida in particular and Earth in general] is my home. This is where I belong" (*Cocoon*). Ramirez never has the chance to live in America in a manner which coincides with Bernie's statement. The police literally tip their hats to O'Brian; the *Cocoon* screen writers figuratively tip their hats to clichéd science fiction language: Jack Bonner bids the senior citizens who leave his boat and join the aliens' adieu with these words: "May the force be with you." In contrast, the illocutionary force is not with removed American Indians and with removed Ramirez. Laws which deny their full humanity force them to leave their home.

"The Chronicle of the Space Traders" adroitly addresses the plight of removed people in terms of extraterrestrial abduction — and economic motivation. Delgado and Stefancic, in this essay's epigraph, equate Bell's story with the Trail of Tears. In addition, the appearance of the word "chronicle" in a science fiction story's title immediately evokes Bradbury's *The Martian Chronicles*. Bell creates a thought experiment involving what would happen if extraterrestrials wanted to buy all the black people in America. He posits that seemingly peaceful and powerful outer space aliens would offer Americans gold and clean nuclear power in exchange for all American black people. White American legislators pass a constitutional amendment to make the sale possible. Borders are closed; black people cannot escape to Mexico or Canada. Like Ramirez, they complacently prepare to be expelled. They face an *On the Beach* end of their world:

Crowded on the beaches were inductees, some twenty million silent black men, women and children, including babes in arms.... The inductees looked fearfully behind them. But, on the dunes above the beaches, guns at the ready, stood U.S. guards. There was no escape, no alternative. Heads bowed, arms now linked by slender chains, black people left the new world as their forebears had arrived [Bell 73].

Ramirez is an inductee of their ilk.

Brooklyn Law School professor I. Bennett Capers discusses "Space Traders" in terms of how newness relates to law and society: He mentions "Bell's use of narrative to talk about law in new ways, and to expose law in new ways. To expose society as well, and say the unsaid "(Capers 7). Ditto for Bradbury. In 1947 no one else wrote fiction about undocumented Mexicans; no one else at the time created literature about how the law functioned in relation to them. Bradbury predicted the future in terms of Arizona's racist law directed against Latinos; "Never" narrativizes this future vision which came true during Brewer's regime.

Bradbury, more specifically, predicted the future in terms of Arizona's controversial law SB 1070 (the Support Our Law Enforcement and Safe Neighborhoods Act), the broadest and most onerous anti-immigration measure ever proposed in American history. The law stipulates that it is a misdemeanor crime for an alien to be in Arizona without carrying required documents. Police determine an individual's immigration status during a "lawful stop, detention or arrest." Bradbury' s prediction is prescient to the extent that when Nina Perales, the Mexican American Defense Fund National senior counsel, argued against SB 1070 during a Columbia University Law School debate, she spoke in a manner analogous to a literary critic commenting on "Never." She spoke as a rhetorical daughter of Bradbury: "Perales said local police would be able to form a reasonable suspicion that certain Latinos — who make up 25 percent of Arizona's population — lack authorization to be present in the U.S., based solely on sight, as the law requires.... Perales ... views the law as a "'very strong attack on the civil rights of Latinos'" (Debate). The police treat Ramirez in the manner Perales describes.

In addition, Bradbury's "Never" can function as a counter attack to the assault on Latinos Perales argues against. She explains that she has been attacked because of her views. When she was told to go back to Mexico where she came from, she responded that she was born in Queens (Debate). She provides a real-world example of how the clichéd "go back to where you came from" insult is science fictional. A person who was born in Queens obviously cannot possibly emanate from Mexico. What is less obvious and absolutely shocking is the notion that deporting Mexicans, relocating Indians, and enslaving Africans may be less fantastic than trading American blacks to extra-terrestrials. Delgado and Stefancic make this point in relation to "Space Traders: "Bell's scathing skepticism thus finds ample support in our history. Indeed, the space trade might in some respect be even easier to carry out than African slavery or Indian relocation" (Delgado and Stefancic). If Earthlings meet visitors from the stars, trading minorities to them could become as normal in America as the pie whose odor entices the police in "Never" (Bradbury 108). And when people of color line up on the beach waiting to be taken away from Earth, white Americans might respond with the aforementioned complacency O'Brian's son manifests when he sees Ramirez being expelled (Bradbury 110). One day white Americans might "cry all the way to the bank" after they sell all American minority groups to extraterrestrials. Forced to embark on this potential new future Trail of Tears, the expelled people will literally cry all the way to a galaxy far, far away.

Delgado and Stefancic provide a more detailed explanation of how Capers' term "bridge," articulated in relation to imaginative and legal narrative, applies to "Space Traders":

> Bell's bleak Chronicle ... [is an] examples of storytelling, an emerging form of legal scholarship.... We believe that legal storytelling is a necessary transition between a more universalistic, static view of law and politics that prevailed until recently, and one more suited to our times.... In literature and the social sciences, the assumption that one "true" understanding of meaning or culture is possible has been vigorously challenged.... Legal storytelling is a means by which representatives of new communities may introduce their views into the dialogue about the way society should be governed. Stories are in many ways more powerful than litigation or brief-writing and may be necessary precursors to law reform [Delgado and Stefancic].

"Never" is "legal story telling" which is applicable to the early twenty-first century and is prescient about border crossing in relation to undocumented Mexicans. Bradbury uses subtle alien abduction science fiction to challenge a true understanding of meaning in culture in relation to undocumented Mexicans. Ramirez introduces non-racist views which are pertinent to how Arizona should presently be governed. "Never" is a powerful precursor to contemporary immigration law reform in Arizona.

Despite the affinity between "Never" and Arizona's troubling immigration situation, the story has not received pervasive media attention. Not so for "Space Traders." Conservatives called attention to a 1991 Columbia University protest in support of Bell's fight for a more diverse law school faculty. They chastised Obama for publically putting his arm around Bell at this public event — and circulated the picture of him doing so (Shapiro). This is how a conservative commentator lambasted Bell's science fiction story: "'Space

Traders' captures the stupidity, paranoia, and shameless race-hustling of the people that Obama embraces.... It's disgusting. It's revolting" (Schlichter). The commentator apparently does not like "Space Traders." I believe that he would not think twice about selling minorities to extraterrestrials. In the manner of Brewer chastising Obama on the tarmac, "Never" points a reprimanding finger at this commentator. Bradbury insists that racist law and diatribe must not fly.

Conclusion: Mr. Ramirez Is Science Fiction

Throughout his career, Bradbury brought science fiction to bear upon the literary mainstream, acted to quell the marginalization of science fiction. In *Shadow Show*, a collection of stories whose authors Bradbury influenced, editors Sam Weller and Mort Castle comment upon how Bradbury affected the canon by not adhering to separation edicts between literature and genre fiction: "He published in *Weird Tales* and *The New Yorker*.... With a creative output encompassing groundbreaking works of science fiction, universally recognized tales of fantasy, and award-winning realist contemporary prose, Ray Bradbury has spent his entire career ignoring and blurring the boundaries between genre and literature.... Over the course of his acclaimed career, Bradbury has charted and forged his own path, altering and expanding the canon ad infinitum" (Weller and Castle 1). Bradbury has fought against "textism," my term for discrimination against certain forms of imaginative discourse. Bradbury, like Ramirez, is a foot soldier in the war against marginalization.

Mars is the West. Arizona is Mars (vis-a-vis the Sonoran Desert acting as a template for Bradbury's personal vision of Mars). Another assertion needs to be stated: Ramirez *is* science fiction. Ramirez allegorically represents science fiction as a ghettoized, marginalized, expelled, and abducted from the canon, literary Other. Ramirez, cast as an allegorical figure, lacks a first name. Although Mr. Ramirez is no first nameless planet Vulcan denizen like Mr. Spock, it is logical to see him as a representation of science fiction.

First nameless Mrs. O'Brian and the completely nameless police also have their allegorical roles to play. Boarding house owner O'Brian represents the Caucasian mainstream literary canon. Ramirez is at once welcomed within and excluded from her boarding house. Similarly, the canon at once awards token inclusiveness to Bradbury and expels the preponderance of science fiction works. The fact that even marginally included figure Ramirez is ultimately cast asunder shows the precarious position of Bradbury as a pioneer of his own altering and expanding canonical path. The police represent the conservative critics who enforce the rules about what can and cannot be canonized.

"I'll See You Never" in its entirety adheres to this allegorical scenario. The entire story uses its own textuality to knock down the border wall separating science fiction from the mainstream; "I'll See You Never," a story oozing with subtle science fiction, was published in *The New Yorker*—despite the fact that many genre fiction detractors would never wish to see science fiction located within this august publication's rarefied fiction space. In 2012, *The New Yorker*'s science fiction issue included a story by Bradbury called "Take Me Home." Bradbury would certainly concur with designating *The New Yorker* as a proper home for science fiction.

Ruben Martinez, the author of *Desert America: Boom and Bust in the New Old West*, says that "the West is the future" (Martinez, *Smiley*). Inclusion — the end of the racism that excludes Ramirez as well as the textism that excludes science fiction — is the future. From the standpoint of the mid–twentieth century, Bradbury foresaw this ultimate future social, legal, and generic border crossing. In relation to prescience and depth, Bradbury is Super Border Crosser.

With regard to the 2012 presidential election results, I see Bradbury waving his finger in the face of Governor Jan Brewer. This imagined sight is of course at once science fictional and most definitely not subtle.

Works Cited

The Andy Griffith Show. CBS. 1960–1968. DVD.

Bell, Derrick. "The Chronicle of the Space Traders." *The Derrick Bell Reader.* Eds. Richard Delgado and Jean Stefancic. New York: New York University Press, 2005, 57–73. Print.

Blazing Saddles. Dir. Mel Brooks. Perf. Cleavon Little, Gene Wilder, and Slim Pickens. Warner, 1974. DVD.

Bradbury, Ray. *Fahrenheit 451.* Illustrated by Joe Mugnaini. New York: Ballantine, 1953. Print.

_____. "I See You Never." *The New Yorker.* 8 Nov. 1947. 108–110. Print.

_____. *The Martian Chronicles.* Garden City, NY: Doubleday, 1950. Print.

_____. "Take Me Home." *The New Yorker.* 4 and 11 June 2012. Print.

Brody, David. "Conservative 'Superhero' Brewer Turns Up Arizona Heat." CBN. 16 Aug. 2012. n.d. Web.

Capers, I. Bennett. "Derrick Bell's Children." *Columbia Journal of Race and Law.* 2012. 1 Dec. 2012. n.d. Web.

Cocoon. Dir. Ron Howard. Perf. Don Ameche, Wilford Brimley, and Hugh Cronyn. Twentieth Century–Fox, 1985. DVD.

"The Debate Over Arizona's Immigration Law: Necessary or an Excuse for Racial Profiling." *Columbia Law School Journal.* 1 Nov. 2010. Web.

Delgado, Richard, and Jean Stefancic. "Derrick Bell's Chronicle of the Space Traders: Would the U.S. Sacrifice People of Color If the Price Were Right?" *University of Colorado Law Review.* 62. 1991. 1 Dec. 2013. Web.

Ellison, Ralph. *The Invisible Man.* New York: Random House, 1952. Print.

E. T.: The Extra-Terrestrial. Dir. Steven Spielberg. Perf. Drew Barrymore and Peter Coyote. Universal Pictures, 1982. DVD.

The Help. Dir. Tate Taylor. Perf: Emma Stone, Viola Davis, and Octavia Spencer. Dreamworks SKG, 2011. DVD.

Ibsen, Henrik. *A Doll's House: A Play in Three Acts.* 1879. Boston: W. H. Baker, 1890. Print.

Kafka, Franz. *The Metamorphosis.* Leipzig: Kurt Wolf Verlag, 1915. Print.

Der Kaiser von Kalifornien. Dir. Luis Trenker. Perf. Luis Trenker, Viktoria von Ballasko, and Werner Kunis. Luis Trenker, 1936. DVD.

"Let That Be Your Last Battlefield." *Star Trek.* Episode 70. NBC. 1966. DVD.

Martinez, Ruben. *Desert America: Boom and Bust in the New Old West.* New York: Metropolitan /Holt, 2012. Print.

_____. Televised Interview. *The Tavis Smiley Show.* 24 Aug. 2012.

McNeill, Joe. *Arizona's Little Hollywood: Sedona and Northern Arizona's Forgotten Film History 1923–1973.* Sedona: Northedge, 2010. Print.

Michaud, Jon. "Ray Bradbury in *The New Yorker*." *The New Yorker.* 6 June 2012. Web.

Millhiser, Ian. "10 Worst Things Arizona's Racist Sheriff Joe Arpaio Has Done." *AlterNet.* 10 May 2012. Web.

Preston, Julia. "Young Illegal Immigrants Jump at a First Chance." *New York Times.* 16 Aug. 2012. A1, A14. Print.

"Republicans, Unplugged." Editorial. *New York Times.* 7 Nov. 2012. 8 Nov. 2012. Print.

Rich, Frank. "Mayberry R.I.P." *New York Magazine.* 30 July 2012. 18, 20–24. Print.

Rodriguez, Roberto. "Arizona: Indian Removal or Modern-Day Reducciones" *Dissident Voice: A Radical Newsletter in the Struggle for Peace and Social Justice.* December 31, 2010. n.d. Web.

Schlichter, Kurt. "Derrick Bell's 'Space Traders' Review: Racist Paranoia ... and George Clinton's Disembodied Head." *Breitbart TV.* 8 Mar. 2012. 20 Oct. 2012. Web.

"Sedona, Arizona." *Wikipedia.* 12 Mar. 2012. 1 Dec. 2012. Web.

Shapiro, Ben. "Obama: 'Open Up Your Hearts and Your Minds' to Racialist Prof." *Breitbart TV.* 7 Mar. 2012. 2 Oct. 2012. Web.

Shute, Nevil. *On the Beach.* New York: William Morrow, 1957. Print.

South Pacific. 1949. Dir. Joshua Logan. Music Richard Rodgers. Lyrics Oscar Hammerstein II.

Star Trek. NBC. 1966–1969. DVD.

Star Wars. Dir. George Lucas. Perf. Mark Hamill, Harrison Ford, and Carrie Fisher. Lucasfilm, 1977. DVD.

Thelma & Louise. Dir. Ridley Scott. Perf. Susan Sarandon, Geena Davis, and Harvey Keitel. Pathé, 1991. DVD.

Tiptree, James, Jr. "The Women Men Don't See." *Warm Worlds and Otherwise.* New York: Ballantine, 1975. Print.

The Twilight Zone. CBS. 1959–1964. Image Entertainment. DVD.

Wall, Wendy. *Inventing The American Way: The Politics of Consensus from the New Deal to the Civil Rights Movement.* New York: Oxford University Press, 2008. Print.

Weller, Sam, and Mort Castle. *Shadow Show.* "Introduction." New York: HarperCollins, 2012, 1–7. Print.

Wells, H. G. *The Invisible Man, a Grotesque Romance.* New York: Harper, 1897. Print.

"You've Got to Be Carefully Taught." *South Pacific* libretto. Music Richard Rodgers. Lyrics Oscar Hammerstein II. 1949. Print.

Bradbury's
Survivance Stories

Grace L. Dillon

We are one race of many fantastic parts, each needful of the others' survival, each wanting to know the other." — Ray Bradbury, *A Feasting of Thoughts, a Banqueting of Words: Ideas on the Theater of the Future*

There has been a centuries-long conflict between the wretched of the earth and those who ruled and exploited them. Does anyone imagine that this situation has ended? — Howard Winant, *The New Politics of Race*

When I was a child, I spoke as much Finnish as I could capture from the pacifist-anarchist community where my father, mother, six brothers and sisters and I attended open meetings to debate scripture and the latest news out of *Suomen Kommunistinen Puolue*, and as much Anishinaabemowen as I could gather from my grandfather, an Ojibwe who cooked for the lumberjack camps during timber harvest and who vexed my parents whenever we visited by fishing Eskimo Pies from a glossy white fridge that had a bullet hole straight through its door. But mostly I spoke the lingua franca of the Cold War era; *nin jaganashim*, in other words. This all happened in the Upper Peninsula of Michigan (which is not *really* Michigan) and not so long ago, though the U.P., back then anyway, must have slipped time in an effort to remain quiet and feral, while electric metropoles like Cheybogan, Peshtigo, Petosky, and others tempted us to cross borders. But we never did. Civilization might as well have been 65 million miles away.

It was a frontier, no different from the beauteous frontier of the mythical American West, except that snow stood in for sand and chimerical whiteness trumped bona fide burnt sienna and brown. Without technologies like

television and cinema, we lived like eighteen-hundred-something homestead-
ers making a go of it at the end of an alternate Oregon Trail. So we read,
sometimes by candle and lantern light, like those pioneers of old; we played
at *indians* in the woods, pretending to be like our grandfather and grandmother and *omishomissan gaie okomissan gaie od anike-omishomissan gaie od
anike-okomissan*. At a very young age, I mitigated the isolation of my snowy
frontier by reading books borrowed from my parents' library and from my
grandfather's library, books borrowed from the pacifist-anarchist Finns in the
nearest faraway town; I read Aristotle, Plato, and Dante, Dostoevsky, Jane
Austen, Milton, C. S. Lewis, E. Rice Burroughs — anything I could get my
hands on, all before I was twelve. One day, my grandfather handed me a copy
of *Dandelion Wine*.

After that, the Martians came.

Today it is easy to unwrap allegories inside Bradbury stories. Everyone
agrees that the Martians are like *indians* and that the Earthmen are like white
men manifesting their destinies in a fiction that existed before the age of
(post)colonial theory. As I grew older, I began to hear stories of how Mr.
Bradbury explicitly explained his plan to refashion the Niña, the Pinta, and
the Santa Maria in the guise of silver space ships — I even came across verbatim
transcriptions where Bradbury says of the *Chronicles*, "I pointed out the problems of the Indians, and the western expansionists" (qtd. in Wolfe 110).

All can agree that Bradbury's Mars is like the Western American frontier,
one possible setting for first contact narratives that juxtapose native and
invader, colonized and conqueror, and that this conceit reflects a longstanding
tradition in science fiction. "Ray Bradbury's *The Martian Chronicles* (like
countless other space-colonization novels) portrays frontiersmen from Earth
encountering alien civilization clearly modeled on those encountered by Europeans in the 'New World,'" according to David Mogen (159). Gary K. Wolfe
concurs, "This focus is not, of course, unique to Bradbury; Bradbury merely
provides what may be one of the clearest links between the traditional frontier
orientation of much of American literature and the attempts to extend this
orientation into new worlds, which is characteristic of a great deal of science
fiction" (104–105). Patrick B. Sharp writes, "Bradbury used the frontier landscape to question notions of cultural and racial superiority" (223).

Today when I juxtapose Bradbury's Mars with stories of what Bradbury
might be teaching us about the inevitability of space colonization as the next
step in the progress of human civilization, or about the efficacy of space race
when expensive problems need to be fixed right here on home, or about the
implications of settler-*indian* (Vizenorian "*i*") frontier contact for the history
of democracy in the United States, or about how Martian-settler relations

invoke Cold War praxis, or about how nuclear holocaust can achieve ameliorating effects, or about how Martians are actually human dreams ... I think about playing *indian* in the U.P. woods, about reading *The Martian Chronicles* to my sisters and brothers late into the night when twenty-foot snowdrifts isolated our farm and we couldn't get to meetings until a thaw, and about my grandfather, and about my father, and about being *indian*, and about those Bradbury stories where distinctions between Earthmen and Martians blur, where Martians, *Nanabozho nâssa ijinagwad*, morph themselves into othered selves, *bejig kéma gaié nabané*, to placate Earthmen, where Earthmen become Martians, where Martians may have been Earthmen all along—"Dark They Were and Golden Eyed," for instance, and "The Third Expedition," "The Martian," "The Million-Year Picnic."

Wayne L. Johnson writes, "The Martians' ability to change their appearance is something of a survival mechanism" (36).

Gerald Vizenor (Anishanaabe) writes, "Survivance is an active sense of presence, the continuance of native stories, not a mere reaction or a survivable name. Native survivance stories are renunciations of dominance, tragedy, and victimry" (*Manifest Manners* vii). "Survivance" is an aesthetic response to the extirpation and genocide of Indigenous peoples by Euro-Western explorers and empires that began with sixteenth-century foraging in what (to them) constituted a "new world" in the Americas and that continues in what (to them) constitute "third worlds" today. Vizenor explains, "Native American Indians have endured the lies and wicked burdens of discoveries, the puritanical destinies of monotheism, manifest manners, and the simulated realities of dominance, with silence ... and the solace of heard stories" (*Manifest Manners* 4). While "survivance" as applied by Vizenor and others focuses on the Native American experience in North America, analogous thinking is pervasive among other modern cultures that have experienced trauma and loss. Survivance resembles the related concepts of "creative masochism" (Tatsumi), "creative defeat" (Shigeto Tsuru), "the mental history of failure and defeat" (Masao Yamaguchi), and "the strategy of being radically fragile" (Seigo Matsuoka) that Japanese intellectuals have used to characterize their nation's cultural and psychological response to the post–World War II occupation period, when Euro-Western agents of imperialism appropriated and hybridized Japanese culture (Tatsumi 3).

If Bradbury's analogies teach us anything about the historical experience of Indigenous, First Nations, and Native American peoples, they teach survivance.

Survivance. Not survival. At first glance, the term survivance might seem to connote survival, *nin ishkone*— specifically, the survival of Indigenous peoples in the face of colonization, victimization, and attempted dominance first by European and then by American settlers. Ernest Stromberg writes, "While 'survival' conjures images of a dark minimalist clinging at the edge of existence, survivance goes beyond mere survival to acknowledge the dynamic and creative nature of Indigenous rhetoric" (1).

Vizenor elevates survivance from the status of a mere label of experience to the level of ontology. Rather than thinking of survivance as a way to describe historical behavior (as in "the Cherokee who survived the Trail of Tears were settled in Oklahoma"), survivance implies the complex totality of sentient being. Vizenor calls it a "practice" in contrast to "ideology, dissimulation, or a theory" ("Aesthetics" 11). In effect, survivance is a way of life, what many Indigenous scholars refer to as "Indigenous ways of knowing." Most importantly, survivance establishes Native identity *in the present*, as opposed to viewing Native experience as a relic of the past, consigned to museum exhibits and to the nostalgic longing for a return to the noble, savage identity dissimulated in many seminal and commercially successful science fictional contact narratives in the guise of an alien race: from the Na'vi that inhabit James Cameron's Pandora, for example, back to the red Martians of Helium in Edgar Rice Burroughs' Barsoom books.

Viewed through this lens, Bradbury's Martian-*indians* no longer suffer erasure as a "lost civilization" while privileging invading Earthmen (even sad and guilty ones) as conquers or colonizers.

Consider the Bitterings in "Dark They Were and Golden Eyed" (1949), anthologized in *A Medicine for Melancholy*. An Earth family arrives on Mars as part of a colonial expedition, learns later that Earth has been ravaged by nuclear war ("No more rockets to Mars, ever!"), and processes their now utter isolation in differing ways until mother, children, and, finally (reluctantly), father ultimately "go native," transforming into the Martian race whose cultural memory dwells in the abandoned indigenous marble villas, in the canal waters, and in the surrounding hills, *manito* haunting alien human imaginations.

Dialogue bald-facedly makes the allegorical connection plain for readers who otherwise might miss it:

> "Colonial days all over again," [Harry Bittering] declared. "Why, in another year there'll be a million Earthmen on Mars. Big cities, everything! They said we'd fail. Said the Martians would resent our invasion. But did we find any Martians! Not a living soul! Oh, we found their empty cities, but no one in them. Right?" [Bradbury, *Medicine* 95].

Elsewhere Harry underscores the association between his invasion of Mars and nineteenth-century Manifest Destiny on Earth by lamenting his failure to follow best practice in settler etiquette:

[T]he Earthmen had felt a silent guilt at putting new names to these ancient hills and valleys.... The American settlers had shown wisdom, using old Indian prairie names: Wisconsin, Minnesota, Idaho, Ohio, Utah, Milwaukee, Waukegan, Osseo. The old names, the old meanings [Bradbury 97, 98].

Harry's vacillation between exuberant colonial pride and what can best be described as white guilt is largely overlooked by commentators. In *White Awareness: Handbook for Anti-Racism Training*, Judith Katz writes, "Feelings at the unconscious level include fears and fantasies related to racism. These fears and fantasies are a result of personal experience, as well as stereotypes and myths about Third World people with which they have been indoctrinated" (94).

This characterization certainly applies to Harry, who is overcome with trepidation at the Bittering's initial arrival on Mars ("At any moment the Martian air might draw his soul from him, as marrow comes from a white bone" [94] and thereafter simply frets (*Alone, thought Bittering. Only a thousand of us here. No way back. No way. No way; Bittering wandered into the garden to stand alone in his fear; The fear was never gone. It lay with Mr. Bittering and Mrs. Bittering, a third unbidden partner at every midnight talk, at every dawn awakening* [95]).

Harry's paranoia reaches extremes as he fantasizes the familiar adventure trope of cannibals hiding in the native landscape: "What would happen to him, the others? This was the moment Mars had waited for. Now it would eat them" (97). And "because the cannibal flourishes in a climate of frozen isolation, confronting the monster in ourselves and in our culture begins to break down the experience of separation," writes Deborah Root, "imagining other people as deadened objects becomes less appealing, if we can bear to look in the mirror" (205).

> "Here you are, Harry." Sam handed him a pocket mirror. "Take a look at yourself." Mr. Bittering hesitated, and then raised the mirror to his face.
> There were little, very dim flecks of new gold captured in the blue of his eyes.
> "Now look what you've done," said Sam, a moment later. "You've broken my mirror" [Bradbury 100].

Underscoring the racialization of Earthling-into-Martian transformation, Harry measures his wife's prolonged transformation in terms of darkening skin color: "Dark she was, and golden, burnt almost black by the sun." Throughout his existence as an Earthman settler, Harry is beset by feelings of helplessness, isolation, and fear.

> Staring at the mountains wildly he thought: *Are you up there? All the dead ones, you Martians? Well, here we are, alone, cut off! Come down, move us out! We're helpless!*; Mr. Bittering felt very alone in his garden under the Martian sun, bent

here, planting Earth flowers in a wild soil; Mr. Bittering put his hand to his head. He thought of the rocket, himself working alone, himself alone even among his family, so alone; The fear would not be stopped. It had his throat and heart. It dripped in a wetness of the arm and the temple and the trembling palm [98].

The adversary he so fears is the prospect of change, a term that is introduced at least a dozen times in the story. Earth seeds planted in the soil of the family's alien garden undergo genetic alteration (*Do you see? They're different. They've changed! They're not peach blossoms any more!* [98]). Renewing the theme of cannibalistic consumption, whereby the eater is altered by the spirit of the thing he eats (*Now [Mars] would eat them*), Harry fears the metamorphosed carrots, radishes, and peaches that grow in garden: "We must get away," said Bittering. "We'll eat this stuff and then we'll change — who knows to what. I can't let it happen" (99). In short, Harry Bittering is obsessed with the fear of change:

> In the Earthmen's settlement, the Bittering house shook with a feeling of change....
> If I lie here long enough, he thought, the water will work and eat away my flesh until the bones show like coral. Just my skeleton left. And then the water can build on that skeleton — green things, deep-water things, red things, yellow things. Change. Change. Slow, deep, silent change [Bradbury 101, 103].

Bradbury imaginatively constructs racial unity as a metamorphosis of a white American into the unknown Other that he fantasized and unconsciously feared. Perhaps the Other that Harry has in mind never existed, really: "But did we find any Martians! Not a living soul!" Notably, Harry is the only settler among the one thousand, including his wife and children, who fears changing the way he sees people. — His son eagerly wants to change his human name from "Tim" to the Martian language, "Linnl." His wife remains nonchalant about her and the children's altered bodies; memory of her former self seems to have vanished:

> "Cora, how long have your eyes been yellow?"
> She was bewildered. "Always, I guess."
> "They didn't change from brown in the last three months?"
> She bit her lips. "No. Why do you ask?"
> "Never mind."
> They sat there.
> "The children's eyes," he said. "They're yellow, too."
> "Sometimes growing children's eyes change colour" [103].

Mrs. Bittering's assertion that changing eye color indicates *growth* suggests that Harry has much catching up to do if he wants to retain his Martian family. The prominent emphasis on change begs the question of what, precisely, is changing, or, put differently, of how we are able to measure it. The change from Earthling into Martian fundamentally is an exercise in racial formation, expressed in terms of skin color and other genetically modified physical characteristics.

As the thousand individual colonists adapt, *Kitchimokomamens, Kitchimokomanikwens, Kitchimokomanikwe,* all including Harry's family reveal an easygoing demeanor that deserves some attention. Racially stereotyped language punctuates descriptions of their new state of being — *Kitchimokoman* — and fearing the imagined Martian menace early in the story, Harry asserts a set of middle-class American values as safeguard against hostile natives: "We're clean, decent people" (96). As the Earth settlers transform more completely into Martians, their behavior is described in terms of laziness and indifference: "Men stood in the open door and talked and joked without raising their voices. Once in a while they gave him a hand on lifting something. But mostly they just idled and watched him with their yellowing eyes" (101). Harry focuses good old American ingenuity on building a rocket that can take everyone back to Earth, yet he receives only the "reluctant help of three indifferent men" (101). These idle comrades advise *mañana,* urging him to forget worry and work until autumn: "Their voices were *lazy* in the heat." Even décor reflects the lure of indolence: "'I've some ideas on furniture for the villa,' he said, after a time. 'Big, *lazy* furniture'" (106).

The story essentially narrates Harry's anxiety about *losing* his anxiety about completing the rocket that could preserve the former Earthling identity and sustain the othering of Mars as *not home* and of Martian racialization as *other than.* The Bitterings' final break with Earth and white identity is illustrated in microcosm when Harry leaves the settlement cottage for the marble ruins of the Martian villas: "Looking at the small white cottage for a long moment, he was filled with a desire to rush to it, touch it, say goodbye to it, for he felt as if he were going away on a long journey, leaving something to which he could never quite return, never understand again." The long journey begins with nostalgic longing for a former state of being, literally a skin that he is shedding, *gichi-mookomaan,* as the cottage, *nin wâbishkis,* proxies for the lost America of a dying Earth, *Gaa-waabaabiganikaag* — soon enough, within five years, to be precise — American Earthman Harry Bittering no longer exists, the settlement town remains "empty," and a newly arrived expedition finds "native life in the hills," presumably Harry, his family, and the original settlers whose race has been completely remade.

"Indian-hating identified the dark others that white settlers were not and must not under any circumstances become," writes Richard Drinnon (xxvii).

Renewing racially intonated language, the narrative casts a young lieutenant in the cycle of first contact; he defines "native" identity in terms of skin color: "Dark people. Yellow eyes. Martians. Very friendly." While the lieutenant is assured of amicable relations with the locals, appeased because they seem to catch onto the English language facilely (for why would the conqueror deign learning the language of the soon-to-be subjugated?), the captain's reply hints at a colonial character: "'Dark, eh?' mused the captain. 'How many?'" (108). While it is possible that the captain is simply curious about Martian demographics, one gets the sense that "dark" means "dangerous" on Mars once again, and that the captain immediately sizes up the Martians as a martial adversary, a commercial property, or both.

"The modern epoch was founded on European imperialism and African slavery," writes Winant. "Both these systems were organized racially. The theft of labor and life, of land and resources, from millions of Africans and Native Americans, and from Asians and Pacific Islanders, financed the rise of Europe.... Conquest, imperial rule, and the chattelization of labor divided humanity into Europeans and others" (205).

The longstanding cycle of Euro-American empire repeats with the arrival of the post-war colonizers five years after nuclear holocaust has changed the Bitterings' point of view to yellow, *nind osâwis gaie nind osâwa*, five years after the news of the bombs began to blacken them, *nin makatéwitchige*—Ferocious and unending cultural and psychic energies were expended to sustain this schism [between Europeans and other], which was also constantly challenged and undermined in innumerable ways," Winant continues. *Pitchâ babamadizwin. Pitchâ chibimoodaywin.* Harry's long journey out of the white settler cottage to which he can never return is renewed in the figure of the lieutenant whose transformation is beginning as this story ends: "The lieutenant snapped his gaze from the blue colour and the quiet mist of the hills far beyond the town. 'What? Oh, yes, Sir'" (109).

What had the captain been instructing him to do? In the end, it won't have made any difference.

If we extrapolate the western American frontier from Bradbury's Mars, it is easy to analogize Earth's colonization with white settlement of the West and to read Bradbury's Martian stories as challenging and undermining the ferocious and unending cultural and psychic energies that were expended to sustain the schism between white and Indigenous peoples, *nawaii waiâbishki-wedjig gaie bemâdisidjig bejig gaie bemâdisidjig nabané.*

Akhi nin adjinikas. "Manifest Destiny" was, of course, a coinage, not an invention. Sacvan Bercovitch points out that the Puritan founders sought to re-enact the biblical story of Exodus and made their *chibimoodaywin* migration about conquest and occupation rather than emancipation (qtd. in Spanos 127). Edward Ingebretsen writes, "Manifest Destiny could be read onto new-world geographies partly because its terms had already been established as a moral geography by which to map the wild terrain of the soul" (200). "At our country's founding," writes Gary P. Stewart, "Americans embraced a sense of the nation's universal mission and manifest destiny" (59).

"Manifest Destiny proclaimed the Messianic mission with its accompanying myth of the 'promised land,' and the terror of white supremacy," according to E. San Juan, Jr. (3). "The idea of innate Anglo-Saxon superiority was nurtured by, and became an integral part of, American racial ideologies of the late eighteenth and nineteenth centuries," writes Audrey Smedley. "It also became part of American mythology.... Indeed, the myth was at the heart of the doctrine of Manifest Destiny, by which some white Americans expressed belief in themselves as a "chosen people" destined to rule and civilize others, according to Smedley (188).

"Manifest destiny has always been a bloody and disastrous notion. In its American manifestation it has led to the killing of millions of Native Americans, Mexicans, and Filipinos," writes Lawrence Davidson. "What was originally only an alliance between God and America's continental destiny, has now become God's alleged assertion that American manifest destiny is synonymous with the world's destiny" (169).

"Manifest Destiny would cause the death of millions of tribal people from massacres, diseases, and the loneliness of reservations. Entire cultures have been terminated in the course of nationalism. These histories are now the simulation of dominance.... The postindian simulations are the core of survivance ... the postindian conversions are in the new stories of survivance over dominance" (*Manifest Manners* 4).

"Dark They Were and Golden Eyed" erases white supremacy and ameliorates Manifest Destiny by imagining racialized *becoming* in place of racialized *othering*. There really are no Martians. There is only us. This message of unity, which might strike us, even today, as wishful thinking at best and as hallucinatory in practice, brings *The Martian Chronicles* to an end:

> The night came down around them, and there were stars. But Timothy couldn't find Earth. It had already set. That was something to think about.
> A night bird called among the ruins as they walked. Dad said, "Your mother and I will try to teach you. Perhaps we'll fail. I hope not. We've had a good lot to see and learn from. We planned this trip years ago, before you were born. Even if there hadn't been a war we would have come to Mars, I think, to live and form our own standard of living. It would have been another century before Mars would have been really poisoned by the Earth civilization. Now, of Course — "

They reached the canal. It was long and straight and cool and wet and reflective in the night.

"I've always wanted to see a Martian," said Michael. "Where are they, Dad? You promised."

"There they are," said Dad, and he shifted Michael on his shoulder and pointed straight down.

The Martians were there. Timothy began to shiver.

The Martians were there — in the canal — reflected in the water [Bradbury, *Martian*, 181].

"Dark They Were and Yellow Eyed," "The Million-Year Picnic," "The Third Expedition" et al. (all chronicles of Martian metamorphosis) are mixedblood messages and survivance stories. Gerald Vizenor describes his own Anishinaabe-French-Swedish *indian* identity as mixedblood/crossblood and characterizes his own work as "encountering a mixedblood experience in a creative way, to give consciousness to crossblood experience, to create a consciousness of crossblood identity" (qtd. in Coltelli 112). This project is an act of survivance. The policies of Manifest Destiny established Indian identity in terms of blood quantum even though for peoples like the Anishinaabeg, "Percentage of Indian and white blood was not a determining factor in distinguishing a mixedblood.... For the most part the distinction was cultural" (*The People* 107). Manifest Destiny strategized robbing Native Americans of the right to decide who they are and how they choose to define themselves; blood quantum legislation imagined Indians would breed themselves out. "The practice of determining tribal identities by geometric degrees of blood, or blood quantums, as if blood could be measured in degrees, has elevated a racist unscientific method to the level of a federal statute," writes Vizenor. "Elected officials expected the tribes to vanish ... certain that in one or two generations tribal cultures would no longer exist" (*The People* 106).

"The mixed-blood person has the power to expose *mishi nimakinago* constructed nature of Indian identity, to prove the difference between blood and culture," writes Deborah L. Madsen (41). Vizenor calls upon mixedbloods to create "a new consciousness of co-existence" and to "swim deep and around through federal enclaves and colonial economic enterprises in search of a few honest words upon which to build a new turtle island" (*Earth Divers* ix–xi). "This is a confrontation in so many ways," he says. "It's an international confrontation, it's a confrontation of American racialism because of the genetic categories of who's Indian, and I'll not allow the world to deny my experience just to fulfill some genetic category" (Coltelli 112).

Nind anishinâbew, nin wâbitchiia.

Gerald Vizenor is a mixedblood trickster prophet, *Neegoniwabungigaywin*, who commands white tropes, *enallage*. He spells *indian* using a lowercase "i" and italic font to draw attention to the strangeness of the word. "Indians" don't exist. "The word Indian, and most other tribal names, are simulations in the literature of dominance" (*Manifest Manners* 10–11).

> The American settlers had shown wisdom, using old Indian prairie names: Wisconsin, Minnesota, Idaho, Ohio, Utah, Milwaukee, Waukegan, Osseo. The old names, the old meanings [Bradbury *Medicine* 98].

Ray Bradbury is a mixedblood European American, *nigân win dibâdjim gedijiwebak bidâdjimotage gaie*. "In recounting his own mixed European ancestry," writes Jonathan R. Keller, "Ray Bradbury offered these private thought in an undated high-school diary entry: 'That's the one thing I like about being an American. You have so many bloods and types mixed into you it is impossible to brag about one's racial credentials, one just confusedly gives up and says, Hell. I'm an American. Isn't that enough?'"

"Ray Bradbury does not displace the issue of American racism from a representation of our real, lived culture to a pretend culture on another planet with others, that is, aliens," writes Ellen Bishop. He "brings us down to Earth in order to emphasize the social, political, and psychological effects of racism on the 'master' class" (87). Eller writes, "Bradbury touches on all the capital crimes that can result from bigotry" and creates white characters that transform racially so that they resemble those they have "so terribly wronged" (235). Speaking of *The Martian Chronicles*, Bradbury once said "I was warning people ... I was *preventing* futures."

Win nigamis. Win niganâdjim, imagining the old names, the old meanings. His survivance stories advocate a mixedblood message of racial diversity.

Ray Bradbury died on Tuesday, June 5, 2012, according to most reputable sources.

In its obituary, the *Indian Today* Media Network repeated the Harper-Collins vision of Bradbury's Mars.

> "Bradbury's Mars is a place of hope, dreams and metaphor — of crystal pillars and fossil seas — where a fine dust settles on the great, empty cities of a silently destroyed civilization," reads the description on his official website from his publisher, HarperCollins. "It is here the invaders have come to despoil and commercialize, to grow and to learn — first a trickle, then a torrent, rushing from a world with no future toward a promise of tomorrow. The Earthman conquers Mars ... and then is conquered *by* it, lulled by dangerous lies of comfort and familiarity, and enchanted by the lingering glamour of an ancient, mysterious native race."

"This may or may not have been influenced by his wife's Cherokee heritage," the *Indian Today* Media Network goes on to say. "Her grandmother was Cherokee, according to the site's entry about Marguerite Bradbury, who died in 2003."

Sam Weller confirms the ancestry of Marguerite Susan McClure: "She came from a rich genealogical background.... Her grandfather had married a full-blooded Cherokee Native American in the late 1800s."

I accessed the story by Sam Weller and many others when I was asked to write this essay on how Ray Bradbury shaped the way that I imagine Indigenous futurisms.

The site included a panel of pictures of Marguerite Susan McClure, Ray Bradbury's Cherokee wife.

Waiâbishkwid!

I thought that, or something like it, immediately. In that split second, I recognized myself as a *bitterling*. Not an *Earthling*. Not a *Martian*. In that instant, the spirit sank heavy into the marrow of my bones.

On September 20, 2012, in a televised debate between incumbent Massachusetts Senator Scott Brown and Elizabeth Warren, the senator said, "Professor Warren claimed that she was a Native American. A person of color. And as you can see, *she's not.*"

I watched that debate during the time that I was working on this chapter. And I considered the words of the prophet.

Something was going to happen.... It was coming nearer.... At any moment it might happen.

And then it happened.

Works Cited

Bishop, Ellen. "Race and Subjectivity in Science Fiction: Deterritorializing the Self/Other Dichotomy." *Into Darkness Peering: Race and Color in the Fantastic.* Ed. Elisabeth Anne Leonard. Westport, CT: Greenwood Press, 1997. 85–104. Print.

Bradbury, Ray. *The Martian Chronicles.* New York: Bantam, 1962. Print.

_____. *A Medicine for Melancholy.* New York: Bantam, 1960. Print.

Coltelli, Laura. "Gerald Vizenor: The Trickster Heir of Columbus: An interview." *Native American Literatures Forum* 2–3 (1990–91): 101–16. Print.

Davidson, Lawrence. "Christian Zionism as a Reflection of American Manifest Destiny." *Critique: Critical Middle Eastern Studies* 14.2 (Summer 2005): 157–169. Print.

Demy, Timothy J. *Politics and Public Policy: A Christian Response: Crucial Considerations for Governing Life.* Grand Rapids: Kregel Academic & Professional, 2000. Print.

Drinnon, Richard. *Facing West: The Metaphysics of Indian-Hating and Empire Building.* Norman: University of Oklahoma Press, 1997. Print.

Eller, Jonathan R. *Becoming Ray Bradbury.* Urbana: University of Illinois Press, 2011. Print.

Indian Today Media Network. "Martian Chronicles Author Ray Bradbury Dies at 91." June 6, 2012. Web.

Ingebretsen, Edward J. *Maps of Heaven, Maps of Hell: Religious Terror as Memory from the Puritans to Stephen King.* Armonk, NY: M.E. Sharpe, 1996. Print.

Johnson, Wayne L. "The Invasion Stories of Ray Bradbury." *Modern Critical Views: Ray Bradbury.* Ed. Harold Bloom. Philadelphia: Chelsea House, 2001. 9–22. Print.

Katz, Judith H. *White Awareness: Handbook for Anti-Racism Training*. Norman: University of Oklahoma Press, 1978.

Madsen, Deborah L. *Understanding Gerald Vizenor*. Columbia: University of Southern Carolina Press, 2009. Print.

Mogen, David. "Native American Visions of Apocalypse: Prophecy and Protest in the Fiction of Leslie Marmon Silko and Gerald Vizenor." *American Mythologies: Essays on Contemporary Literature*. Eds. William Blazek and Michael K. Glenday. Liverpool: Liverpool University Press, 2005. 157–167. Print.

Root, Deborah. *Cannibal Culture: Art, Appropriation, & the Commodification of Difference*. Boulder, CO: Westview Press, 1996. Print.

San Juan, Jr., E. *Cultural Studies: Critiques of Multiculturalist Ideology and the Politics of Difference*. Durham: Duke University Press, 2002. Print.

Sharp, Patrick B. *Savage Perils: Racial Frontiers and Nuclear Apocalypse in American Culture*. Norman: University of Oklahoma Press, 2007. Print.

Smedley, Audrey. *Race In North America: Origin and Evolution of a Worldview*, 3d ed. Boulder, CO: Westview Press, 1998. Print.

Spanos, William V. "Edward W. Said and Zionism: Rethinking the Exodus Story." *Boundary 2* 37.1 (2010): 127–66. Print.

Stromberg, Ernest. *American Indian Rhetorics of Survivance: Word Medicine, Word magic*. Pittsburgh: University of Pittsburgh Press, 2006. Print.

Tatsumi, Takayuki. *Full Metal Apache: Transactions Between Cyberpunk Japan and Avant-Pop America*. Durham: Duke University Press, 2006. Print.

Vizenor, Gerald. "The Aesthetics of Survivance." *Survivance: Narratives of Native Presence*. Ed. Gerald Vizenor. Lincoln: University of Nebraska Press, 2008. 1–24. Print.

_____. *Earthdivers: Tribal Narratives on Mixed Descent*. Minneapolis: University of Minnesota Press, 1981. Print.

_____. *Manifest Manners: Narratives on Postindian Survivance*. Lincoln: University of Nebraska Press, 1994. Print.

_____. *The People Named the Chippewa: Narrative Histories*. Minneapolis: University of Minnesota Press, 1984. Print.

_____. "Trickster Discourse: Comic Holotropes and Language Games." *Narrative Chance: Postmodern Discourse on Native American and Indian Literatures*. Ed. Gerald Vizenor. Albuquerque: University of New Mexico Press, 1989. 187–211. Print.

Weller, Ray. "Marguerite Bradbury: 1922–2003." *Ray Bradbury Official Site*. Web.

Winant, Howard. *The New Politics of Race: Globalism, Difference, Justice*. Minneapolis: University of Minnesota Press, 2004. Print.

Wolfe, Gary K. "The Frontier Myth in Ray Bradbury." *Modern Critical Views: Ray Bradbury*. Ed. Harold Bloom. Philadelphia: Chelsea House, 2001. 103–24. Print.

A "Night Meeting" in the Southwest

Hospitality in The Martian Chronicles

ADAM LAWRENCE

> Beyond the objective, which is always already correlative to a prior "aim" and intention to discover — behold an other that *reveals itself*, but that does so precisely in surprising the intentions of subjective thought and eluding the transcendental synthesis. An exceptional idea of the Infinite that has escaped being, and of a presence stronger and more venerable than the totality. An idea that cannot, by virtue of the "ontological argument," be locked within the totalizing look, nor to some other world, nor some empty heaven. — Emmanuel Lévinas, *Alterity and Transcendence*

Much of the negative criticism of Ray Bradbury's *The Martian Chronicles* has emphasized the book's failure to depict the Red Planet plausibly and scientifically; in the sixty years since the book's publication, critics have continually cited this weakness as a sign of Bradbury's nostalgic, inward-looking vision. Back in 1956, for example, Damon Knight made the following observation in his short essay "When I Was in Kneepants: Ray Bradbury": "wherever he is required to invent anything — a planet, a Martian, a machine — the image is flat and unconvincing. Bradbury's Mars, where it is not as bare as a Chinese stage-setting, is a mass of inconsistency; his spaceships are a joke; his people have no faces. The vivid images in his work are not imagined; they are remembered" (4). About twenty years later, George Slusser argued that "the main thrust [of Bradbury's vision] is never forward to Utopia, but backward, toward some golden age or American Eden, to a place of childhood innocence, toward lost harmony with nature" (4). As recently as 2011, Eric Rabkin concluded an essay by proclaiming, "In *The Martian Chronicles*, Ray Bradbury will live forever and generations will say, reading him in whatever form, that there the American myth comes clean again, small town life welcomes us all, and his Mars, undoubtedly, is heaven" (103). The theme in all three criticisms is self-reflexivity: Bradbury apparently invents worlds that do not estrange but rather reaffirm a comfort zone.

To begin with, it is hard to deny that there is a certain flatness to some of Bradbury's landscapes, but Bradbury's "Mars" in particular is flat for two reasons: it functions as a mirror, reflecting back the beliefs, ideologies, preoccupations, and obsessions of those who wish to imagine "space" or the conquering of it in the name of progress; it also resembles the bleak, desert landscape of Arizona, where Bradbury lived, briefly, in the mid–1920s and early 1930s (Reid 1–2), and where he developed his early impressions of Southwestern indigenous culture. Related to this flatness is a certain opaque sense of identity, which has been attributed to some flaw in Bradbury's writing but which is actually the consequence of a distorted mirror image: if his characters "have no faces," it is often because they are hiding their true form, for the sake of protecting or preserving identity. It is certainly true that both the Martians and the Earthlings in Bradbury's book view each other rather conservatively at times (Mucher 177), relying on a sort of Platonic essentialism that dictates an eternally unchanging image of an immutable type.[1] For example, the Martian patriarch Mr. K. feels that he has grasped the essence of the "American astronaut," as derived from his wife's erotic dream; so he, like countless Martians after him, proceeds to eliminate the Nathaniel Yorks who will inevitably invade Mars. However, Bradbury clearly laments this view, and demonstrates another approach to self-other relations, expressed through visionary characters such as Spender, Wilder, Tomás Gomez, and the apparitional Martians who attempt to communicate with the Terran visitors at various points.

While *TMC* does feature Bradbury's (in)famous small-town nostalgia (in scenes where a suburban American neighborhood has been seemingly transported to an alien planet), it also demonstrates the poisoning effects of a romanticism that can lead one culture to impose itself on another, obliterating a civilization in the process. Early stories in the collection demonstrate Bradbury's attempt to conceptualize "Mars" as an indigenous culture that undergoes radical changes as the result of colonization. But despite these instances of racial intolerance and miscommunication, and despite the fact that the original destruction of the Martian culture has made "contact" nearly impossible, a later tale, "Night Meeting," emphasizes the importance of hospitality and peaceful cultural exchange. The story features the dream-like encounter between a human, Tomás Gomez, and a Martian, Muhe Ca, along an "ancient highway." Their meeting involves a series of misses: they are face to face but cannot touch each other; objects they hold have no substance for each other. But while they become disheartened by the conflict of worldviews, they manage to form a bond on the basis of their mutual loneliness. Although Tomás identifies himself as a "colonist" from Earth, his name, along with the description of his features, link him to Latino or Hispanic culture, which has suffered various forms of racial and social oppression in the United States. Moreover, this fictional night meeting between two strangers is Bradbury's gesture of hospitality to both the Southwestern culture he knew and future civilizations (or planets) that might suffer as the result of other colonizing missions.

While the frontier motif is clearly significant in *TMC*, the book also contemplates the ethical dilemma of invasion, assimilation, and hospitality. In "Night Meeting" Bradbury moves away from violence and negation and towards a philosophical contemplation of the self-other encounter; the story characterizes hospitality as a form of *substitution* in which the identity of the self is challenged and, in a number of ways, transformed by the call of the other whose presence demands sensitive contemplation. According to Walter Mucher, *TMC* participates in a "Late Modern" trend of evaluating the "spatiotemporal self," a key component of Edmund Husserl's phenomenological analysis of the "subjective act of self-definition" (172). Emmanuel Lévinas, who is not mentioned by Mucher, also considers this self that seeks to articulate its existence, but he goes further than Husserl by questioning the very violence implied by one's teleological search for self: the so-called *being-in-the-world* is necessarily disturbed by its proximity to others who refute the supremacy of the self and of totality. Moreover, particular portions of Lévinas's work mesh well with Bradbury's theme of presenting and estranging the human spatiotemporal self-assurance. The philosophical evaluation in *TMC* was inspired by Bradbury's sense that the expansion of the West and the destruction of indigenous culture was in itself a "science fiction story" (qtd. in Wolfe 104)—a temporal disruption of an environment, leading to an irrevocable change, but also an ethical call for sympathy and hospitality. However much critics have come to see *TMC* as a nostalgic yearning for days of innocence and for an Edenic return to the agrarian pioneer settlement era, the course of the narrative implies that Bradbury was looking for *something new*: the "Night Meeting" in the Southwest/Mars is the product of this philosophical vision.

The "Metaphysical Desire" and "Substitution": The Philosophical Scaffolding of TMC

Such a philosophical reading is warranted since *TMC* is structured on a metaphysical collision: two worldviews, two sets of voices are competing for primacy. However, contrary to some interpretations of the book, Bradbury does not ultimately subscribe to the belief that American identity was somehow rooted in the settler's experience of developing a democratic, individualist society through a primordial struggle with a bleak desert or wilderness landscape.[2] While some characters, such as Sam Parkhill, clearly identify the colonization of Mars as a natural or inevitable process, related to "the law of give and take" (Bradbury 134), others, like Jeff Spender, explicitly condemn the invasion of Mars or, like Tomás Gomez, open themselves up to an encounter with alterity. In her contribution to this collection, Gloria McMillan discusses how university students have responded to the motif of conquest, particularly in the sequence "And the Moon Be Still as Bright." The American identity, according to the frontier myth, is only possible through the firm grasp of the land, and yet it is precisely the *failure* to grasp that Bradbury seeks to underscore, particularly in "Night Meeting." Read through Lévinas, we could view this beautiful tale as the desire to disavow knowledge — not so much information or intelligence, as vision or awareness — the very structure of *knowing* that grasps the other before contact even occurs. This sense of knowing is exemplified in the practice of classifying different genera in nature; it is certainly apparent in the very goal to "understand" Mars: in both cases, "vision dominat[es] the process of becoming" (Lévinas, *Alterity* 11). "Night Meeting" implies a critique of both colonization and the primordial instinct to know and see that drives the mission to Mars. This particular "chronicle" constitutes the optimum experience of the self-other relation, free of violence and hatred: the encounter is peaceable, beautiful, and exemplary of an ethical relation that exists nowhere else in the book.

Walter Mucher's article "Being Martian: Spatiotemporal Self in Ray Bradbury's *The Martian Chronicles*" highlights the self-other encounter in "Night Meeting" and other sequences, although specifically through Husserl's spacetime phenomenology. According to Mucher, *TMC* "reflects the Late Modern's incursion into a psychological and phenomenological humanism in which, in their search for a new self, the protagonists re-create a world of multiple readings which re-trace their exploits, moving forward while continuously looking back over their own experiential shoulders" (171). In light of the many stories in which this "search for a new self" is challenged, it seems quite appropriate to view Bradbury's "chronicle" as an account of the *failure* to account for the "other." While the characters themselves might wish to construct a linear story of their progress, the encounter with an other (planet) reflects back the violence of their intentions, disrupts the traceable flow of time, and places them face-to-face with their own limit, their own mortality. Despite the growing sense that Martian culture has been replaced by Earth culture, the conclusion of Bradbury's book implies that the human visitors to Mars have themselves been *substituted* for something else.

According to Lévinas, substitution is dependent upon my awareness of the other's proximity to me, my consciousness that the other is not reducible to images or themes (*Otherwise* 100) but is, in fact, a real presence. This relation between a self and an Other is an existence necessitated by immediacy, which, through my primordial instinct to claim an identity, I try to ignore. In this state of egoism I "live from..." the texture of the world around me, including the soil, water, and air, and I find "nourishment" in the very energy that comprises the world and the others that populate it (*Totality* 110–111). The "metaphysical desire," however, "tends towards *something else entirely*, toward the *absolutely other*" (33; original emphases): this is a desire that does not attempt to absorb the other but, in turning towards it, turns away from the self, from the enjoyment of totality. The "absolute other" is not the "other" that I *think* I see, and the "other" in which I find nourishment, but rather the other that is still to come. Further, this desire toward the "absolutely other" takes me away from the place that I call home. As Lévinas elaborates,

> The metaphysical desire does not long to return, for it is desire for a land not of our birth, for a land foreign to every nature, which has not been our fatherland and to which we shall never betake ourselves. The metaphysical desire does not rest upon any prior kinship [33–34].

The "I" in this scenario becomes an exile, removed from the state of "living from" or knowing a territory, and estranged from a state of knowing itself. More than this, once I have made this sojourn, I can never return, never remove myself from this foreign land. Further, my movement toward the other in this case is not based on a prior filial connection, or familiar friendship, but on an entirely new relationship with the absolutely foreign and unfamiliar "stranger." While Lévinas uses the analogy of exile here, he lays great emphasis on the actual experience of a self-other relation, an experience that radically displaces my previous knowledge of otherness, foreignness, and foreign lands.

The parallels between Lévinas's ethical philosophy and science fiction are apparent in the basic notion of a "desire for a land not of our birth," although it is clear that many of the astronauts in Bradbury's book are really looking for reflections of themselves. Nevertheless, *TMC* traces the instances where the metaphysical desire creates a sense of exile and estrangement; in such scenarios, the self does not seek out the other with specific intentions or preconceived ideas, but listens and waits. As Lévinas describes, the "call" of the other is not simply a form of speech but the possibility of contact: "The Other — the absolutely other — paralyzes possession, which he contests by his epiphany in the face" (*Totality* 171). On the one hand, Lévinas speaks of a face, an expression, and a promise of speech, and on the other, a touch, a grappling, and a loss of sensation. In this scenario, the incessant need of the other constitutes a "persecution" of my self-centred ennui (*Otherwise* 124) and an infinite and arduous call for a responsibility to every other person. I am summoned and "inspired" (114), dislodged from my previous separation from the other, from my belief in his invisibility, from my enjoyment of him through images and themes, and brought into full contact with him. However, a full response here is not anything like action but rather complete passivity: I am detained. Lévinas states that infinite responsibility "commands me and ordains me to the other, to the first one on the scene, and makes me approach him, makes me his neighbor [....] [The demand] provokes this responsibility against my will, that is, by substituting me for the other as a hostage" (11). We can understand this otherwise radical claim as a restatement of the "metaphysical desire," which "approaches me not from the outside but from above" (Lévinas, *Totality* 171). Some of the language here evokes the religious notion of a divine invasion; however, Lévinas is describing a physical and primordial contact that happens to be *inspired* by a metaphysical desire. Despite the astronauts' impression in *TMC* that they are dreaming or seeing apparitions, the most striking occasions of the self-other encounter are rendered through the bodily sensation of touch, caress, and genuine astonishment — all signs of what Lévinas calls "substitution," in which the self is overwhelmed by the presence of an Other that cannot be pre-determined.

Ethical Substitution *in* The Martian Chronicles: "Ah Yes, That Other Over There"

We can find initial parallels to this brief sketch of Lévinas's ethics in numerous scenes where Bradbury's Martians and Earthlings view each other only as alarming or nourishing dreams, and where — especially in the case of the Earthlings — the *other* place serves either as a mirror for the Ego or a negation of the Ego's dreams, rather than a disorienting displacement that leads to a new relationship with the "alien." We might consider this state as being *prior to* the "metaphysical desire," where the self-absorbed Earthling refuses to open himself up to a land not of his birth.

The type of "Mars" that each group of Earthlings meets depends upon the spirit behind the visit: because the first several expeditions are driven by egomania, Mars often appears to be a reflection of the *known* landscape. Although we do "see" Mars through the eyes of Mr. and Mrs. K. ("Ylla"), the discovery of a new planet and culture seems less important to the first astronauts than the acknowledgment of their accomplishment. The dilemma of hospitality, as presented in "The Earth Men," is the fundamental reliance upon response time: humans identify hospitality as an immediate action; one is hospitable when one responds instantaneously. This explains the crew's disappointment when their arrival is greeted with indifference: as far as the Earthmen are concerned, the Martians are behaving *in*hospitably. When Captain Williams appears suddenly at the door of Mrs. Ttt, she appears to behave rudely, slamming the door in his face. "'See here!' cried the man when the door was thrust open again. He jumped in as if to surprise her. 'This is no way to treat visitors!'" (Bradbury 17). Although we eventually discover that the inhabitants do not believe the astronauts are "real" but rather mentally deranged Martians, the captain nevertheless fails to even consider the possibility that the entire mission constitutes an invasion of privacy, a potential destruction of the environment, and a military threat. However, if the American astronauts fail to pull back from their egoism, the Martian psychologist who eventually diagnoses the men as insane fails to see them through anything other than his pre-conceived theory: to the Martians at this point, the Earthling other cannot exist as anything but a hallucination. So the communication breakdown and the failure of contact can be attributed to egoism on both sides; the destruction of peaceable communion is consummated when the psychologist shoots the four astronauts and then himself.

The members of the Third Expedition behave more cautiously than their predecessors, but the discovery that Mars looks a hell of a lot like Green Bluff, Illinois (Bradbury 35) implies that they, too, have been unable to free themselves from the frontier ideology that the strange elementary world is for their consumption and nourishment. The Earthlings discover that their old friends, family, and even their homes have been reproduced here on Mars. Far from reflecting Bradbury's nostalgia, "the similarity between Earth and Mars is treated ironically, with the intention of making the reader realize and be shocked in their naïve expectations" (Martín-Albo 106). Whether through actual colonization or egoistic projections (which, according to Lévinas, would amount to the same thing), the Martian landscape has been transformed from sparse desert to lush small town, complete with small brick houses, tall maples and churches (Bradbury 33). The Martians do discover that, like Mars, Earth has no future: Mars is now a necessary escape route for a culture on the verge of destroying itself. However, Martian culture, too, is on the wane since it has been uprooted in order to successfully transplant Earth culture. As we discover in a later sequence, "The Martian," the natives of this planet have begun assuming human form. In "The Third Expedition," Captain Black does not yet have proof of this shape shifting, but theorizes the possibility that the Martians have used telepathy to reproduce human forms and culture in order to lure humans to their destruction (46–47). He then becomes afraid for his life, wondering if his supposed brother will "change form, melt, shift, and become another thing, a terrible thing, a Martian. It would be very simple for him just to turn over in bed and put a knife into my heart" (47). Like the other fantasies, this paranoiac one comes true: Black jumps up out of bed and tries to leave the room but, we are told, "never reached the door." The final few short paragraphs (47–48) describe in spare chilling language the death of sixteen men (the exact number of astronauts of the third expedition), their funerals, and a final dirge. Here again an opportunity for fellowship, communion, and hospitality ends in violence and death, but Bradbury suggests that the Earthmen may have brought this upon themselves.

As we discover, the human impostors act purely on the imagined projections of the Earthlings: when an astronaut begins to think of his family, they suddenly appear; when he begins to remember specific details about his parents and siblings, they act accordingly; and if he suspects that they are not really his family but "terrible" things, Martians, they once again follow through on his worst fears. As Gary Wolfe argues, Bradbury shows the consequences of relying on past logic to make future judgments: "It is this persistence of the past, this trap of the old values of civilization, that initially destroys the unprepared explorer on the alien frontier" (113). Human morality, bound as it is to the dichotomy of good/evil and the instinct to repress imagination and speculation, hollows out the future like the bleak and bare Martian landscape. The wish to shatter the illusion of peace, hospitality, and friendship indicates something of the Cold War tenor of Bradbury's time and the "precariousness of human existence in an atomic age" (Hoskinson 349): to Captain Black, these "friends" are actually Martians (reds, Commies) in disguise, waiting to pounce on us in our most vulnerable moments. While it may be right to assume that the Martians in this tale are ironic representations of egotistical behavior, the Earthmen also mistake an ethical gesture for an aggressive one: Martians have substituted their entire culture, their own identity, in order to establish a community. The mournful tone of the final section of the story is not simply an imitation of human emotion but the sadness at the loss of friendship and communion.

By the time we reach "Night Meeting," the visitors have finally received a response to their demands, but not before they have radically altered the Martian environment. This is to say that, like the European explorers of the New World, the aggressive demand for hospitality overruns the possibility of *further* hospitality: Martian culture has perished. The colonization of Mars, then, is a situation where the guest has become a host but fails to take responsibility for this new role. In Lévinas's terms, Mars serves the purpose of nourishing the dreams of Earthlings, and cannot be of any use unless it accommodates these big, heavy dreams. However, Bradbury wishes to modify this approach to otherness, particularly in episodes where a character opens himself up to a "metaphysical desire" and, more significantly, to "substitution."

In contrast to the early stories, "Night Meeting" presents the scenario in which a colonist is content to *receive* Mars and its foreignness rather than impose a pre-conceived fantasy (like the men of the "Third Expedition"). The title of the story itself implies that it does not give primacy to illumination and vision; the protagonist, already in a land that is not of his birth, will grope his way blindly in order to find another kind of *seeing*: through the eyes of another — the ghostly apparition of a Martian who, despite his revenant form, insists on the reality of his presence. Seeing a small, insect-like craft hovering before him, Tomás Gomez hails the figure in a nervous but unsuspicious gesture of welcome. It is important that, unlike previous men who walk the Martian landscape, Tomás carries with him no paranoia, no weapons, but rather the willingness to embrace the strange:

> Tomás raised his hand and thought Hello! automatically but did not move his lips, for this *was* a Martian. But Tomás had swum in blue rivers on Earth, with strangers passing on the road, and eaten in strange houses with strange people, and his weapon had always been his smile. He did not carry a gun. And he did not feel the need of one now, even with the little fear that gathered about his heart at this moment [Bradbury 81].

It is notable that Tomás does not reference the familiar environs of Earth but rather its "strange" aspects: he is used to being unused to others, and yet his approach is openness and a readiness to accept difference. His name, along with the brief reference to his "brown hands" (79), implies his association with other marginalized cultures in the United States: the subtle message here is that, while Tomás is apparently a representative of "the Future" (85), the fate of the Martians echoes the fate of Southwestern inhabitants whose colonial past is obliquely referenced.

The "fear" that Tomás experiences is appropriately "little" since it has not been enhanced or exaggerated by egoism. The very spirit of this encounter is, according to Lévinas, just as it *ought* to be: in the form of a blessing and a welcome:

All encounter begins with a benediction, contained in the word "hello"; that "hello" that all *cogito*, all reflection on oneself already presupposes and that would be a first transcendence. This greeting addressed to the other man is an invocation. I therefore insist on the primacy of the well-intentioned relation toward the other. Even when there may be ill will on the other's part, the attention, the receiving of the other, like his recognition, mark the priority of good in relation to evil [*Alterity* 98].

Tomás, who has been advised earlier that evening by an old gas attendant to be open to surprises and to accept Mars for "what it is" (Bradbury 79), does not presume that the Martian approaching him has evil motives. His "well-intentioned" gesture of saluting the stranger can be contrasted with Sam Parkhill's paranoid and aggressive reaction in "The Off Season," when the Martians approach him in their sand ships: "I don't like strangers. I don't like Martians, I never seen one before. It ain't natural" (134). In contrast to Sam, who obsesses over land ownership and familiarity, and who prefers to shoot first, Tomás is ready to accept the unfamiliar and chooses to smile instead.

While the identity of the Martian is already pre-determined by his dark skin colour and golden eyes (features emphasized in the earlier sequences), the ensuing exchange is a defamiliarizing experience for both human and alien. For example, Tomás offers a coffee to Muhe, but when he hands over the cup it passes right through the other's hand and spills on the ground. They are able to communicate, once Muhe uses telepathy to learn Tomás' language; but they *see* essentially different things: they live in different chronotopes. Tomás sees his Green City, a colony established one year before by Earthlings, while Muhe sees his Eniall Mountains, which have stood for countless generations; Tomás sees the ruins of Martian civilization, while Muhe sees a flourishing city, with "canals [...] full of lavender wine" (Bradbury 83). Making full use of his poetic skills, Bradbury constructs an achingly beautiful scene where two strangers first try to welcome each other, but cannot actually make contact, and offer sustenance, but fail in the transaction. The two men insist on the presence and substance of their home cities, but fail to even establish this. Like Lévinas, Bradbury is emphasizing that one's selfhood is only confirmed by an Other's presence, and that confirmation does not establish, legitimize, or prioritize the self but, on the contrary, puts its authority into question. As Mucher notes, in his philosophical analysis of this story, "Each represents the other's reality by projecting its negation unto the other" (182). On the one hand, both the offering of verbal communication and sustenance (in the form of a steaming cup of coffee) fails because each man exists on a different plane. However, while each may not be able to see what the other sees, they can see each other, even if they see *through* each other. From a philosophical point of view, the other sees through the illusion of the self's supremacy, at the same time that the self needs the other to confirm the illusion. This type of exchange is hinted at in "The Earth Men," where the astronauts' feat of scientific progress is diagnosed as hallucinatory projections (Bradbury 27–30). Martians see psychosis, where the Earthlings see real, sane accomplishment: a successful voyage to Mars.

There is no question, then, that, in *TMC*, Bradbury sympathizes more with the Martian civilization, which consistently exposes the flaws in both the rational-technological frame of mind and the romantic illusions associated with space exploration and colonization. This is not to say that the Americans fail in their attempt to establish settlements but rather that their self-constructed narrative of settling another "Wild West" (in the "final frontier") underscores all the more their imperialistic motives. Tomás's exchange with Muhe reveals the reality of Earth's destruction of Martian culture as well as the illusion of Earth's supremacy and authority. Mars is a curious hybrid of Martian and Terran (American) influences; the very landscape of Mars maps both colonization and a lingering doubleness or hybridity. As Homi Bhabha describes, the "civilizing mission is threatened by the displacing gaze of its disciplinary double" (Bhabha 86). Earth has always been here (Mars), which means that it has never been there in reality: it has been a projection of Earth culture. As the man from the third expedition surmises, this constructed culture provides a way of assuaging the acute sense of loneliness of living on Mars and the longing for Earth (Bradbury 39). Muhe's insistence that his culture is alive is not so much an illusion that Martian culture still thrives so much as the illusion that Earth's culture thrives *on its own*.

As a stylistic feature, Bradbury uses recurring tactile imagery to underscore the theme of loneliness and estrangement. When the two men comprehend that their worldviews have been undermined, they experience a cold feeling: "an ice was in their flesh" (84). As the conversation switches from debate to thoughtful conjecture, each man admits that he has recently felt cold when walking along this road, as if he were the last man alive on this world (85). For each man, the presence of the other is estranging, but this experience binds them. The greatest moment of disillusion is also the greatest moment of fellow-feeling: "it was like talking to an old and dear friend, confiding, growing warm with the topic." When they "agree to disagree" (86), this concession is not simply a cliché but the acknowledgment of the (un)condition of their friendship: it is a transference that does not deprive the other of his selfhood even while it does not prioritize it. Muhe's and Tomás's beautiful misunderstanding reminds us that hospitality is infinite *because it can never really (fully, completely) be offered.* The host is already overcome by his sense of absence; the other makes him disappear by his dominant presence. The master of the house has lost his authority completely.[3] Muhe may not be "real" in the sense that Tomás is used to, but neither are the fantasies about humanity's dominance in the universe. As Mucher notes, "it is not the Martian who is the Other, as Earth would have us believe. Rather, it is the intruding Earthness, which shows its otherness previously concealed by its imperialistic superiority" (182).

"Night Meeting" evokes a whole series of philosophical questions about the ethical dimensions of response time — or the interval in which a request waits to receive an answer — as well as the problems of perception. Given the recurring tension between reality and dreams in *TMC*— of instances where an Earthling sees one thing that is a hallucinatory projection to a Martian — it is apparent that Bradbury is interested in probing the ways in which Americans perceive the world, or worlds, around them. As it appears to the Men of the third expedition, Mars is very similar to Illinois (Bradbury 38). Actual Martian culture is perceived only as dead, as having passed on, according to the members the fourth expedition ("June 2001:— And the Moon Be Still as Bright"). As team doctor Hathaway reports to Captain Wilder, the Martians died of contact: "chicken pox" (50). This, of course, is reminiscent of the native experience in North America. But the specific disease in *TMC* is the very contagious virus of loneliness, depression, and paranoia.

Yet, it would be inaccurate to say that the disease — the psychosis, the contamination of a culture — leads to a blindness, or rather that the failure to communicate and come to terms with disparate worldviews is necessarily the result of blindness. On the contrary, it is *vision*— dominant and overriding — that corrupts the first four expeditions on Mars; it is vision that prevents rather than promotes an ethical relation between self and other; it is vision, moreover, that insists on this dichotomy of self/other, with the Self capitalized and dominant, over the lower-case and passive other. "Ethics," Lévinas argues, "is an optics. But it is a 'vision' without image, bereft of the synoptic and totalizing objectifying virtues of vision, a relation or intentionality of a wholly different type" (*Totality and Infinity* 23). Such a passage seems to resonate well with science fiction, which, before and after existential phenomenology (Husserl, Heidegger), has concerned itself with parallel realities and universes, and the defamiliarizing or estranging effects of (time) travel. Moreover, the "optics" that Lévinas speaks of resembles that of the astronaut who time warps from one dimension to another; the result is that new and old worlds collide and cause a momentary obfuscation of vision. To return to Bradbury, space travel may have a certain vision in mind, and it may hope to perceive Mars, for example, as a totalized entity already plotted on the Earthling's map, but this vision is diffracted or refracted by the presence of another culture. So, Mars, as Captain Williams discovers in "The Earth Men," is actually the planet "Tyrr" (Bradbury 17). In "Night Meeting," the very condition of the separation between Tómas and Muhe is their mutual blindness: they cannot see the objects of each other's civilization. Yet, their mutual blindness also questions the supremacy of one dominant vision, or of vision, period.

Bradbury suggests that neither sight nor communication can suffice to form an ethical relation: contact — physical, concrete, and intimate — is the very condition of any "relation." He underscores this point in the repeated reference to both the cold and warm feeling each man experiences throughout the exchange. In the first instance, Muhe tosses a knife in the air for Tómas to catch and, like the coffee cup, it passes right through the other's hands. When he bends to pick up the knife he discovers he still cannot touch it and recoils "shivering" (82). This, of course, anticipates the later observation by each man that the coldness settling on him makes him feel as if he were "the last man alive on this world" (85). This coldness indicates the absence of the touch, of contact, the chilly shadow of a past intimacy, which is no more. As Lévinas has noted, "proximity" still allows for that space, for that interval in the exchange, in which the other can be free to move forward and back, even while it also initiates the moment of contact (*Otherwise* 81–83). Moreover, accepting or receiving the other means also opening oneself up for a *new* intimacy. Consider the following, striking passage:

> Now he [Tomás] looked at the Martian against the sky.
> "The stars!" he said.
> "The stars!" said the Martian, looking, in turn, at Tomás. [...]
> You could see stars flickering like violet eyes in the Martian's stomach and chest, and through his wrists, like jewelry. [...]
> They pointed at each other with starlight burning in their limbs like daggers and icicles and fireflies, and then fell to judging their limbs again, each finding himself intact, hot, excited, stunned, awed, and *the other, ah yes, that other over there*, unreal, a ghostly prism flashing the accumulated light of distant worlds [Bradbury 82–83; emphasis added].

By all appearances, this is an erotic description of the anticipation of contact where each man views the other as a stunning piece of cosmic energy, twinkling and flashing in this mere fragment of time; where each man finds himself disarmed — "hot, excited, stunned, awed" — by the beauty of the other man. It is certainly the most sexually suggestive of all "encounters," with the exception of Mrs. K's erotic dreams of the American astronaut in "Ylla." But, while Mr. K. pre-determines the evil of the other by imagining conspiracies, Tomás arms himself with only a smile, clearly delighted, if disarmed, by the attractive other. More so than any other story, "Night Meeting" attains the optimum level of Bradbury's philosophical exploration. The difference here is that there is no longer a collision of worlds: two worlds enter each other's sphere in a brief moment of union.

Both Bradbury and Lévinas criticize the human capacity to hierarchize into right and wrong, self and other, being and not being. The "otherwise than being" of Lévinas's ethics refers to the entity that cannot be extrapolated with our current language: the "other" is otherwise and still to come. It is noteworthy that while Tomás exclaims, "Good lord, what a *dream* that was," Muhe *thinks*, "How strange a *vision* was that" (86; emphasis added). The subtle difference is a crucial one: Muhe's reaction seems to imply that there is something *prophetic* in the encounter, that there may be more "night meetings" to come; even while Tomás's interpretation dis-establishes the very notion of a "real" Self: the Martian was, simply, a "dream." Ethics for Lévinas is not the reversal of roles —*you* now become the aggressor — but the relinquishing of the power to *be* aggressive, to kill another. Morality, on the other hand, seeks to punish or overthrow the other in the name of some idea of justice. *TMC*, in turn, seeks to find an alternative to this morality. The early stories, as it has been shown, offer instances where such an attempt fails: self and other, human and alien are in violent conflict. The possibility of Earth (and an Earthling visitation) is frequently met with suspicion and death. Mars, we discover, is only possible — palatable, that is — through an "Earthian logic" (173). However, "Night Meeting" offers the first conceptualization in the book of an alternative: a scenario where the self is overcome with awe and is, in a manner of speaking, exchanged for the other and worshipped in turn.

Conclusion: Mars as Mirror

As Howard Hendrix, George Slusser, and Eric Rabkin note in their preface to a recent study on Mars in science fiction, "Whenever we look at Mars, we are looking at the mirror of our own cultural dreams and concerns" (2). There is plenty of evidence that Bradbury was pointing the "mirror" at his fellow Americans — but not simply to criticize their imperialist fantasies of conquering another "red" culture. Contrary to Slusser's argument from the 1970s, the vision of Mars that we get in *TMC* expresses the deeper wish for a utopian environment free of pollution, crime, and war[4]; in addition, Mars presents a specific *ethos* that contrasts sharply with American "values" — even the ones that Bradbury himself usually celebrated. To begin with, the ugly side of the mirror is surely most evident when the men of the Third Expedition see a transplanted pre–World War II suburbia; we might view this as Bradbury at his most saccharine. However, it is clear that these staid American values pose the biggest threat because the "Dream" is so big, so smothering, that it seems to colonize on its own; the dream is an essence, a gas, that leaks off the first rocket that lands on Mars and poisons the environment with its "frame cottages," "roofs with shingles," "green shades," "flowerpots and chintz and pans" (Bradbury 78). Mars, of course, is analogous to American indigenous cultures that have suffered from the same big dream; this is the "dream" that Canadian poet Gwendolyn MacEwen warns about in "Dark Pines Under Water" (1972) — the kind of dream in which the "explorer" sinks into the "new world" he himself has concocted and transforms the landscape irrevocably.

There is no truly bright side of the mirror in *TMC*; Bradbury realized the falsehood of trying to put a positive spin on the colonization and decimation of an entire culture. But there are characters who serve as ethical visionaries in the book: Wilder, Spender, and Tomás Gomez each, in their own way, give back reflections of a more culturally sensitive and flexible American response to otherness and the consequences of cultural genocide. To be sure, there are the crude and crass Parkhills and Teeces, along with the arrogant and paranoid astronauts from the first three expeditions who think they are visionaries but suffer from species chauvinism. Nevertheless, the book does end with the sense that the new human inhabitants of Mars have imbibed the message Parkhill scoffs at: *you* are the Other now. For the entirety of the book, humans react out of fear of their own mortality and extinction — the thought that they might be just one culture/species, that they, too, could lose their home planet. The human species — until the very final chapter, "The Million-Year Picnic" — fails to see that the Martians are hosting them, are making gestures of hospitality, and are allowing them to find a new life at the expense of their own.

While Rabkin is certainly correct that small towns function "as the models of community" in the early sequences of the book, the violent and tragic conclusions to these encounters hardly recommend them as ideal models, or even as examples of "community" that Bradbury felt should be translated universally. However much "small-town" life had been practically a genre for Bradbury in his early years (Rabkin 97), he seems to have altered this view significantly in *TMC*. The poetic homage to the dwindling crystal cities in Mars and the symbolic image of "Martian dust storms [...] tearing away the plastic walls of the newer, American-built city that was melting down into the sand, desolated" (Bradbury 156), reinforces that the ideal itself was crumbling in Bradbury's mind. As Mucher notes, "the end of the Martian race becomes the subliminal catalyst that foresees the end of the Human race"

(181). Again, it partly comes back to the Arizona connection: Bradbury had first-hand knowledge of the effects of the white American assimilationist ideology and how it just did not suit the Southwest environment. The implicit representative of this ethical warning is Tomás, who shares the legacy of the human imposition of "Earthian" values but who also critiques the specifically white American imposition of values.

According to Rabkin's interpretation, the destruction of one American culture on planet Earth does not eliminate the "American myth" (103) but, on the contrary, necessitates the need to rehabilitate the old frontier vision that apparently had reached its "golden years" in the 1950s. To what degree has American life been reborn on Mars? It is more accurate to say that the book chronicles the failure of this project, however much we are meant to sympathize with the characters, like Hathaway in "The Long Years," who use their technical wizardry to rebuild American towns from memory. The *lament* is evident — richly and poetically rendered in such chapters as "The Third Expedition," "The Settlers," "The Green Morning," and "The Silent Towns"; but the *critique* is still implied in the symbolic references to the "dead American town" in "The Long Years" (164) and to the burned-black suburban households in "There Will Come Soft Rains." One of Bradbury's messages seems to be that the American space program and its competition with other superpowers tainted simple American life exhibited in cheerful family dinners, parades, ice cream parlors, hotdog stands, and good old fashioned movies and music. But another message seems to be that the transplantation of all these good things, while it may have a good intention, can lead to disastrous consequences; again, we cannot miss the *other* lament in the book: that for a foreign, indigenous culture.

It is quite apparent that, by the time we get to "The Million-Year Picnic," the original mission to Mars has radically changed into a search for community, friendship, communion, and an embrace of otherness. The desire for otherness is frequently revealed to be a fetishistic or imperialist intention to overcome the landscape, to consume it, and to take pleasure from its exotic qualities; to put it in Lévinas's terms, "Knowledge is intentionality: act and will [...] an 'I want' and an 'I can' that the term intention itself suggests" (*Alterity* 14). But the desire expressed by "Dad" in the final story is of a different order, and is comparable to Lévinas's "metaphysical desire" (*Totality* 33–34). While Mucher reads *TMC* via Husserl (with whom Lévinas was taking issue at various points in his writings), we should still see the validity in Mucher's concluding statement about how the mission to Mars has been modified: "This 'desire' which, from a beginning, is represented as a desire to impose Earthness upon Mars, has now been transformed into a desired fulfillment of abandoning one identity for another" (184). The "substitution" motif is complete when, in the final scene, the Earthlings become "Martians"—just as the Martians had shucked off their bodies and identities in previous sequences. Again, far from seeking to recreate Earth on Mars, it is clear that the family represents a new order of humanity rather than "continuations of the Old Order" (Mucher 185). Perhaps we can view Tomás Gomez as one of the progenitors of this new order. He follows the old gas attendant's advice to "take Mars for what she is" (Bradbury 79). As a result, Tomás does not find someone with whom he can claim "prior kinship" but rather one who *could* be called "brother" out of hospitality, out of kindness, and out of an embrace of the "other standing over there."

Notes

1. Stephen Jay Gould discusses this notion in contrast to the Darwinian emphasis on variation: "in Plato's world, variation is accidental, while essences record a higher reality; in Darwin's reversal, we value variation as a defining (and concrete earthly) reality, while averages [...] become mental abstractions" (41). As he writes later on, in his discussion of the "bare bones" of natural selection, "Offspring vary among themselves, and are not carbon copies of an immutable type" (138).

2. According to Gary Wolfe, this is American historian Frederick Jackson Turner's "thesis," which Bradbury was apparently echoing throughout TMC (110–11). There is much evidence, however, that Bradbury was parodying this premise about an Edenic return to pioneer days.

3. In "Hostipitality" (2000), Jacques Derrida reinforces the inherent problem of a hospitality bound by conditions: "[the] law of hospitality [...] violently imposes a contradiction on the very concept of hospitality in fixing a limit to it, in de-termining it: hospitality is certainly, necessarily, a right, a duty, an obligation, the greeting of the foreign other [l'autre étranger] as a friend but on the condition that the host, the Wirt, the one who receives, lodges or gives asylum remains the patron, the master of the household, on the condition that he maintains his own authority in his own home" (4; original emphasis).

4. More recently, Ángel Mateos-Aparicio Martín-Albo has argued that viewing Mars from the native inhabitants' perspective "allows Bradbury to create a poetic and utopian vision of the Martians and of the Martian landscape which increases the sense of loss when that civilization is destroyed by the human colonists" (111).

Works Cited

Bhabha, Homi. *The Location of Culture.* New York: Routledge, 1994. Print.
Bradbury, Ray. *The Martian Chronicles.* Toronto: Bantam, 1982. Print.
Cohen, Richard. "Foreword." *Otherwise Than Being, or Beyond Essence.* Trans. Alphonso Lingis. Pittsburgh: Duquesne University Press, 1999. xi–xvi. Print.
Derrida, Jacques. "Hostipitality." *Angelaki: Journal of the Theoretical Humanities* 5.3 (December 2000): 3–18. Print.
Gould, Stephen Jay. *Full House: The Spread of Excellence from Plato to Darwin.* Cambridge: Belknap, 2011. Print.

Hendrix, Howard V., George Slusser, and Eric S. Rabkin, eds. "Preface." *Visions of Mars: Essays on the Red Planet in Fiction and Science.* Jefferson: McFarland, 2011. 1–7. Print.

Hoskinson, Kevin. "*The Martian Chronicles* and *Fahrenheit 451*: Ray Bradbury's Cold War Novels." *Extrapolation* 36.4 (Winter 1995): 345–59. Print.

Knight, Damon. "When I Was in Kneepants: Ray Bradbury." *Modern Critical Views: Ray Bradbury.* Ed. Harold Bloom. Philadelphia: Chelsea House, 2001. 3–8. Print.

Lévinas, Emmanuel. *Alterity and Transcendence.* Trans. Michael B. Smith. New York: Columbia University Press, 1999. Print.

_____. *Otherwise Than Being, or Beyond Essence.* Trans. Alphonso Lingis. Pittsburgh: Duquesne University Press, 1999. Print.

_____. *Totality and Infinity: An Essay on Exteriority.* Trans. Alphonso Lingis. Pittsburgh: Duquesne University Press, 1969. Print.

MacEwen, Gwendolyn. "Dark Pines Under Water." *The Harbrace Anthology of Literature,* 4th ed. Ed. Jon C. Stott, Raymond E. Jones, and Rick Bowers. Toronto: Nelson, 2006. 345. Print.

Martín-Albo, Ángel Mateos-Aparicio. "The Frontier Myth and Racial Politics." *The Postnational Fantasy: Essays on Postcolonialism, Cosmopolitics and Science Fiction.* Ed. Masood Ashraf Raja, Jason W. Ellis, and Swaralipi Nandi. Jefferson: McFarland, 2011. 100–24. Print.

Mucher, Walter J. "Being Martian: Spatiotemporal Self in Ray Bradbury's *The Martian Chronicles.*" *Extrapolation: A Journal of Science Fiction and Fantasy* 43.2 (Summer 2002): 171–87. Print.

Rabkin, Eric. "Is Mars Heaven? *The Martian Chronicles, Fahrenheit 451* and Ray Bradbury's Landscape of Longing." *Visions of Mars: Essays on the Red Planet in Fiction and Science.* Ed. Howard V. Hendrix, George Slusser, and Eric S. Rabkin. Jefferson: McFarland, 2011. 95–104. Print.

Reid, Robin Anne. *Ray Bradbury: A Critical Companion.* Westport, CT: Greenwood Press, 2000. Print.

Slusser, George Edgar. *The Bradbury Chronicles.* San Bernardino: Borgo, 1977. Print.

Wolfe, Gary K. "The Frontier Myth in Ray Bradbury." *Bloom's Modern Critical Views: Ray Bradbury.* Ed. Harold Bloom. Philadelphia: Chelsea House, 2001. 103–24. Print.

Illustrating Otherness
Crossing Frontier's in Ray Bradbury's The Illustrated Man

Francisco Laguna-Correa

Ray Bradbury haunts me. The first encounter that I had with the American author was during my childhood in Mexico City. When I was born, my father was a door-to-door book salesman whose best client was himself: he bought encyclopedias, literary anthologies, and book collections, arguing that those "treasures" were going to be one day the inherence of his newborn son. Among all of those books, there was, indeed, a Spanish edition of *The Martian Chronicles*, with a gray cover featuring an illustration of what apparently was a rocket traveling towards a red planet. It was in those "chronicles" where I first found that Martians were not green nor had antennae coming from their heads, but that indeed they were brownish and looked akin to human beings. Many years later, when I was starting to acquire books avidly following the lead of my father, I found with an ambulant book vendor outside of a subway station a Spanish edition of *The Illustrated Man*. This was my second encounter with the American science fiction author, which complemented the hypothesis that I created in my childhood after reading *The Martian Chronicles*. I was, in the imagery of Bradbury's text, something close to a Martian and, if a human, one living in a past, bucolic, picturesque, and rural time. This was conflictive to me as I used to think about the United States in a similar way that Bradbury represented Mexico. The United States was in my imagination the land of *The Old Man and the Sea* and the novels of John Fante, a rural or semi-rural place where people made exhausting commutes to and from their homes and where people struggle with solitude and natural forces, such as overly cold winters and incredibly strong animals.

During those years, my readings of Friedrich Nietzsche and the fact of having grown in a very big metropolis like Mexico City made me look at nature and weekend escapades to the surrounding bucolic towns with a strong sense of romanticism, as if the future of human existence and the collective spirit was in Nature and not in the city. We as humans, as Nietzsche would suggest, were to return to solitude and stillness to find and free ourselves; something like what William Butler Yeats tells us, not without a sense of frustration, in his poem "The Lake Isle of Innisfree":

> I will arise and go now, for always night and day
> I hear lake water lapping with low sounds by the shore;
> While I stand on the roadway, or on the pavements grey,
> I hear it in the deep heart's core [31].

Nietzsche, I believed, was a humanist thinker able to recognize that societies were getting corrupted under utilitarian and positivistic principles. By going back to Nature, somehow, this corruption was to be reverted, allowing us to recover our lost ability to look at the world with all of our senses and with a constructive innocence.

The Illustrated Man left me with a similar feeling and with the certainty that Ray Bradbury was a kind of humanist reminding us — warning us sometimes with hidden desperation (of more peaceful and romantic times. Bradbury, I thought, was telling us that those times were attainable and closer to us than it seemed. *The Illustrated Man*, and more precisely two of its stories, was a door to look at Mexico, my own country, in a self-reflective and inquiring way. Moreover, this self-reflectivity was also a pathway to a dystopian representation of the United States and its society and present — future? — spiritual struggles.

This essay is an attempt to articulate this self-reflectivity and the representation of otherness, which, in my case, was the representation of the United States and the American society. Therefore, this essay is about the reception of two of Bradbury's short stories, "The Highway" and "The Fox and the Forest," by a Mexican reader who has indeed read them on both sides of the frontier. I should say that *The Illustrated Man* that I met in Mexico was exclusively in Spanish, while in the United States it has been solely in English. Writing this essay has been a conciliatory reflection, thus allowing both my Spanish and my English Bradbury to meet and become more conscious of each other.

Those Who Drive and Those Who Walk: Am I the Other or Are They the Others?

When I first arrived to the United States, I was driven from the airport to my new home in suburban Portland through an endless highway flanked by trees, rain, and darkness. I had heard that Americans were humans with four wheels attached to their bodies, but I never thought that this statement could be as serious and truthful as it became. Soon after my arrival, I learned that I could not do much where I was with my two legs. I found out that Americans do drive a lot, despite the distance that keeps them away from their destiny; it could be as far as another state or as close as the store down the street. I mention all of this because driving is at the core of "The Highway."

This short story is about a man and a woman, Hernando and his wife, who live in a rural setting next to a transited highway (could it be a road between Nogales and Tucson?). One rainy day cars stop driving through, and Hernando gets the feeling that something really bad has happened. Suddenly cars start coming again, but at such speed that it is impossible for Hernando and the people in the cars to establish any sort of communication. When the highway becomes empty again and it seems that no one else would come, a muddy and "thirsty" convertible shows up and it approaches Hernando. Behind the steering wheel there is a young man, accompanied by five young women, all of them seem distressed, and do not care about getting their hair and outfits wet. Bradbury adds to this detail, "None complained, and this was unusual. Always before they complained; of rain, of heat, of time, of cold, of distance" (40). These young people ask Hernando desperately for water, but not to drink it, but to feed the radiator of their car. When Hernando tells them that there was a lot of traffic a few minutes ago, adding that: "It all goes one way. North" (41), all of the passengers start crying. Hernando inquires about the reason for their sadness. The driver, surprised, tells Hernando, "It's happened" (41). Hernando finishes pouring the water in the radiator's car, and calmly asks again what is going on, arguing that he did not hear the first time. The driver, close to breaking down, informs Hernando that the end of the world is coming, that an atom war has started; then the car rolls away heading north. Hernando walks back home and, when his wife asks him what has happened, he replies, "It's nothing" (42). Then he goes back to work in the field next to his donkey, wondering about what they mean when they say "the world."

This story, despite its simplicity and brevity, stresses social aspects regarding otherness representation that deserve a closer examination. First I would like to point out how Bradbury draws the idealization of the United States–Mexico frontier as one exempted of the worries and dangers of Modernity. There is a double pace in the story suggested by both Hernando and the cars. On the one hand, Hernando represents a sort of timeless time, closely related to Nature, which makes him owner of a romantic wisdom and craftiness. On the other, we are presented to a vertiginous time that does not stop, that goes north escaping from the inevitable end of the world. "The Highway" itself is the space in which these two times collide, and just like in any collision, there are traces left behind. Bradbury reminds us of the relation between these two types of time through the inclusion of two objects. The first is a tire that "had come into the hut with violence one night, exploding the chickens and the pots apart" (39). The car from which this tire came ended deep under a river nearby Hernando's house and the highway. This tire announces the intrusion of Modernity into Hernando's life, an intrusion that presents itself with an explosion and destruction. Bradbury, looking at this encounter from a humanist perspective, allows Hernando to make up something constructive out of this collision: "The following day he had carved the shoe soles from tire rubber" (39). The second object that Bradbury includes is a keystone to understand how the natural time that Hernando represents is a remedy to solve the anguish that the world's end brings along. When the young people from the convertible asked Hernando for water, "he returned with a hub lid of water. This, too, had been a gift from the highway. One afternoon it had sailed like a flung coin into his field, round and glittering. Until now, he and his wife had used it for washing and cooking; it made a fine bowl" (40). The hubcap eventually became the utensil to pour water into the radiator of the car, thus allowing the young people to keep going north as the world gets closer to its end by an atomic war.

It is meaningful and also conflictive that Bradbury introduces the hubcap as a gift from the highway, as the hubcap becomes the object of encounter, of collision, between Modern and Natural time. It is a gift to both Hernando and his wife, but it also becomes the salvation of the young people traveling in the car. Bradbury seems to suggest that there is an implicit cyclical process within Modernity in which the causes and the effects reside in the products of Modernity. If we are to concede that Modernity is its own source of conflict, as the atomic war suggests, we are to concede also that Modernity may become its own salvation through the intercession of Hernando and his natural environment: he is crafty — creative as it is used in Spanish — and his craftiness allows him to make a bowl from a hubcap. Within the epistemological construction of Modernity, a hubcap left in the middle of a highway is an object without a content of "being," which is to say, trash. Being creative, or crafty, is at the core of Platonic *poiesis*, as this process transforms something that "it is not" into something that "it is," and the vehicle of this transformation is one who is "indeed mad or devoid of logic and rationale knowledge, but from an archaic perspective they are, like the prophets, touched by the 'sacred disease,' divine vehicles to be treated with veneration and fear" (Spariosu 23).

Whereas Plato believes that this vehicle is a poet, a rhapsodist in fact, Bradbury frames Hernando as this vehicle, whose "natural knowledge" makes him play the role of a messenger that links Nature — water — with Modernity — a car's radiator.

Ranajit Guha has framed temporality in two extremes, modernity and postmodernity (Mignolo 424), and this framework also works in Bradbury's "The Highway," with the only variation that the American author builds temporality between the extremes of Modernity and Nature. Even the very last question brought up by Hernando, who wonders about what do "they mean" when they say the world, becomes suddenly an ideal epistemological state of mind, in which the incapacity to understand the loss of material "beings" arises as a spiritual salvation. Furthermore, Bradbury reverts to Domingo Faustino Sarmiento's nineteenth century dichotomy between civilization and barbarity. According to Sarmiento, an influential Argentinian positivist who became president of Argentina, education and scientific progress were the keystones to transition from a natural state — barbarity — to a civilized one — Modernity. In Bradbury's short story, the components of this dichotomy have their roles inverted, and Modernity becomes a glimpse of destruction and social regression — barbarity; meanwhile Nature represents construction and human preservation.

Despite the humanist and idealistic configuration of Bradbury's "The Highway," there are a few aspects that we should examine closer in terms of otherness representation. It stands out in this short story that the main characters, from both Natural and Modern space, are men. It is clear throughout "The Highway" that men have the questions and the answers, regardless of the fact that women are a majority. In the case of Hernando, his wife stays inside the house while he is the one going outside. It is through this contact with the "outer world" that Hernando is able to formulate to himself an ontological question which suggests self-awareness: "What do they mean, 'the world'?" becomes the criticism of Modernity, as this question implies that not everyone is living in a Modern time, and, furthermore, not everyone needs to live within Modernity as understood by most Western societies. We should not forget, though, that Bradbury is a writer of metaphors, and as such he might be implying something else by creating a gender distinction between Hernando and his wife regarding their space of social interaction. It has been widely stereotyped that Mexican immigrants in the U.S. tend to be young men coming from rural areas, while women stay at home awaiting their return and the novelties that they may be bringing with them. This image of the immigration process is fairly clear in "The Highway," Hernando is not only the one going outside and witnessing how four-wheeled humans escape north, but he is also the one who brings the novelties — trash susceptible to be transformed into something useful(to his wife's indoor space. While "The Highway" may be interpreted as a metaphor of the inevitable collapse that Modernity will produce in "the world," thus requiring an alternative space to return to more Natural and constructive times, Bradbury himself may not agree with this configuration. In a 2002 interview with Jonathan Eller, Bradbury did not think that the craftiness of rural Mexican people to transform trash into something useful was a desired direction to take. The American author remembered his first trip to Mexico back in 1945, mentioning that

> everywhere you went, the ... things you threw away were the things they picked up. Going from Guanajuato, ... we saw a crashed airliner by the side of the road. They'd never taken it away. Too much bother. But the ants were taking it away. Like those films — you see the ants, the leaf ants, they're picking up bits of leaves, and they're walking and walking. Well, this airliner was invaded by ants. You pass by, and there are peasants coming to get a piece of aluminum or an engine part or a piece of glass. That airliner will be gone a year later. You don't bother to take it away. The people will take it away [124].

With his friend Grant Beach, Bradbury made a road trip to Mexico between October and November of 1945; in the next subchapter I will examine this experience in more depth. At this moment I would like to point out from Bradbury's statement his insistence to distinguish between "You" and "The people," thus questioning to what extent Bradbury's humanism is an inclusive epistemological construction in which the "We" has already transcended the world's ideological and material divisions. Otherness is implied, nonetheless, by this nominal differentiation. Even though the trip of Bradbury and Beach to Mexico exposed both of them to a complex and diverse array of people, from urban and rural places, the American author and his friend did not record the complexity of the Mexican society as experienced during their trip. Their eagerness to look at Mexico as an exotic and pre–Modern country kept them away from realizing that Mexico by the mid of the twentieth century was becoming a Modern and progressive nation rapidly becoming the economic and cultural leader of the entire Latin American region. Prior to the 1950s, the Mexican society experienced drastic changes, ranging from the social revolution of 1910, the nationalization of oil in 1938, and the consolidation of an educated and wealthy middle-class that was growing and becoming a social actor advocating for the modernization of the country. From a humanist approach, it could be claimed that Bradbury missed the opportunity to represent Mexico in a loyal and objective way, thus dissolving some of the negative and unfounded stereotypes — i.e., an exotic, rural and poor place inhabited by an uneducated population whose higher aspiration was emigrating to the U.S.— that the idea of Mexico aroused, and sometimes keep arousing, in the English-speaking readers.

Furthermore, Bradbury's assertion underlines an issue that is at the core of Modernity, and more specifically between the relationship that the U.S. has established with Latin America during the last century and up to our days. It is no secret that the U.S. exports harmful electronic waste to Latin America, besides forcing this region to become a manufacturing space in which a lack of environmental restrictions, tax exemptions, labor exploitation, and the continuous mediation of the World Bank and the IMF permit the U.S. to pollute the environment and deteriorate social conditions in Latin American countries, all in the name of progress and material accumulation (GAO). It is also no secret that American corporations are hesitant to take responsibility for the environmental devastation that these countries are suffering. Bradbury's anecdote about the airliner seems to have inspired "The Highway." Hernando is one of those ants, a peasant grabbing pieces of the trash that Modernity leaves behind, that Americans leave behind under the assumption "*You* don't bother to take it away. *The people* will take it away." The desperate run of "Modern" individuals towards progress does not allow them to realize that they are trashing the highway on their way north. Perhaps, someone like Hernando, a human who camouflages himself with Nature, will take care of it, will transform the trash into something useful. However, Bradbury does not consider that the agency of empowerment required to take care of "those things," let's say policy changes and environmental protection, is neutralized by the influence and self-importance of Modernity. Bradbury does not believe that those peasants are "taking care" of the airliner due to their dexterity and craftiness, but solely due to their poverty. Yet, even though we may deny it, those human beings, women and men, have the skills, the creative minds, and the imagination that Modern people have already lost. This does not neutralize or alleviate social inequalities and economic injustice; however, craftiness and creativity are both human assets that deserve to be acknowledged, as well.

The "Other" as a Source of Uncertainty

As I mentioned before, between October and November of 1945, Ray Bradbury and Grant Beach made a road trip from Los Angeles to Mexico, "in Beach's late–1930s V-8 Ford sedan, heading east all the way across southern Arizona, New Mexico, and Texas to the border crossing Laredo. They proceeded into Mexico through a great swarm of locusts that seemed to underscore the completely alien nature of the adventure in Bradbury's mind" (Eller, *BRB*, 119). This adventure, as told by Eller and remembered by Bradbury, was traumatic and shocking for the American author.

Through his experience living in Los Angeles, Bradbury had created an idea of Mexico based on the contact that he had established with the so-called Mexican Americans from Los Angeles.[1] Bradbury had set up a working space in a tenement at 413 North Figueroa, in downtown Los Angeles, which was owned by the mother of Grant Beach. "Bradbury's family had lived a few miles south and west of these neighborhoods throughout his high-school years, in generally white working-class neighborhoods. Now he was writing and sometimes living above streets where a largely Mexican American population also included Chinese, Filipinos, and other Asians" (Eller 54). Therefore, the expectations that Bradbury had about Mexico during that trip were challenged in ways that *The Illustrated Man*'s author was not expecting at all.

Bradbury was going to Mexico with the purpose of fitting his experience *a priori* about Mexico in one way or another. According to Jonathan Eller, one of the first narrative memories of Bradbury's trip to Mexico, dated October 26 of 1945, was intended as the opening of a novel concept titled *The Fear of Death Is Death* (Eller, *TLF*, 365). This is the way it begins:

> You go into Mexico, and there it is, the smell of death. It is there with the smell of church incenses and the cookings of many foods. You live in an effluvium of death. The air is one part melancholy. The air is one part dirge.... It drips from the eaves of your window on rainy Mexico City afternoons and it is in the opening groan of the door, and everybody sings and there is bright dancing, but, nevertheless, you are living with death.
>
> You feel it when you are once over the border, it is there and nothing you can do with the throttle or money or your mind will put it away from you [Eller, *BRB*, 121–122].

Eller justifies Bradbury's aesthetic predisposition towards death by revealing that the main goal of the trip was to buy "tribal" masks and to witness the November 2 celebration of "El día de los muertos" (Day of the Dead) in the isle of Janitzio in Pátzcuaro, in the state of Michoacán. Eller himself, while he is describing Bradbury's journey to Mexico, makes evident his lack of knowledge about the country that borders the U.S. to the south. He misspells toponyms and names, and deforms the sense of Mexican cultural features, such as the Day of the Dead, which Eller attributes to a sort of pagan celebration in which Mexicans indeed display a ritual for Death itself. It is understandable that coming from a Protestant tradition, both Eller and Bradbury found a celebration that mixes pre–Hispanic and Catholic traditions shocking, in which most Mexican people remember their relatives who have passed away. Many other details, some bigger than others, escape Eller's study regarding Mexico. It is clear that Bradbury was going to Mexico looking for a story about death and this predisposition prevented him from getting to know Mexico as it really was, rather than as he wished it to be.

Furthermore, these *a priori* expectations deprived Bradbury of recognizing the progressive and Modern aspects of Mexico, such as the increasing presence of women in public offices (Porter 42). Perhaps, by noticing this aspect of Mexican society, Bradbury would have felt inspired to make Hernando's wife from "The Highway" go outside to the road, as well. Also, after the Mexican Revolution and since the 1920s, Mexico City became the most important cultural center of Latin America, bringing intellectuals, artists, and writers from the entire American continent and Europe. Furthermore, during these decades the Mexican muralist movement flourished, gaining international recognition for Mexican painters such as Diego Rivera, David Alfaro Siqueiros, and José Clemente Orozco. Bradbury does confess to Eller that while in Mexico City the science fiction writer "spent most of his time seeking out the murals and paintings of José Clemente Oro[z]co, David Alfaro Siqueiros, and Diego Rivera" (*BRB* 121), adding that "he was fascinated by the Church of the Blessed Virgin, where worshippers approached the altar on their knees" (121). Needless to say that the name of this "church" is not what Eller mentioned or Bradbury remembered.... But it is more important to point out that the idea and inspiration of an "illustrated man" could have come from the murals and paintings that Bradbury saw in Mexico City. All of these painters/ muralists were funded by the Mexican government, under the assignment that their work reflected the struggle of Mexico to acquire and maintain its independence from foreign nations (such as Spain, the United States, and France), as well as the depiction of the search of national identity throughout Mexican history, often representing past, present, and future Mexican society from a Marxist perspective.[2] Another detail of these murals is that they often feature humans in movement, with plenty of stories, colors, and historical clues surrounding them, thus bringing in front of the audience a multi-diegetical experience; for these reasons, it is not impossible to believe that Bradbury's encounter with Mexican modern paintings was the source of inspiration for *The Illustrated Man.*

However, all of these details escape Eller's study and Bradbury's memory. Furthermore, when Eller mentions Bradbury's shock at encountering immigration in Los Angeles and poverty in rural Mexico, he seems to deny the almost coetaneous effects that the Great Depression produced in terms of internal migration and widespread poverty in the United States. This mechanism of denial of our own social inequalities and economic unfairness by pointing out the inequalities and economic struggles of others is a strategy of Modernity to allocate economic, social, and individual value based on cultural discrimination (Harris 81) and through coloniality practices (Ahmed 77). Through this mechanism, the Other becomes always an entire social group, not an individual, therefore creating a disadvantageous relation with power and agency of power for an entire collective. In this regard, Eller mentions that while in Mexico Bradbury:

> Was also troubled by the intercultural tension he was sensing almost every day in Mexico. It really didn't matter if the contact was urban or rural — there was always, it seemed, an underlying coldness that was all the more chilling because it was not personal at all. Throughout his career, he would write stories in response to twin tragedies of poverty and racial bias. But Mexico almost overwhelmed him, and the only way to deal with the experience was to write [121].

It is paradoxical and interesting how Bradbury experienced himself what he recognizes as "cultural bias" against his whiteness. The feeling of being suddenly the Other made him resent and feel overwhelmed by Mexicans. Bradbury and Eller did not consider the fact that the so-called Mexican American War of 1847, orchestrated under racial and Manifest Destiny ideologies, is remembered in Mexican collective memory as the United States Intervention, which produced the loss, under very unfair circumstances, of more than half of the national territory, including the current states of Arizona, California, New Mexico, and Texas. Furthermore, there were other personal factors that triggered Bradbury's negative experience while in Mexico. We should not forget that he was traveling with his friend Grant Beach, and we should not also forget that their friendship ended while they were in Mexico. Eller mentions that between Bradbury and Beach there were rising interpersonal tensions, such as the following fragment evidences:

> It began with Beach himself, who projected an almost constant ill humor. He did not have Bradbury's ability to converse with new acquaintances; furthermore, Beach had been sick with strep throat through much of the trip, and he expected Bradbury to find him medicines and doctors along the way. He also expected Bradbury to handle all of the room arrangements and service the car in each town, even though Bradbury did not speak Spanish and had never driven an automobile [121].

These interpersonal circumstances may better explain Bradbury's stress and sensitivity to an alleged "intercultural bias," as it probably was very frustrating to deal with all of those responsibilities without speaking any Spanish. His expectations of being received in Mexico with arms wide open and the deference that he thought an American deserved was worsened by the fact that his exotic ideas of Mexico did not quite match his experience, and not speaking

Spanish only increased his desperation during his two-month Mexican journey.

Bradbury ended leaving Beach alone in Mexico City with his Ford and his strep throat, and made his way back to Los Angeles on his own: "Bradbury arrived in Los Angeles [on Tuesday, November 26] and explained the situation to Mrs. Beach. Grant continued on in the Ford with the rest of the baggage and purchases; along the way, he pulled to the side of a bridge crossing and threw Bradbury's typewriter into a river" (Eller, *BRB*, 125). The idea of taking pieces from Bradbury's typewriter lying in the bottom of a river resembles "The Highway." This could easily be a metaphor to explain the literary influence that Bradbury has left in Latin America — including, of course, Mexico — mostly among Mexican young authors from the 1950s and 60s who read avidly *The Martian Chronicles*.[3]

Taking into consideration the shocking experience that Bradbury had in Mexico, and following Eller's lead that the "only way to deal with the experience was to write," we could suggest that both "The Highway" and "The Fox and the Forest" may be considered stories in which Bradbury deals with that experience. In "The Highway" the image of the Mexican peasant getting pieces from what Modernity leaves behind its way appears. Furthermore, the fact that Hernando reacts solicitously and with no hesitation to the request for water from the young American may be a representation of how Bradbury wished that Mexicans could have reacted to his own requests. Eller mentions that Bradbury had to take care of the maintenance of the Ford V8 even though he did not know much about cars. It is possible that while in Mexico, and with the language barrier, Bradbury had a frustrating experience with the Ford V8. By representing Hernando as an acquiescent and serviceable man, Bradbury uses his literary writing as a cathartic channel to alleviate some of his frustration. Also, the representation of women in the story seems to have a relation with the attitude that Grant Beach assumed during the road trip. In the story, those accompanying the driver request special care from him. It seems that "The Highway" is both a reflection about the dangers of Modernity and a cathartic exercise for the author to lighten himself from the stressing experience of his journey in Mexico next to Grant Beach.

"The Fox and the Forest" may also be interpreted as a direct reflection of his road trip to Mexico in 1945. The plot of the story is not complicated. William and Susan Travis are a married couple from the year 2155. William works for a factory that makes atomic bombs, where he performs an essential role in their manufacturing. The year 2155 is not a good year to be alive, since there is war, slavery, and a generalized unhappiness. In an attempt to escape from their apocalyptic 2155, William and Travis traveled in time — a sort of vacation — back to 1938 Mexico, where they believe that peace, simplicity, and happiness can be found. When it seems that they have been able to run away from their time, the 2155 police show up to take them back to the future, thus frustrating the couple's escapade. This narrative has a very pessimistic focus, and Bradbury, as in "The Highway," evokes the nostalgia of the old happier times (Garci 305–06).

Despite the fact that the story draws on the past, 1938 Mexico, as the place to pursue happiness and a peaceful state of mind, the story features a series of morbid and even grotesque images regarding Mexican scenery and society. Immediately, in the beginning of the story, we encounter the following images: "Then rush on hot wires to bash the high church tower, in which boys' naked feet alone could be seen kicking and re-kicking, clanging and tilting and re-tilting the monster bells into monstrous music. A flaming bull blundered about the plaza chasing laughing men and screaming people. The bull passed, carried lightly on the shoulders of a charging Mexican, a framework of bamboo and sulphurous gunpowder" (114–15). To a Mexican reader, it may be odd and unnecessary to index the charging man carrying the flaming bull as a Mexican; since the action is taking place in Mexico, it is absolutely natural that there are indeed Mexican people in Mexico. Through the accentuation of the "Mexicanness" of the man, otherness is established since the beginning of the story to distinguish among "us" and "them." This also underlines the fact that for Bradbury not everyone is sharing a common experience; whereas Americans are in the middle of an atomic war, Mexicans are supposed to be immersed in a time without worries or urgencies. Adding to this, it is meaningful, as in "The Highway," that Mexican people are represented as closer to Nature either from spiritual or cosmetic reasons. In Bradbury's description of this man, otherness is represented through an almost mimetic relation between Natural forces, such as fire and a bull, and the Mexicanness of the man: natural forces, animal forces, and Mexicanness constitute the representation of the Other since the beginning of this story.

"The Fox and the Forest" story in *The Illustrated Man* does include a spin in terms of otherness representation, as Bradbury makes the Travis couple be recognized as outsiders themselves. Nevertheless, in Bradbury's eyes, the Travises, though they are white Americans, do not become an Other in front of Mexican people, which should be the most natural case scenario. In opposition to "The Highway," in this story women acquire a bit more of a voice; however, men still are the ones who rule and exercise their power. In this regard, Susan Travis is the one who first recognizes a familiar, but, nonetheless, outsider who is haunting them:

As they passed the café entrance Susan saw the man looking out at them, a white man in a salt-white suit, with a blue tie and blue shirt, and a thin, sunburned face. His hair was blond and straight and his eyes were blue, and he watched them as they walked.

She would never had noticed him if it had not been for the bottles at his immaculate elbow; a fat bottle of crème de menthe, a clear bottle of vermouth, a flagon of cognac, and seven other bottles of assorted liqueurs, and, at his finger tips, ten small half-filled glasses from which, without taking his eyes off the street, he sipped, occasionally squinting, pressing his thin mouth shut upon the savor. In his free hand a thin Havana cigar smoked, and on a chair stood twenty cartons of Turkish cigarettes, six boxes of cigars, and some packaged colognes [Bradbury 115].

Such a character would stand out in Mexico or anywhere else in 1938 or 2012. We should not forget, as did the Travis couple, that this man came from the future, a time devoted to war and destruction, in which enjoyment and leisure are not for everyone. It would seem that the power to index otherness in Bradbury's story is an exclusive prerogative of white people. The blonde white man that Susan Travis recognizes as an Other would produce the same impression in a Mexican individual; however, in the entire story there is not one single mention or implication that such a character may possibly appear also to the eyes of Mexican people as a disruptive Other.

The ambivalence towards Mexican people acquires a higher tone with the inclusion of the American motion-picture company which is filming on location. The encounter between the crew and the Travises is smooth and does not involve the tension that they experienced while meeting Mr. Simms, the white blonde man who smokes and drinks as if the world were coming to an end and who they believe is coming from 2155 to take them back to work. It is definitely strange, and problematic, how the Travises get a sense of normality and affinity with the crew. The director welcomes the Travises with a meaningful and self-explanatory statement regarding Mexican people:

"American tourists!" he cried. "I am so sick of seeing Mexicans, I could kiss you." He shook their hands. "Come on, eat with us. Misery loves company. I'm Misery, this is Miss Gloom, and Mr. and Mrs. Do-We-Hate-Mexico! We all hate it. But we're here for some preliminary shots for a damn film. The rest of the crew arrives tomorrow. My name's Joe Melton. I'm the director. And if this ain't a hell of a country! Funerals in the streets, people dying. Come on, move over. Join the party; cheer us up!" [121].

It is due to the loud and crude way of expressing himself that Mr. Melton gains the trust of Mr. and Mrs. Travis. This encounter is problematic because the Travis' chose to travel to 1938 Mexico to escape from their inhuman time, and yet they passively and silently agree about the "Do-We-Hate-Mexico!"

anthem. The Travises get to believe that by staying close to the film crew they will be able to dodge Mr. Simms, who has already approached the couple to let them know that there is not any way to escape from 2155. In a brief article by Kent Forrester, attention is brought to the fact that in *The Martian Chronicles* there is a clear ambivalence towards Martians, which is articulated through the plot and the ideas that Bradbury forces upon his characters. Forrester believes that "under the influence of Bradbury's plots, the Martians kill. Under the influence of his 'neo-humanism,' we are *told* that the Martians are cleaner and nicer than we are" (52). This same ambivalence prevails in "The Fox and the Forest" at different levels and in both Mexicans and Americans.

It is unclear if the Travis couple's desire to escape 2155 is for very individualistic and hedonistic reasons or because they are in fact a couple of humanists against war and the developing of atomic bombs; however, Bradbury does suggest that William and Susan Travis possess a deeper sense of humanity and morality than, for instance, both Mr. Simms and Mr. Melton. The ambivalence that Forrester's article underlines regarding Martians also fits the Travises, as William, in a desperate attempt to escape from Mr. Simms, decides to kill him by hitting him with a car. This scene is perhaps more shocking that the idea of a half–Mexican and half-flaming bull; through this scene, we recover the image of Americans as half-human and half-machine:

> Mr. Simms was seated there, his neat legs crossed, on a delicate bronze bench. Biting the tip of a cigar, he lit it tenderly. Susan heard the throb of a motor, and far up the street, out of a garage and down the cobbled hill, slowly, came William in his car. The car picked up speed. Thirty, now forty, now fifty miles an hour. It was rushing sixty miles an hour, straight on for the plaza. "William!" screamed Susan. The car hit the low plaza curb, thundering; it jumped up, aped across the tiles toward the green bench where Mr. Simms now dropped his cigar, shrieked, flailed his hands, and was hit by the car. His body flew up and up in the air, and down and down, crazily, into the street [123–24].

William becomes a killer, thus matching the profile of the Martian drawn by Forrester; Americans can kill in both 2155 U.S. and in 1938 Mexico. By this point of the story, the reader has collected enough elements to conclude that the Travises will not be able to get away from 2155. Despite the fact that William has killed Mr. Simms during daylight and in front of a crowd, he will not be held responsible by the Mexican authorities. Bradbury attributes the impunity of William's crime to either the inefficiency or the corruption of the Mexican authorities, most likely the latter, as Bradbury draws an eloquent painting of this situation: "They came down the Official Palace steps together, arm in arm, their faces pale, at twelve noon. '*Adiós, señor*,' said the major behind them. '*Señora*.' They stood in the plaza where the crowd was pointing at the blood" (124). This last brushstroke of the crowd pointing at the blood of Mr. Simms exacerbates the impunity of the crime. Following Bradbury's axiological system in which Others have little to do against Modernity and its rule, William and Susan Travis will be held responsible for escaping their time and killing Mr. Simms only by their own comrades. To the surprise of the couple, Mr. Melton and the film crew — as well as Mr. Simms — were all secret agents commissioned to take them back to 2155.

The end of the story has a cinematic touch, as the members of the crew and the Travises are altogether in Mr. Melton's room, who reveals to the couple that they are also agents from 2155. William, to whom the killing of Mr. Simms has given the courage to do anything in order to escape, takes his gun out and fires it while the crew manages to restrain him. The manager of the hotel urges them to open the door, claiming that the police will come soon. That is when "a camera was carried forward. From it shot a blue light which encompassed the room instantly. It widened out and people of the party vanished, one by one" (127). It would seem that everything was just a film, a mere representation extracted from two different types of reality, which are the United States of 2155 and the rural Mexico of 1938.

This last image of the camera shooting a blue light that made everyone vanish inside Mr. Melton's room may be interpreted as well as a metaphor. Bradbury could be either criticizing the representation that the Hollywood industry was spreading of American characters, or he could be also suggesting that after all, every representation of an Other may be an illusion that does not completely match social reality. Regardless of Bradbury's intention with this last beautifully composed metaphor, the idea of representation is a vital element of "The Fox and the Forest." Following Forrester's proposal regarding the ambivalence of Martians, this story, just as "The Highway," both criticizes and celebrates Modernity. On the one hand, the criticism of the effects of war and the development of atomic bombs is condemned by Bradbury, but, on the other hand, by idealizing Mexico as a backwards, close to Nature, non–Modern space, Bradbury draws a conflictive representation of Mexicanness. It seems that the Bradbury's work evidences both the gains and the losses of Modernity and progress.

This American author is indeed a sort of neo-humanist, one who is witnessing with concern how mechanization and the Western idea of progress are becoming a menace to humanity, but in his own process of resistance to Modernity, he does not quite understand the Other; instead, and regardless of this limitation, Bradbury idealizes them and proposes their space, their territory, their way of life, as an alternative to Modernity. Nevertheless, this alternative approach to Modernity seems to frame the Other, in this case, Mexican people, as citizens without an equal status.

Notes

1. This is another way to represent the Other. By imposing a hyphen between the demonym "American," a distinction is also imposed between what it is completely and exclusively American and what it is not.

2. The painters who joined the artistic movement called "Muralismo mexicano" were distinguished for their leftist, prominently Marxist, ideologies. According to the article "El muralismo y la Revolución Mexicana" by Luz Elena Mainero, muralismo "is a sort of denunciation painting with a huge charge of socialist ideology, given the fact that the themes that it features are of a revolutionary nature, such as elevating class struggles and denouncing oppression, for this reasons it is a type of painting characterized by its acute social content." *Translation by the author.*

3. The first Spanish edition of *The Martian Chronicles* (*Crónicas marcianas*) was published in Buenos Aires, Argentina, in 1955, with a prologue by prominent Argentinian writer Jorge Luis Borges, who wonders: "What this man from Illinois has done, I ask myself, when closing the pages of his book, to produce in me such horror and solitude when I think about episodes of the conquest of another world." Borges, surprisingly, first learned to read in English and was a great reader of its literature, to such extend that the first time that he read *Don Quixote* by Miguel de Cervantes, it was in an English edition. *Translation by the author.*

Works Cited

Ahmed, Sara. *Strange Encounters: Embodied Others in Post-Coloniality.* New York: Taylor & Francis, 2000. Print.

Bradbury, Ray. *The Illustrated Man.* New York: Doubleday, 1951. Print.

_____. *The Martian Chronicles.* New York: Doubleday, 1958. Print.

Eller, Jonathan R. *Becoming Ray Bradbury.* Urbana: Illinois University Press, 2011. Print.

_____, and William Touponce. *Ray Bradbury: The Life of Fiction.* Kent, OH: Kent University Press, 2004. Print.

Finn Dominguez, Maria. *Mexico in Mind.* New York: Vintage, 2006. Print.

Forrester, Kent. "The Dangers of Being Earnest: Ray Bradbury and *The Martian Chronicles.*" *The Journal of General Education*, Vol. 28, No. 1 (Spring 1976): 50–54. Print.

Garci, José Luis. *Ray Bradbury. Humanista del futuro.* Madrid: Editorial Helios, 1971. Print.

Harris, Cheryl. "Whiteness as Property." *Identities: Race, Class, Gender, and Nationality.* Ed. Linda Martín Alcoff and Eduardo Mendieta. Oxford: Blackwell, 2003. 75–89. Print.

López Castro, Ramón. *Expedición a la Ciencia Ficción Mexicana.* Mexico City: Editorial Lectorum, 2001. Print.

Mignolo, Walter. "Coloniality of Power and Subalternity." *The Latin American Subaltern Studies Reader.* Ileana Rodríguez, ed. Durham: Duke University Press, 2001. 424–44. Print.

Porter, Susie. "Empleadas públicas: normas de feminidad, espacios burocráticos e identidad de la clase media en México durante la década de 1930." *Signos históricos*, No. 11 (Jan.–July 2004): 41–63. Print.

Spariosu, Mihai. *Mimesis in Contemporary Theory—An Interdisciplinary Approach: The Literary and Philosophical Debate.* Amsterdam: Josh Benjamins, 1984. Print.

United States Government Accountability Office (GAO). *Electronic Waste. EPA Needs to Better Control Harmful U.S. Exports Through Stronger Enforcement and More Comprehensive Regulation.* Aug. 2008. 11 Jan. 2013. Web.

Yeats, William Butler. *Collected Poems.* London: Wordsworth Editions, 2000. Print.

Loss in the Language of Tomorrow
Journeying Through Tucson on the Way to "Usher II"

AARON BARLOW

When Ray Bradbury refers to "realism" in his story "Usher II" in *The Martian Chronicles*, he's not referring specifically to the historical "school" of Stephen Crane and William Dean Howells but to the opposite of the imaginative. His "realism" extends far beyond the writers of the end of the 19th century but also includes many of those of his parents' generation, authors who loomed over younger writers, dark clouds whose rains kept away the fancy of the sun. At least, that's how Bradbury might have seen the situation.

Bradbury's personal vision of realism also includes what was once the new type of academic consideration of literature, the work of the New Critics who, in the mind of romantics like Bradbury, stripped everything away from stories leaving only "text," ink on paper. These movements are gone, now, or have been consumed in new movements or are appearing again in new forms. But they were once quite strong. Caught up in the mania for science and its reproducible results, they seemed to aim to produce an objective writing and both objective reading and criticism, all removed from vagaries of personality — be it that of writer, reader, or critic.

Bradbury, even as a young man, was having none of it. Certainly not while he was preparing his first book in the late 1940s.

Later, in a 1997 introduction to that book, *The Martian Chronicles*, Bradbury tells us, in italics, to keep away from him the type of thing I am doing here, right now, by writing this (and that you are complicit in, by reading).

105

In keeping with his general outlook on life, he didn't say don't do it, just that he didn't want to know about it. Perhaps it's only fair to have waited until he was dead, including it in a memorial volume not for him, but for all of us who have been influenced by him. After all, he knew that the "how" of his craft is important but also that concentration on that "how" rather than on the "doing" itself could kill his ability to draw on the inner unknowns that allowed him to write. It was a personal thing.

Still, his directive reminds me, in a way, of the plaint in T.S. Eliot's "The Love Song of J. Alfred Prufock," where the narrator grumbles:

> And when I am formulated, sprawling on a pin,
> When I am pinned and wriggling on the wall,
> Then how should I begin
> To spit out all the butt-ends of my days and ways?
> And how should I presume?

Bradbury explains his refusal to hear analysis of his work, to look at it (and himself) sprawled like a butterfly on Eliot's pin: "by pretending at ignorance, the intuition, curious at seeming neglect, rears its invisible head and snakes out through your palmprints in mythological form" (xi–xii). Otherwise, if he did look, like Prufrock he would be stifled. He would not have then presumed.

In addition, Bradbury has also written, "Early on, in and out of high school, and standing on a street corner selling newspapers, I did what most writers do at their beginnings: emulated my elders, imitated my peers, thus turning away from any possibility of discovering truths beneath my skin and behind my eyes" (viii). Once he found his voice, pulling it out from inside himself, he never did have to bow or to hesitate. Doing so, he knew, might even have caused him to be silenced forever.

For he *did* presume and wanted to stick with simply that, in all its complexity. He had turned to himself, finding not butt-ends but astonishment. And so I, too, presume, writing my essay about him from inside of me, emulating Bradbury, perhaps, but not obeying him. He would, I hope, appreciate that.

In some respects, it doesn't surprise me that Bradbury should have made the discovery of the self hiding inside the skin to the possibility of writing well, that he should have found the curiosity that made him resonate so well with readers. He grew up, he says, on myths, fables, and science fiction — but (and we should be grateful for this) when a "mature" reader or writer should shed these childish things in favor of modernism and the idea of replicable results, he faltered. Realism: that's what adults read and write, he surely heard … and literary criticism, well, that, I am sure he also heard, dealt with the words on the page, ones that could be examined, counted, and considered, all with the idea of coming up with an indisputable conclusion. The story, to use a phrase of his, would be thus trapped on paper, making the tales, like his own description of his early work, "lifeless robots, mechanical and motionless" (viii). If he could not have gotten beyond that, of course, if he could not have slipped around the influence, he never could have become Ray Bradbury, successful author.

Nothing overtly personal should be involved in "real" writing, he surely heard (or imagined he heard), certainly nothing imaginary — and no romance. "'Oh, realism! Oh, here, oh, now, oh hell!'" (167). The words Bradbury placed in the mouth of William Stendahl in "Usher II" must have come from his own heart. Stendahl's triumph, we readers intuit, was also his own.

That line, coming from Bradbury's heart, certainly pierced mine. I've quoted it often, and in contexts from the political to the personal. To me, it is perhaps the most memorable line of 20th century American fiction. The words are a cry against order, against knowing too much, and against "deciding" that the imaginative is not real and that art is merely a craft of building. They are a cry against the death of wonder, both in reading and in writing; they buck the trend represented by the midcentury mindset where the precision of Hemingway ruled and writings of that new type of "literary criticism" that had to be about things, about "texts" and not about people.

The self was taken out of the equation along with all of those emotions, suspicions, guesses, and secret hopes that the world has always hidden much more than it revealed but that the self contained and does reveal. Objective truth, in the modern world, seemed to be all that mattered, and all that could not be found if the personalities of writers and critics interfered with the quest.

So, out they go!

Bradbury bucked the trend. Or what he saw as the trend. He just couldn't do it, couldn't let go.

What made him different? What allowed him to maintain his grip on the elusive visions of past, present, and future that he saw as all rolled into one, visions that would prove so vital to his writings and to their continued life? He writes that, while producing a staged version of *The Martian Chronicles* in the early 1980s, he saw an exhibition of artifacts from Tutankhamen's tomb — and saw in them his own Mars. Later, watching his Mars performed, he saw King Tut in it: "before my eyes and mixed in my mind, old myths were renewed, new myths were bandaged in papyrus" (x–xi). What made him able to see so much and so many similarities in, often, what appeared to be so little and so different?

The answer, as far as I can tell, lies in two experiences of his, at least. The first was the learning of the nature of language itself, an experience of reading. Language is a repository of the past just as it is a tool of the present and a foretelling of the future. Most of us forget that, seeing the words we use as only things, concrete things that we build with. Through reading, Bradbury had learned that they were much more, that their abundance takes them far beyond their application on the page or in speech. He learned this once and for all, he says, through Sherwood Anderson's *Winesburg, Ohio* with its "dozen characters living their lives on half-lit porches and in sunless attics of that always autumn town" (viii).

The second experience was his encounter with the "New West" during his periods in Tucson, Arizona, while his family was engaged in a movement that would, ultimately, take them from Waukegan, Illinois to Los Angeles, California. It was in Tucson, certainly, that he learned that the fabulous worlds he had already been reading about so often weren't really simply creations of the mind — he discovered that they could be *real*. Even amid the new and modern buildings — just like the new buildings all over the country — and the new inhabitants (including his family), the signs of another Tucson remained, signs of the desert, the Spanish, and the Pima. Bradbury must have seen worlds on worlds there, in an Arizona fast transforming itself almost as completely as Bradbury's settlers would transform Mars.

Tucson, in 1930, had grown by 50 percent in the Roaring Twenties just ended and was over four times as large as it had been at the turn of the century. It had solid stone buildings identical to the new ones of the East and a "forward-looking" attitude even as the Great Depression was starting. The past of Native Americans, Spanish, and Mexicans was receding into the tomorrow of an American modernism quite in keeping with the rest of the nation. Yet the old could still be seen even as it disappeared around rebuilt corners, and the romance of it must have still shone brightly for a boy from the staid and (certainly to him) old-fashioned Midwest, one who could still imagine the legendary "Old West" of horses and steam engines in this "New West" where automobiles and airplanes were fast bringing in the homogeneity his imagination had so recently left behind. Still, no matter how much he longed for the mystery of the past, the older vision of trails of romance was indeed fast being replaced by the constraining highways of realism.

Tucson was also a *new* new world, and not just to the young Bradbury. To a young transplanted Midwesterner, it was a strange and fabulous combination of both past and coming future. It was, at twelve, Bradbury's real-life Mars ... even if a fading one, an imaginative one, and an appearing one.

The Mars he imagined, Tucson, one of the new worlds he had reached, was myriad and was tailored by the books he had been reading, including the Edgar Rice Burroughs' John-Carter-of-Mars series. The seventh of the tales, *A Fighting Man of Mars*, appeared in book form in 1931, when Bradbury was eleven and just when his family was to-ing and fro-ing from Tucson. But Bradbury had been reading other things as well, the stories of L. Frank Baum's Oz, a world as fanciful as Burroughs' Mars (maybe more so), Lewis Carroll's wonderland, even curiouser and curiouser. And he was reading of Kipling's India, and Poe's dreary shades and oppressive monuments. And more. Tucson must have represented all of these — and it must have excited and disappointed him as its realities were experienced and new doorways were both opened and closed.

It was a wonderful age in Tucson for Bradbury to be a reader, eleven was, with twelve being, perhaps, even better. Sometime in the 1950s, Peter Graham, an editor at *Void*, a small science-fiction fan magazine, apparently coined an appropriate phrase for part of what Bradbury was experiencing two decades earlier: "The golden age of science fiction is twelve." Perhaps it's also the golden age for *all* reading — or the start of one, especially for those who massage their reading into writing, something Bradbury, even at that young age, had begun to do. It was an inspiring age, and unique (or seemed so, to each reader). Though it started with others, the writers, it always ended up with oneself, the most important reader. Bradbury claims that

> by giving romance and adventure to a whole generation of boys, Burroughs caused them to go out and decide to become special. That's what we have to do for everyone, give the gift of life with our books. Say to a girl or boy at age ten, Hey, life is fun! Grow tall! I've talked to more biochemists and more astronomers and technologists in various fields, who, when they were ten years old, fell in love with John Carter and Tarzan and decided to become something romantic [Weller].

He's right, though the kids didn't become only scientists and technologists. Burroughs and the others led me and thousands of others far removed from the lab to adventure, too — to a life that, for me, included four years in Africa and a great many different sorts of exploration before I settled into an academic career. Bradbury, once a fellow follower himself, led others — including me — to new words and worlds. When I was in my teens, I devoured his books, especially *Fahrenheit 451*, for I was crazy for words. Just like the John Carter books were mine alone, or so I had thought a few years earlier, Bradbury made me wild to go to new private places, or to explore the new places I was already going. Like Bradbury's at that age, my family bounced around a great deal.

The landscape of twelve, for me, was the mountains of North Carolina, another place of past and prologue, and then the wats, the temples of Thailand, where different pasts and futures also collide. For Bradbury, the landscape was Tucson, as golden as any place imagined in science fiction yet sometimes deceptively barren, just as is the Mars of John Carter — or the later Mars of Bradbury himself. The parallel was probably immediately clear to the young reader, as was excitement at the encounters with the unknown, both in life and in fiction. John Carter's Earth, Dorothy's Kansas, and Bradbury's Waukegan were all where one came *from*; Mars and Oz and Tucson were where one was going. It was exciting to get there, though the excitement was tempered by the past, by "home," though it was also sometimes disappointing for entirely different (and unique) reasons. Certainly, as Bradbury would say many years later, "everything went into ferment that one year, 1932, when I was twelve" (Weller). Tucson had to have been a major part of that ferment.

But that new world, for all its mystery, proved more dreary than Mars for John Carter or Oz for Dorothy. That's the problem with reality. On its own, it has no imagination. Excitement is brought to it — it does not exist in it. Exploring Tucson must have showed Bradbury that much of it wasn't even new at all, but had been imported from the old, from back east of the Mississippi, on its arrival obliterating all but trace elements of the unknown grandeur Bradbury had expected to find. Modernism, with its straight lines and determined visions, had arrived in the same boxcars. The lesson Bradbury took away as he watched the new land a-building was one he carried into his own writing.

Building or not, 1932 was a low point for the modern era. Cracks were appearing as cheap foundations became evident: it was the depth of the Great Depression. Tucson's growth spurt was gone, not to appear again until the 1950s. Hope for the future, there still was (this was America, after all), but it was tempered by a gritty realism that threatened to dash all dreams against dust storms and empty factories. There had to be more, Bradbury may have thought as he looked around at all the contradictions. And there was, but it came from an ephemeral source, one that could not be measured and examined. Like Dorothy, he had to find it within himself— and, like Dorothy, he did, though it did not take him back to Illinois, his own Kansas. Instead, it took him forward. Ultimately, it took him to Mars.

The two distinct (though merging through the growing of American commonality) physical worlds of Waukegan and Tucson, along with the dying Arizona past, the harsh present, and the emerging and imagined glittery future, may also have been the genesis of what Bradbury would later call "a ricochet vision" (Weller) a way of looking ahead to see what's behind — or vice versa. A way of looking over to see under — and vice versa. A way of looking backward

and forward to see what's here now. Making it even more complicated, Bradbury was moving through the landscape, too, something of a ricochet himself.

The objects of vision, too, ricocheted. "Wild West" heritages competed
with the "New West" of oil, machines, and money creating their own double
visions of past and future, or of past covering future (or vice versa), both
being real and, as Bradbury was surely discovering, both also fake. Just two
years after the he left Tucson for good, settling with his family in Los Angeles,
the Johnny Mercer composition "I'm an Old Cowhand (from the Rio Grande)"
laughed at the juxtaposition old and new in the West and became a hit. It
includes these lines:

> We know all the songs that the cowboys know
> 'Bout the big corral where the doggies go;
> We learned them all on the radio!
> Yippie yi yo kay ay.

Yippee, indeed. Even the songs and the cowboys themselves were creations
of the entertainment industry, Bradbury would discover as he explored the
environs of Hollywood, creatures of the myth-making machinery.

Sometimes it must have seemed as though all that remained of the old
was its pelt, now draped over a new and mechanical body. Even though there
was real romance in the past of the Southwest, it too had fallen into the wheels
of the dynamo and, no matter how much he might want to try, Bradbury
must have known he could not reclaim it — part of the reason, I think, for
the pervasive, though often unspoken, sense of nostalgia in a lot of his work,
nostalgia not for a particular past, but for attitudes of discovery and amaze-
ment that should live on even when one necessarily turns to the future but
that so often don't, that nostalgia for the age of twelve.

Though he did not stay there long, what Bradbury learned in Tucson
around that absolutely critical age of twelve colored all that he would later
do — in terms of writing, at least. In terms of words, Tucson taught him what
could have been, what was, and what could be. That it did so on top of the
reading that the kid was already doing made it possible for Bradbury to grow
to become a rare voice in American literature, an omnivoice that seemed at
once only influence and beyond influence. A ricochet writer, but one with
understanding that ricochets can still hit. Better than almost anyone else, he
understood that the language of tomorrow always includes the past, no matter
how "forward facing" we may pretend our thoughts to be. The real language
of tomorrow, after all, includes recognition of all of the lost pasts, even those
it has rolled over or that it had turned into the material of its own amusement.
Perhaps Eliot, again, at the start of "Burnt Norton," has expressed it best:

> Time present and time past
> Are both perhaps present in time future,
> And time future contained in time past.
> If all time is eternally present
> All time is unredeemable.

Only language redeems the past.

What Bradbury was learning, and what stayed with him, was that the key to great writing is a sense of wonder — both for reader and writer — and that words are the key that unlocks it. The realism and the modernization that was becoming Tucson were, as he may have seen it, also entailing the leaving of wonder behind. In writing, it left the past in favor of words as things instead of keys and its modernization, too, was an acquired taste, though not one, he must have discovered, that he cared to quest. He hinted as to why, in that interview years later: "It started with Poe. I imitated him from the time I was twelve until I was about eighteen. I fell in love with the jewelry of Poe. He's a gem encruster, isn't he? Same with Edgar Rice Burroughs and John Carter" (Weller). Realism strips away the gems, leaving not Mars, not Oz, and not even Tucson with its ghosts of Native Americans and Spaniards. Leaving only the rigidity of the railroad line.

The realism Bradbury saw strips away childhood and the best of writing. All good writing, he might have argued, is made for children: "Edgar Allan Poe, Herman Melville, Washington Irving, and Nathaniel Hawthorne. All these people wrote for children. They may have pretended not to, but they did" (Weller). Tucson, too, was made of magic for children — but it was being paved for adults.

The writers who Bradbury claimed wrote for children managed to maintain passion for words and for stories as passages from one person to another, maintaining it throughout their creative lives. He emulated them, though probably without making the conscious choice: "My passions drive me to the typewriter every day of my life, and they have driven me there since I was twelve" (Weller). And it was not just for the writing, but for the telling implied, for the talking. For the communication.

Bradbury, in his attitude and passion as a storyteller, always reminds me of Samuel Taylor Coleridge's ancient mariner:

> He holds him with his glittering eye —
> The Wedding-Guest stood still,
> And listens like a three years' child:
> The Mariner hath his will.

This is the storytelling that had also entranced Bradbury, and that he then learned to use to entrance others. But there's more: "I just can't imagine being in a world and not being fascinated with what ideas are doing to us" (Weller). It's not just the tale, but the concepts behind them that make some stories so devilishly attractive. And it's not just the landscape that does the same, but the world around it. The creation.

And the fun. Writing is "the exquisite joy and madness of my life, and I don't understand writers who have to work at it. I like to play. I'm interested in having fun with ideas, throwing them up in the air like confetti and then running under them" (Weller). If that makes him childish, Bradbury seems to be saying, so be it. The adults and their serious creations, after all, so often turn out to be bores.

Though he had such a vibrant literary past to play amongst, and could see science fiction, just born, beginning to shake itself off, stand up, and look around, the primary focus of the major artists of "real literature" of his youth was continuing to move in another direction, just as the country was, a direction of realism and confinement. As he grew older and his own readings broadened, Bradbury probably began to look at his elder, more successful contemporaries (contemporaries of his parents, actually) with something of a sinking feeling. Hemingway had become the model, with nary a smile, in a world stripped of romance and wonder.

I am reminded, here, of William Butler Yeats's "The Second Coming," though of it, too, stripped down, its religious meanings taken away:

> The Second Coming! Hardly are those words out
> When a vast image out of Spiritus Mundi
> Troubles my sight: a waste of desert sand;
> A shape with lion body and the head of a man,
> A gaze blank and pitiless as the sun,
> Is moving its slow thighs, while all about it
> Wind shadows of the indignant desert birds.

Reading was being pared down, and the writer was now becoming the creature of the blank gaze, the readers nothing more than indignant desert birds. What was coming again wasn't just made new (to steal from Ezra Pound) but was destruction of the old as the new claimed the old as its raw material, claiming it because it had been there before. Tucson, with its storied past, must have seemed emblematic of just this sort of change.

To make matters worse, no longer, in realism, was a story expansive, a starting point for the imagination. The New Critics, the university wardens of all that was "real literature," were making it a prisoner to the text — a text no longer the living embodiment of a writer's passion but a thing on a page meant mainly to be examined and evaluated. An exercise for the mind, not a joy.

Just as Bradbury was starting to write seriously, W.K. Wimsatt and Monroe Beardsley published an article in *The Sewanee Review* entitled "The Intentional Fallacy" which was a slap on the wrist to anyone reaching to move beyond the text to try to add imagination and human interaction back in — to return to the telling of a story and to the listening, the reading. They even go so far as to denigrate the importance of what the writer may have set out to do, writing that "the design or intention of the author is neither available nor desirable as a standard for judging the success of a work of literary art" (Wimsatt). Neither, then, is design or intention on the part of the reader. It's the thing alone that counts, not what was meant, not what was received.

Oh, what a bore! A work of literature is nothing more than squiggles on paper? An inert "thing?" "Judging a poem is like judging a pudding or a machine. One demands that it work. It is only because an artifact works that we infer the intention of an artificer. 'A poem should not mean but be'" (Wimsatt). Well, then, let it work. Let it be. But why read it?

Certainly, Wimsatt and Beardsley, as representatives of the New Critics and many of the attitudes of major writers of the day, had taken all of the fun away from reading, making the text simply mechanical instead of magical:

> The day may arrive when the psychology of composition is unified with the science of objective evaluation, but so far they are separate. It would be convenient if the passwords of the intentional school, "sincerity," "fidelity," "spontaneity," "authenticity," "genuineness," "originality," could be equated with terms of analysis such as "integrity," "relevance," "unity," "function"; with "maturity," "subtlety," and "adequacy," and other more precise axiological terms. In short, if "expression" always meant aesthetic communication. But this is not so [Wimsatt].

Personally, I'll take the vague terms over axiological precision any day. Give me the genuine sloppiness of spontaneity over the mature function of integrity. The values I want to study aren't embedded in the text, but in the author and in his or her interactions with the reader. I think that Bradbury would agree. But, the scholars say, "critical inquiries, unlike bets, are not settled in this way. Critical inquiries are not settled by consulting the oracle" (Wimsatt).

Why does that make Walt Whitman come to mind?:

When I heard the learn'd astronomer;
When the proofs, the figures, were ranged in columns before me;
When I was shown the charts and the diagrams, to add, divide, and measure them;
When I, sitting, heard the astronomer, where he lectured with much applause in the
    lecture-room,
How soon, unaccountable, I became tired and sick;
Till rising and gliding out, I wander'd off by myself,
In the mystical moist night-air, and from time to time,
Look'd up in perfect silence at the stars.

Why? Because, in fact, critical inquiries *are* settled by consulting the oracle ... and the oracle lies within us and in the stars above us.

At the beginning of "Usher II," while quoting the opening lines of Poe's "The Fall of the House of Usher," Stendahl (his name carries a certain irony, for the French writer Stendhal is considered one of the earliest realists) views the house he has paid to have created. "Wouldn't Mr. Poe be *delighted*?" (161) he asks his architect. Rhetorically. The architect, Stendhal knows, has no idea what he has done, merely having followed Stendahl's direction, never having read Poe or even having heard of "The Fall of the House of Usher." Through the architect, Stendahl has created a house not just desolate and terrible, but one that will fall down quite soon, one that will exist (like a story) only in memory — though it will have done quite a bit in the meantime. Like Bradbury's slightly younger contemporary science-fiction writer, Philip K. Dick, Stendahl likes "to build universes which *do* fall apart. I like to see them come unglued" (5). For Stendahl, that's his joy, his revenge against a world bound by realism, a world that will destroy his creation if he does not do it himself. It will do so because the house is, of course, far from what realism is about. Stendahl says, "'It was enough just to be able to create this place'" (168). *That's* the real joy. Given the situation, it has to be. For a romantic like Stendahl, that is, there is really no other option.

The beauty and the irony of what Stendahl has done is that he has turned the mechanical, the modern, and the objective against itself ... or, perhaps, into itself ... by having robots made that look just like the humans that they will replace. He then has happen to them (the humans) what happens to characters in Edgar Allen Poe stories while the robots look on, apparently humans enchanted by what is happening to their supposedly robot doubles. Just as Bradbury probably saw an ersatz and real past, present, and future in Tucson, so it is here, all of them getting mixed up, one with another.

A Mr. Garrett, "Investigator of Moral Climates" (166), arrived earlier in the story to condemn the house, but Stendahl has had him killed by a robot, just after telling Garrett not to be afraid of it. After all, it's just "'a robot. Copper skeleton and all, like the witch. See?'" (168). But "Garrett," who is immediately replaced by a robot Stendahl has prepared, turns out to have been a robot himself, the "real" Garrett only appearing in time to see the 'robots' destroyed toward the end of the story.

In many ways, it is the robots which are realism. Just like the writings of realism, however, they only look real but cover mechanical innards. That's the irony of realism as Bradbury imagines it: art never is real; it only appears real through our imaginative acceptance of it as a stand-in for reality. Bradbury describes his robots in such a way that he makes the parallel clear:

Full grown without memory, the robots waited.... Oiled, with tube bones cut from bronze and sunk in gelatin, the robots lay. In coffins for the not dead and not alive, in planked boxes, the metronomes waited to be set in motion.... There was a silence in the tomb yard. Sexed but sexless, the robots. Named but unnamed, and borrowing from humans everything but humanity [171].

Realism, too, is a borrowing from humanity. Realism, too, can have everything — but humanity. Realism, ultimately, is a fake.

And realism, to add insult to injury, doesn't even require reading, the basic utilization of the art of imagination. Just as the architect at the beginning of the story hasn't read Poe, neither has Garrett, who should know what is happening to him close to the end of the story as he is bricked into the room that will be his tomb:

> "Garrett?" called Stendahl softly. Garrett silenced himself. "Garrett," said Stendahl, "do you know why I've done this to you? Because you burned Mr. Poe's books without really reading them. You took other people's advice that they needed burning. Otherwise you'd have realized what I was going to do to you when we came down here a moment ago. Ignorance is fatal, Mr. Garrett."
> Garrett was silent [180].

The Garretts are what Bradbury had seen proliferating during his childhood, proliferating and then burying what they had never experienced and could not understand — including the mystery of a wonderful and fascinating place like Tucson.

But the past, again, is always in the future and in the present. It is still there, even in Tucson. It cannot be obliterated.

It can, however, as Garrett discovers, obliterate *you*.

Works Cited

Bradbury, Ray. *The Martian Chronicles.* New York: William Morrow, 1997. Print.
Dick, Philip K. "How to Build a Universe That Doesn't Fall Apart Two Days Later." *I Hope I Shall Arrive Soon.* Garden City, NY: Doubleday, 1985. 1–23. Print.
Weller, Sam. Interview with Ray Bradbury. "Ray Bradbury, the Art of Fiction No. 203." *The Paris Review* 192, Spring 2010. Nov. 1, 2012. Web..
Wimsatt, W.K., and Monroe Beardsley. "The Intentional Fallacy." *Sewanee Review* 54, 1946. 468–488. Print.

Bradbury's Mars
Pathway to Reinvention and Redemption

KIMBERLY FAIN

The Martian Chronicles by Ray Bradbury manifests the destruction of a Martian civilization and the attempted (and unintended) extinction of its culture. Through the interweaving themes of nostalgia, reinvention, and redemption, Bradbury reveals the dual identity of Americans as both citizens and descendants of an immigrant legacy. The juxtaposition of these two realities represents a duplicitous tension in contemporary America, as well as in the characters and landscape of Mars. Bradbury's awareness of the dual nature of Americans is reflected in these science fiction tales wherein Mars is the new West. The contemporary American Dream becomes the Martian Dream of the future. By depicting American issues of "inequality, ecology, materialism, and war, he extrapolates an opportunity for Martian colonizers to objectively view themselves through a philosophical prism" (Grimsley 1239–40). The economic opportunity and freedom sought by explores who conquered the New World in the 1500s, and the early settlers who traveled west in the United States during the 1700s and 1800s, is mirrored in the short stories of *The Martian Chronicles*. Ironically, the Third Expedition brings the Chicken Pox epidemic, which kills most Martians prior to the arrival of the Fourth Expedition in the short story "And the Moon be Still as Bright." Similarly, the Smallpox epidemic had a genocidal effect on the Native Americans who came in contact with early European settlers (Hodge 544). Charles Mann, author of the best-selling book *1491* declares that during the pandemics of 1770s and 1780s "disease turned whole societies to ash" (126). Bradbury mirrors some of those disastrous effects in his stories that span from 2030 to 2057, by exploring "the effects of Mars landings and settlement on individual Earth people, and occasionally on the dying Martians themselves" (Abbott 241). Bradbury effectively

117

recognizes and articulates the impact of colonial invasion, the danger of impos-ing predisposed notions, and the genocidal effects of infecting prejudice into an indigenous culture. However, nostalgia for the past may consume a people's present and cause the future extinction of an established civilization.

Bradbury's Early Life in the Southwest

Bradbury's early rearing in Tucson, Arizona, and Los Angeles, California, not only influenced his knowledge of the Southwestern landscape and the rich culture of Native Americans, but provided the metaphor of both the stars in the night sky and the Hollywood stars. When Bradbury attended Los Ange-les high school, his fascination with both celebrity stars and the stars in the cosmos rooted an impression in the young man. He obtained thousands of autographs from A-list film stars, executives, and stars from the golden age of radio (Eller 16). His obsession with the entertainment mediums of "stage, screen, and radio" motivated his pursuit of short fiction classes and one poetry class (16). In *Becoming Ray Bradbury*, Jonathan Eller writes that Bradbury's narratives were derivatives of the golden age science fiction and fantasy pulps of his youth (16). During the fall of Bradbury's senior year, an astronomy class that he attended during the fall of 1937 provided the young man with a working knowledge of the Solar System and the galactic island of stars (Eller 17). Yet, even at this juncture in his life, his focus was on the Red Planet; his most detailed class notes document the lectures he observed about Mars and the twin moons (17). At the age of ten, Bradbury's interest in Mars was birthed by Percival Lowell's *Mars as the Abode of Life* (1910). "[H]is high-school studies provided the basic background necessary to plot the simple planetary adven-tures that mark his earliest professional science fiction" (17). Even at this youth-ful age, Bradbury demonstrated interest in the Red Planet, the fourth dimension, space travel, and time travel (17). Yet, this romantic fascination with the nature of technology surpasses his interest in the fundamental principles of science (17). The author reiterates that Bradbury's "note-taking for Astronomy appears routine, and reflects very little true engagement with the more technical aspects of the course" (17). Undoubtedly, Bradbury didn't need an advanced under-standing of science to create fiction that captivated an audience.

Western Homesteading and Colonizing the Extraterrestrial Frontier

The Martian Chronicles is composed of interconnected vignettes that meander between the genres of science fiction, fantasy, and nostalgic realism

(Abbott 240). Bradbury's work exemplifies his Midwestern upbringing, his futuristic notions, and his personal exposure to California's great transformation amid and subsequent to the Second World War (240). Carl Abbott argues that "Bradbury's mass-market stories evangelized for the high frontier of space exploration and its power to redeem or rescue a troubled and threatened world" (240). Since the 1930s, America's nationalistic efforts fostered the groundwork for extraterrestrial pioneers who reflected values of such folklore heroes as John "Johnny Appleseed" Chapman (240). *The Martian Chronicles* served as an intellectual experiment, examining the responses of middle-class Americans, in the 1940s, and their intuitive ability to thrive on an actual frontier (240–241). In "The Wilderness," the story begins in Independence, Missouri, which was a starting point for the Oregon Trail (Abbott 240). Janice lies in the bed, pondering as she prepares to join her husband on Mars, "Is this how it was over a century ago, she wondered, when the women, the night before, lay ready for sleep, or not ready, in the small towns of the East, and heard the sound of horses in the night and the creak the Conestoga wagons ready to go, and the brooding of oxen under the trees" (Bradbury 158–159). In the midst of the character's nostalgic reflection, she is making a historical allusion connecting the pioneering and homesteading past with interplanetary travel of the future.

Homesteading is a process that is used to settle "empty" or underdeveloped territories, which may be the plains of North America or the envisioned planets of science fiction writers' stories (Abbott 242). This type of agricultural settlement is deeply ingrained in the American history of the Homestead Act of 1862 (242). For individuals who were willing to cultivate and reside on the land for five years, an offer of 160 acres of land was bestowed upon them (242). Thus, the legislation of the Homestead Act and Americans' ingenuity may be credited with developing the western half of the United States (242). A frontier is geographically more than open space on a terrain (Schmalholz 45). Appropriately, the frontier may be construed in terms of a cultural, technological, and social change (Schmalholz 45). Frontier narratives contain many elements; however, terraforming stories focus on the problems of technology, organization, power, and politics (Abbott 242). Problems of technology may be interpreted under the guise of social issues and speculations of prevailing social structures of the future (Shaftel 99). Thus, various stories by Bradbury, such as "And the Moon Be Still as Bright" and "Way in the Middle of the Air" encompass the societal ills that both plagued and triumphed early settler history and the modern milieu of the 1940s and 1950s. Stories that take place on imagined planets are referred to as "terraforming" because they draw on settlement experience, adaption, and the "mythology of the American farm-making frontier" (Abbott 242). Admittedly, Bradbury drew from mythology to create stories about Mars that would prevail over practical and efficient science fiction (Bradbury "Introduction" XI). Bradbury once said, "Science and machines can kill each other off or be replaced. Myth, seen in mirrors, incapable of being touched, stays on. If it is not immortal, it almost seems such" ("Introduction" XI). Bradbury's tales take his readers, on a descriptive and mythological journey that is both historically familiar, yet adventurous in its unearthly nature. Therefore, the evolution of western frontier stories lies in the imagery and mythology of this historical reality (Abbott 243). Thus, science fiction reflects, this pervasive American settlement narrative from the formation of the Old West into the intergalactic future of unknown space exploration (243).

The Smallpox of the Old World Is the New Chicken Pox on Mars

Bradbury reminds his audience that adaptation and assimilation is preferential to imposition of predetermined values and traditions that conflict with an indigenous civilization. In *The Martian Chronicles*, the Chicken Pox epidemic paradoxically mirrors the Smallpox epidemic for the purposes of infusing dramatic irony into the New World. Furthermore, epidemics represent the plague of ignorance and prejudice carried by immigrants from the Old World to Mars. Bradbury utilizes the genocidal effects of pandemic disease to embody the fear and decimation of the unknown. In other words, when a society fears the native, there is a tendency to silence or destroy that indigenous group or civilization. In *The Martian Chronicles*, Chicken Pox represents that pandemic need to cleanse or purify that which a people don't understand. Bradbury challenges his audience to appreciate Mars and to adapt instead of engaging in America's past history of genocide with respect to native populations.

By the 1670s, the newcomers triumphed not only because they outnumbered the natives after the 1616 epidemic, but in 1633 a "third to half of the remaining Indians in New England died" from a Smallpox epidemic (Mann 70). James McKay, a trader, remarked that of all of the Scourges and Plagues that affected the Native American populations, Smallpox caused the most mortality (Hodge 543). Adam R. Hodge, a historian, writes that the Native population was reduced when an "outbreak swept through the northern Plains for eighteen months from 1780 to 1782, approximately forty percent of the region's Native population perished" (543). Smallpox had far reaching effects that didn't sequester themselves to the New England or Northern Plains. Mann asserts that "Smallpox raced along the network through the Great Plains and the Rocky Mountains, ricocheting among the Mandan, Hidatsa, Ojibwe, Crow, Blackfoot, and Shoshone, a helter-skelter progress in which the virus leapfrogged from central Mexico to the shore of Hudson Bay in less than two years" (124). Dramatic changes caused by such epidemics as Smallpox disrupted the intertribal balance of power and socio-economic dynamics between Native groups (Hodge 543). Consequently, the 1780–1782 epidemic shaped the landscape of the United States, thereby granting the government the geographical space and the freedom to explore and conquer that land, with less resistance, which ultimately led to the purchase of that region in 1803 (Hodge 544).

Charles C. Mann presents evidence in his award winning book *1491*, that the Native Americans may have battled epidemics prior to the arrival of the Europeans (122). However, even Mann cannot deny that after the arrival of Europeans, Smallpox decimated native populations by turning cities into ash (126). Furthermore, Smallpox was used as an instrument of war by the United States government. Pulitzer Prize winner, Jared Diamond, author of *Guns, Germs, and Steel* writes that "the skin lesions caused by smallpox similarly spread microbes by direct or indirect body contact (occasionally very indirect, as when U.S. whites bent on wiping out 'belligerent' Native Americans sent them gifts of blankets previously used by smallpox patients" (199). Sadly, more indigenous people died from "Eurasian germs" than on the battlefield from European weapons such as guns and swords (Diamond 210). Undoubtedly, the well-read Bradbury was aware of this tumultuous relationship between the European conquerors and those that were conquered. In *The Martian Chronicles*, Bradbury links past transgressions from westward movement to the arrival of Earthlings on the Martian frontier. In so doing, an opportunity for humanity's redemption presents itself on Mars. Consequently, he builds a metaphorical bridge between the American frontier and the Martian frontier. "Bradbury implicitly compares the interactions between native inhabitants of Mars and Earthlings with the interactions between Native Americans and European settlers" (Schmalholz 45). But, before this future redemption manifests on Mars, the Chicken Pox epidemic reminds us of the dismal and genocidal impact of Smallpox caused by the European settlers. Since native populations had never experienced such a threat, they were demoralized by such mass mortality (Diamond 210), and they did not have the medical experience to quarantine or isolate the sick as Europeans did in Europe (Mann 120). However, during the 1800s the rebel army suffered death from Smallpox, as well (122). As a result of their American birth, they harbored no endemic immunity, which their European ancestors often had garnished due to childhood exposure to that fatal disease (122). Therefore, some may argue that Smallpox is an indiscriminate killer that knows no bounds or racial distinctions. By employing a sense of historical significance, Bradbury uses the Chicken Pox epidemic to demonstrate indiscriminate fear of the unknown and the resulting infectious plague literally and figuratively, threatening to wipeout both the newcomers and the natives in Mars.

The Martian Chronicles *Is the New Western Frontier*

Bradbury incorporates the imagery and the mythology of the western frontier into his futuristic tales of the Martian frontier (Abbott 243). Additionally, the Third Expedition acts as a foreign invader into a Martian town. Inevitably, the reader is assured that catastrophic results will ensue upon the introduction of the alien (Levin and Prizel 253). In the mythic tale "And the Moon Be Still as Bright," it is revealed that the Earthling astronauts from the Third Expedition unintentionally killed the Martians with the Chicken Pox virus. The narrator informs the readers that the Chicken Pox virus "did things to the Martians it never did to Earth Men. Their metabolism reacted differently, I suppose. Burnt them black and dried them out to brittle flakes" (Bradbury 69). Bradbury recognizes that Chicken Pox is "a child's disease that doesn't even kill children on Earth" (70). Nevertheless, the author expects the readers to suspend their disbelief, which is consistent with science fiction principles, to infuse a grand warning to humanity. Therefore, Science Fiction acts as a vehicle to highlight the perils in society by using simplified models (Levin and Prizel 253). In this case, the danger is exploration that has no regard for the indigenous population that exists on a frontier prior to occupation.

Jeff Spender, the protagonist of "And the Moon Be Still as Bright" is a prototypical explorer who is psychologically devastated by the massive deaths of the Martians. He is captivated by the beautiful city and reveres the ancient artifacts in the primordial cities of Mars. On the contrary, the other explorers celebrate upon hearing that most of the Martians have died due to exposure from Chicken Pox. The men begin to roar. "Three of them lined up and kicked like chorus maidens, joking loudly. The others, clapping hands, yelled for something to happen.... The noise got louder, more men jumped up, someone sucked on a mouth organ, someone else blew on a tissue-papered comb" (Bradbury 71). Spender laments that the men were not trained on how to behave prior to occupying Mars. Despite Captain Wilder's consolation that

the Martians were "graceful, beautiful, and [a] philosophical people" that succumbed relentlessly to a "racial death," Spender continues to mourn (Bradbury
75) Spender recoils in revulsion at the vulgarity of the earthmen's crude celebration; he intends to kill each man to prevent further contamination of
Mars (Shaftel 104). In the midst of Spender's attempts to avenge the deaths
of the Martians, he kills six of his fellow astronauts, but he is perplexed when
a fellow explorer, ironically named Cherokee deems him "crazy" (Bradbury
82). Although Spender acknowledges that killing the men is wrong, he is
determined to ruin every exploration for the next fifty years by killing every
member of its crew (Bradbury 90). Bradbury issues a violent warning about
technology and its uses by humankind to destroy rather than conserve. Literary critic Oscar Shaftel asserts that "this vulgar contraposition of technology
to humanistic culture is one expression of scorn for man's aspirations which
bring only destruction" (104). Spender admires the Martians because they live
with nature, know how to coexist with nature, and they failed to become all
men and no animal (Bradbury 90). There are allusions to the theories of Darwin, Huxley, and Freud that have resulted in the mechanization of man at
the expense of religion (Bradbury 90). For instance, Spender approves of the
Martians' theories on the purpose of life, saying to his captain, "'The Martians
discovered the secret of life among animals. The animal does not question
life. It lives. Its very reason for living is life; it enjoys and relishes life'" (Bradbury 91). Even though Captain Wilder tells his crew that he plans to shoot
Spender, Wilder hopes that Spender will escape. Nevertheless, the Martian
sympathizer has no interest in running away. By allowing Captain Wilder to
kill him, Spender transforms himself from a merciless killer to a Messianic
figure for Martian civilization. Captain Wilder is consumed by the overwhelming feeling that he could have saved Spender; therefore, he administers
rites at an honorable burial for him in an ancient Martian cemetery (98).
Furthermore, the captain reinvents himself as the conservator of the Martian
terrain, by punching the disrespectful Parkhill for "shooting out the crystal
windows and blowing the tops off the fragile towers" in the dead cities (Bradbury 98). Ultimately, the captain's retribution against Parkhill invokes the
message from Spender to enjoy life, coexist with nature, and protect the
ancient ruins of Mars (98–99).

Undoubtedly, the short story "And the Moon Be Still as Bright" renders
anti-materialist and anti-technological messages, which was common for science fiction stories written during the Cold War" (Shaftel 105). However,
Bradbury reiterates another message about geographical expansion at the
expense of indigenous civilizations. Mars symbolizes the Native American
territory, which was infiltrated by European colonists seeking land and reprisal

from religious oppression and economic disparity. Ironically, the Earthlings' quest for manifest destiny is a repeat of history that mimics the behavior of their ancestors on Earth. Spender's killing spree is a romantic, albeit gothic, representation of the result of man's carnal survival instincts when confronted with his own intemperate nature. Meanwhile, Sam Parkhill is Spender's foil, symbolizing the genocidal tendency to exploit the deaths of others and to destroy that which is foreign or unknown. Assuming the antithesis position of Spender, Parkhill enjoys conquering and pillaging the Martian landscape after his crewmates' death (Bradbury 99). For people who travel to Mars, the American ideal of the Christ-like redemption is offered to those who repent and desire a new life. Momentarily, Spender becomes enlightened and reborn upon his trip to Mars. Thus, he can no longer cope with man's destructive tendencies, and he becomes all animal to compensate for this imbalance. Despite Spender's efforts to create equilibrium between his humanity and Mars landscape, his naïve comrades cause him to disintegrate into violence within his new milieu. Therefore, death is the only option for Spender's redemption after having a psychotic breakdown. Whereas, Parkhill's character remains flat, static, and monosyllabic in contrast. Despite a unique opportunity for transformation in the New World, there will always be segments of society or individuals, such as Parkhill, who seize power by demolishing what others have built. Yet, through the actions of Sam Parkhill, Jeff Spender, and Captain Wilder, Bradbury reemphasizes man's tragic attempt to reinvent himself in a new land. Through Spender's dire attempts at preservation, the pervasive theme of conservation is reiterated by Bradbury, compelling his audience to acknowledge and respect the indigenous cultures of any region.

Essential to science fiction theory is the presumption of future technology and social structures (Shaftel 99). By examining the history of America, during our years of expansion and advancement post–World War II, Bradbury is able to present his concerns in a materialistic culture. Sam Parkhill survives Spender's execution spree, but in the "Off Season," he reprises his role as the embodiment of the maleficence of man. Shaftel asserts that "much of science-fiction accepts the assumption of our elite and pulp literature alike that mankind is degraded and unregenerate, not only in our own dying culture but by external nature" (99). Parkhill represents the degraded and degenerate part of man that exists in everyone if society allows ignorance, prejudice, and nostalgia to succumb their better nature. According to Parkhill his intentions are pure, he simply wanted to come to Mars like any other "honest enterprising business man" (Bradbury 211). Nevertheless, when Parkhill lands on Mars, he is hell bent on domination by force. Instead of attempting to coexist with the Martians, he tries to make them feel inferior to Earthlings. Spender says proudly to a being behind a blue mask, "'You Martians are a couple dozen left, got no cities, you wander around the hills, no leaders, no laws, and now you come tell me about this land'" (Bradbury 204). When Parkhill steals an ancient Martian ship, he is then approached by a Martian who wants to befriend him in peace. Instead, Parkhill projects his fearful hostility onto the Martian and makes presumptions about the native's intentions. Assuming malicious intent, Parkhill shoots the Martian and flees from his evil deed without regret. Parkhill, who has disappointed his wife, tries to console her by saying that he only wanted a hot-dog stand (Bradbury 211). Consequently, Parkhill values profit at the expense people and nature, which is a materialistic modern value that Bradbury disavows. Parkhill has no intentions of reinventing his life. His nostalgia for the Old World makes it impossible for him to live with or learn from other cultures. The hot-dog stand is a completely unoriginal idea, derivative of street vendors, in his native city of New York. Nevertheless, the smell, the taste of hot-dogs are reminiscent of home, creating a sense of familiarity in an unfamiliar land.

Sam Parkhill continues to be a one-dimensional character that cannot see beyond his own self-aggrandized desires. In one instance, Parkhill represents the American capitalist spirit that strives to be the first and the only one of its kind. Thus, the utopian spirit of science fiction underlies the macabre darkness of Parkhill's motives. Shaftel claims that "even in the most degraded picture of the future we are likely to find reference to man the striver, the poet, the restless pioneer" (100). But on the other hand, Parkhill represents the savage nature of man to capture, steal, or annihilate anything or anyone that interferes with his manifest vision for a new life. Shaftel argues that science fiction authors, such as Ray Bradbury reemphasize the theme that "Cruelty and aggression and conquest are watermarked in man's spirit, and science only intensifies the potential of destruction" (103). However, the inner and external conflicts of the characters in "And the Moon Be Still as Bright" and "The Off Season" embody a common theme in science fiction. Often, there is a struggle between financial interests and noble scientists and colonizers for domination of recently discovered planets (Shaftel 116). Although Bradbury's *The Martian Chronicles* is published in the 1940s, the stories remain relevant because they retain themes of nostalgia, idealism, and capitalism that is still present in science fiction television shows and movies. After World War II, there exists a "liberal humanist tradition" that examines the relationship between the individual and humanity, hearkening the days of when white settlers won the West with a Bible and a gun, purifying and clearing the Promised Land from the "unworthy Native Americans" (Levin and Prizel 252). Although Levin and Prizel criticize this idealized interpretation by 1950s writers, both authors acknowledge that those basic principles are the basis for much of successful post–World War II science fiction and beyond (252). Parkhill's actions demonstrate the recklessness of early pioneers to a landscape and a people they could not comprehend. Thus, he invokes early frontier history by abolishing artifacts, ancient ruins, and people that he deems incomprehensible.

In the controversial 1950 short story "Way in the Middle the Air," Jim Crow–style segregation empowers Samuel Teece, a member of the Ku Klux Klan, with fertile ground to reign terror in the South. Lynchings, poll taxes, and substandard working wages and living conditions compel all of the African Americans in the South to make exodus to Mars, the Promised Land of the future (Bradbury 96). To the same extent that African Americans migrated up north for freedom, post–World War I, due in part to the fear of violence and lynching (Wilkerson 93), Bradbury's scientific twist is hardly an implausible reason for mass exodus to another planet in the future. Bradbury brilliantly depicts interplanetary space rockets traveling to outer space as freedom vehicles, presenting a redemptive life altering experience prior to the advent of the Civil Rights Movement in 1955. Despite social relevance, there are critics who find fault with this satire on racial inequality (Grimsley 1241). Literary critic Shaftel refers to the short story as patronizing, but congruously triumphant in nature (103). While another critic, Paul Youngquist argues that despite the liberal intentions of Bradbury, "Way in the Middle of the Air" is a neocolonial fantasy that reinforces the idea of black separatism toward the distant shores of Mars (335). Perhaps, evacuation and separation are the only tranquil avenues for these characters. Nevertheless, Youngquist acknowledges the tenacious spirit of the African Americans who emigrate from America for a better world in the sky (335). Furthermore, he credits Bradbury for depicting the terrors of racism, but he claims that the story fails to resolve the discriminatory issues it raises (Youngquist 335). Bradbury never shares with his audience the fate of the black characters, except to celestially say that the inhabitants "fled straight up into the blue heavens ... golden bobbins rising in the sky, far away. Leaving flame behind, they vanished" (101–102). Do the rocket ships explode in the sky, sending all of its passengers to heaven? Or do they land safely on Mars? Youngquist takes a more philosophical approach when he states, "Blacks abandon Earth to land-nowhere. They simply disappear into black space, as if the logic of cosmic liberalism can make no room for them in the known universe" (Youngquist 335). The audience is left to wonder, do the African Americans disappear into the dark matter of the universe? But critics must remember that this story operates as a science fiction-fantasy. Although *The Martian Chronicles* is often described singularly as a work of science fiction, Bradbury refers to his interrelated tales as having a binary function as fables with mythological elements (XI). The purpose of "Way in the Middle of the Air" is not to resolve the discriminatory issues broached by the characters, but instead to emphasize that space exploration offers every man, black or white, the opportunity for reinvention in a distant, far off land. In this instance, the story succeeds as a victorious tale of the transformative nature of Mars.

Instead of promoting the virtues of racial integration, perhaps, this story reinforces discomforting generalizations about the Jim Crow South and unintentionally supports black separatism on Mars, reminiscent of the Marcus Garvey Movement of the 1920s. After all, the racist Samuel Teece suggests that the blacks secretly built their rockets in Africa (Bradbury 91). Nevertheless, this harsh portrayal about the demented nature of the authoritarian rule warrants a deeper review. According to Pulitzer Prize winning author Isabel Wilkerson, blacks who were two generations removed from slavery encountered whites in the South who "had grown more hostile to blacks than even their slaveholding ancestors had been" (43). In 1901, the former governor of Alabama, William C. Oates, marveled at the new generation of Southerners 'When the Negro is doing no harm, why, the people want to kill him and wipe him from the face of the earth' (Wilkerson 43). Regardless of whether critics, such as Robert Dominianni dismiss "Way in the Middle of the Air" as "bathetic" due to its melodramatic content (49), the well-read Bradbury presents futuristic technology with a realistic portrayal of the danger blacks faced from the early 1900s to the mid part of the 20th century in the dissident South. The descriptions of a nonviolent revolt are perhaps some of the most eloquent and beautifully composed prose ever written as a precursor to the actual Civil Rights marches of the mid–1950s. The biblical allusions to Moses's exodus out of Egypt and the parting of the Red Sea for the Israelites (*New Living Translation*, Exodus 14.15–18) further the redemptive possibilities of the Martian Dream as transformative in nature in the midst of social injustice. The African Americans of the South walk through water, like the people of Israel did in the Old Testament, unharmed by the river's current, now free from their oppressors (*New Living Translation*, Exodus 14.29–31). Bradbury humanizes his black characters by demonstrating deliverance when the American Dream has been exclusive rather than inclusive. He poetically pays homage to the peaceful protests of freedom fighters. The black marchers represent Bradbury's black river prose motif, breaking free from a levee of racial injustice, signifying the renewal and rebirth of the liberated from their oppressors.

Far up the street the levee seemed to have broken. The black warm waters descended and engulfed the town. Between the blazing white banks of the town stores, among the tree silences, a black tide flowed. Like a kind of summer molasses, it poured turgidly forth upon the cinnamon-dusty road. It surged slow, slow, and it was men and women and horses and barking dogs, and it was little boys and girls. And from the mouths of the people partaking of this tide, came the sound of a river. A summer-day river going somewhere, murmuring and irrevocable [Bradbury 90–91].

The baptismal-like waters flow "on wheels and horses and in dusty shoes" (Bradbury 93), infiltrating the sharecropping shacks, washing the valuables out, carrying the clocks, and curtain roads into the black sea (Bradbury 96). Samuel Teece and a few other white men, sit on the hardware store porch, like anxious hounds (91). The crucial time has come to pass. It's far too late to mend the broken levee of black liberation. As the dark river purifies the streets, transubstantiating with spiritual salvation, subjugated victims of oppression morph into victorious innovators who will orbit into space in self-made rockets, venturing to a new world. Moreover, the black river symbolizes a collective black voice, publicizing, and criticizing the malfeasance of an oppressive Southern white culture.

As signified in African folklore, the *griot, imbongi,* or *maroka* may voice the collective opinion of the people as a musician, poet, or spokesperson in order to moderate a leader's conduct (*African* 87–88). Silly, Samuel Teece's store clerk becomes the Southern black voice, a griot after escaping the gun-filled clutch of Teece. Silly questions the Southern leadership, by asking his former boss what he will do with his nights (Bradbury 99). Satirically, Silly is alluding to Teece's heart-racing activity of picking a sturdy tree and knocking on a shanty door, searching for some black person to lynch (100). After Teece expresses the grievances of his community, the river of black men and women who seek land, opportunity, and freedom carry him off into their rocket ships. Silly disregards the taunting voice of Samuel Teece who sacrilegiously mocks Christianity, the black church, and their mass departure by nick naming their rocket ships God the Son, Holy Ghost, Faith, Hope, and First Baptist Church (99).

When the Homesteading Act of 1862 was signed by Abraham Lincoln, there were some descendants of slaves who along with the progeny of European Americans boldly wanted to live the "quintessential American Dream" (Marquis 10). One hundred thousand African Americans received land grants, much like their Caucasian counterparts, if they moved west and cultivated the land (10). In the future, Bradbury attempts to balance the inequities of the South, by paying homage to the colonial and homesteading past, choosing to make the Martian Dream inclusive rather than exclusive. In *The Martian Chronicles*, interplanetary travel is accessible to all humankind. Much like the black characters living in the 21st century of "Way in the Middle of the Air," when the European colonists escaped religious persecution in the 1600s and the white and black pioneers traveled west in the 1700s and 1800s, there were many redundant questions that begged answers. Youngquist's expectation that this 1950 Bradbury tale should provide a response to the social ills of the world, such as racism, is a burdensome weight to place on an author. But on the other hand, Bradbury does provide a literary retort, even if it makes some critics cringe, that unless a community boldly moves forward into the future, they will never know if they will survive life's perilous adventure. Will there still remain an indigenous population on a distant land, or were they subjected to the genocide by the new arrivals? If there are natives on the planet, will they welcome the new immigrants and integrate them into the new Martian Dream? Did colonizers bring enlightenment on how to assimilate, acculturate in an integrated culture of Earthlings and Martians? Furthermore, did the characters from "Way in the Middle of the Air" take on the identity of their former oppressors in an attempt to empower themselves on Mars? Will the beautiful Martian landscape inspire a new and redemptive change in humanity? Without the self-made spaceships, ironically nicknamed "Holy Ghost," "Faith" and "Hope," the African American community may never have the opportunity to reinvent themselves, like some of their colonial and pioneering ancestors, on Bradbury's Mars of the future.

While the short story "Way in the Middle of the Air" reveals the hazardous pitfalls of humankind's need for dominion over others, "The Million-Year Picnic" offers a pathway to redemption in burning the old and appreciating the new. Juliet Grimsley writes in the *English Journal*, "*The Martian Chronicles* must have been a psychological purge for Bradbury. His vitriolic, satirical philosophy fills many passages" (1242). Despite exposing the evils of mankind, Bradbury encourages his readers to live introspectively by advancing their lives, learning to live a prolific and self-satisfying existence that doesn't involve the destruction of our planet (1242). However, in "The Million-Year Picnic," Bradbury ends *The Martian Chronicles* by giving man a second chance, by saving two "good" families to start the human race over in Mars (1242). The dad sits with his son by a fire, and he relays their cultural heritage on Earth. The audience sees a cremation of an American way of life. Semblances of infrastructure dissolve into ash with the burning fire. By igniting documents such as government bonds, an essay on religious prejudice, and a stock report, which are emblematic of economics, inequality, and war, Bradbury sends the message that Earth has been cleansed from the universe (266–67). With the abolition of government, economic, social, and physical infrastructure, the Earthlings will have a chance for redemption on the Red

Planet. At this moment, Bradbury is aware of his proselytizing tone; therefore, the dad mentions that he was a former state governor, and asks his son to forgive him for the sermonic nature of his speech. Then, the dad refers to the former Earth as a "mechanical wilderness" that consumed people with gadgets. The reader eventually surmises that this obsession with material gain, emphasis on machines, led to the Earth's figurative and literal explosion. The dad says to his son, "Wars got bigger and bigger and finally killed Earth" (Bradbury 267). Yet, Shaftel views Bradbury's ministerial tone as a rejection of modern society by presenting materialism as vulgar (103). However, this moral and self-righteous perspective is parallel to the perspectives of other science fiction giants such as Aldous Huxley (Shaftel 103). In the resolution of the story, there is no nostalgia for Earth's devastation. Although the dad expresses relief and gratitude that he and his family survived the Earth's past transgressions, he believes that "'interplanetary travel won't be back for centuries, maybe never. But that way of life proved itself wrong and strangled itself with its own hands'" (Bradbury 267). When the Dad makes this statement to his son, there is a sense that Earth could have prevented its own internal implosion. In one instance, technology is seen as a savior in the form of interplanetary travel. On the other hand, the demise of Earth by its own hands has momentarily ended space travel. Losing sight of religion and nature, as previously stated in "As the Moon Be Still as Bright," caused man to lose himself in the mechanical wilderness. When the dad says, "You're young. I'll tell you this again every day until it sinks in" (Bradbury 267), he is stressing the intergenerational necessity to teach our children about that which is good, pure, and genuine in life. If leaders, such as the dad of this story, commit themselves to authenticity and compromise for the betterment of humankind, the potential exists for a better world on Earth. But in the event that Earthlings are unable to reconcile their differences, Bradbury offers Mars as rejuvenating way of life for future generations.

The Legacy of Ray Bradbury's Vision

During Ray Bradbury's lifetime, advances in technology contributed to the amazing success of the 1997 Mars Pathfinder mission (Schmalholz 44) and the 2008 Phoenix Mars Lander. Society now had the ability to access data from the Internet about this stunning feat (44). The transcendence of Bradbury's work is that *The Martian Chronicles* alludes to the "frontier issues of today-technological advances, nuclear/biological weapons proliferation, world unrest, and the exhaustion of natural resources — which are the same reasons given in the novel for humankind's move from Earth to Mars" (44). Exciting as this achievement is, in 1976, the Viking I lander, settled in the basin and began taking pictures of the Martian surface (Frazier 51). The sounds and cheers erupted from the Viking Mission Control room once the landing had been verified. Two minutes later, in the press auditorium Ray Bradbury was being interviewed because *The Martian Chronicles* "perfectly epitomize[d] the melding of scientific and human yearnings that carried us inevitably toward Mars" (Frazier 51). Bradbury's noble aspiration to appreciate the natural world through the spirit of exploration was now an imminent possibility (Frazier 51). Ironically, this Viking mission had taken beautiful photos of "avalanche-draped Martian canyons, sculptured mesas reminiscent of Monument Valley" in Arizona and Utah (Frazier 44). Much like the short stories of *The Martian Chronicles*, Mars is imagined by Bradbury as composed of beautiful rocks, hills, and mountains.

In this year alone, the Mars rover captured pictures of spherical rock formations, blister-like bumps called "blueberries" have been detected on the Martian surface (Malik "Strange"). These "blueberry" rock formations were actually discovered in 2004. Yet, scientists continue to study them because they are "consecrations created by minerals in water that settled into sedimentary rock" (Malik). With the knowledge that water once existed on Mars, scientists know that life may exist now or in past centuries on the Red Planet. Later this year, Methane was detected, which means that gaseous residue of long-extinct microbes or even the output of Martian organisms are alive and well today (David). All of the hoopla surrounding new discoveries on Mars, and new insights of older discoveries, would have been glorious for Bradbury. The author died at the age of 91 in Los Angeles, California, on June 6, 2012 (Rogers). He left an impressive legacy of science-fiction that still lives. In his lifetime, Bradbury shared an effective collection of short stories, *The Martian Chronicles*, which highlights the impact of colonial invasion, danger of imposing predisposed notions, and infecting prejudice into an indigenous culture. Bradbury uses characters like Jeff Spender, Sam Parkhill, and Samuel Teece to impress upon society that nostalgia for the past may consume a people's present and cause the future extinction of an established civilization. Meanwhile, characters like the former governor and Silly, demonstrate the ability to capitalize on the future without reservation. The primary message of *The Martian Chronicles* is that humans who integrate into Martian society may achieve transformation and redemption if they respect, settle, and preserve ancient Mars for future generations.

Works Cited

Abbott, Carl. "Homesteading on the Extraterrestrial Frontier." *Science Fiction Studies* 32.2 (2005): 240–264. Web.

Baci, Laura, ed. *African American Literature*. New York: Holt, 1998. Print.

Bradbury, Ray. Introduction. *The Martian Chronicles*. New York: Harper, 2011. Print.

_____. *The Martian Chronicles*. New York: Harper, 2011. Print.

_____. *The Martian Chronicles*, 2d ed. New York: Bantam/Spectra Books, 1979. Print.

David, Leonard. "Mars Methane Mystery: Curiosity Rover May Find New Clues." 23 Oct. 2012. 24 Nov. 2012.Web.

Diamond, Jared. *Guns, Germs, and Steel*. New York: W. W. Norton, 1999. Print.

Dominianni, Robert. "Ray Bradbury's 2026: A Year with Current Value." *The English Journal* 73.7 (1984): 49–51. Web.

Eller, Jonathan R. *Becoming Ray Bradbury*. Urbana: University of Illinois Press, 2011. Print.

Frazier, Kendrick. "The Mars Landing: Just the Beginning." *Science News* 110.4 (1976): 51. Web.

Grimsley, Juliet. "'The Martian Chronicles': A Provocative Study." *The English Journal* 59.9 (1970): 1239–1242. Web.

Hodge, Adam. "Pestilence and Power: The Smallpox Epidemic of 1780–1782 and Intertribal Relations on the Northern Great Plains." *The Historian* 72.3 (2010): 543–567. Web.

Holy Bible, New Living Translation. Ed. Linda Taylor and Shawn Harrison. Wheaton, IL: Tyndale, 1996. Print.

Levin, A. E., and Yuri Prizel. "English-Language SF as a Socio-Cultural Phenomenon." *The Sociology of Science Fiction*. Spec. issue of *Science Fiction Studies* 4.3 (1977): 246–256. Web.

Malik, Tariq. "Strange Mystery Spheres on Mars Baffle Scientists." *Yahoo Online*. 15 Sept. 2012. 24 Nov. 2012. Web.

Mann, Charles C. *1491: New Revelations of the Americas Before Columbus*. New York: Random House/Vintage, 2011. Print.

Marquis, Amy Leinbach. "Chasing the Dream." *National Parks* 85.1 (2011): 10. *History Reference Center*. 22 October 2012. Web.

Rogers, John. "Author Ray Bradbury Has Died in California." 6 June 2012. 25 Nov. 2012. Web.

Schmalholz, Deborah Wielgot. "American Pathfinders: Using Ray Bradbury's 'Martian Chronicles' to Teach Frontier History." *Using Literature to Teach History*. Spec. issue of *Organization of American Historians* 13.2 (1999): 44–48. Web.

Shaftel, Oscar. "The Social Content of Science Fiction." *Science & Society* 17.2 (1953): 97–118.Web.

Wilkerson, Isabel. *The Warmth of Other Suns: The Epic Story of America's Great Migration*. New York: Vintage, 2010. Print.

Youngquist, Paul. "The Space Machine: Baraka and Science Fiction." *Amri Baraka Issue*. Spec. issue of *African American Review* 37.2/3 (2003): 333–343. Web.

The Desert Is Earth and Mars

An Ecocritical, Bachelardian Exploration of "And the Moon Be Still as Bright" and It Came from Outer Space

CHRISTOPHER COKINOS

"...reverie is a consciousness of well-being."—Gaston Bachelard, *The Poetics of Reverie*

A Material Ecocritical Frame

Tucson-based astronomer and photographer Stephen E. Strom has recently offered exhibits in galleries and online that juxtapose images of the terrestrial and the Martian deserts, images that are sometimes difficult to place: At which planet are we looking? The earthly photos are Strom's own and they often present scenes without reference to easily recognized scale; the Martian photographs are from publically available orbiter images stored in the digital archives of both the European Space Agency and the National Aeronautics and Space Administration. Set beside each other, the photographs are a reminder of connections and contrasts between Earth and "the Red Planet." In Strom's words, the images conjure "patterns that reveal sculptural, chromatic, and (implicitly) temporal rhythms. Viewed in totality, they speak to the commonality of physical and geological forces, often acting on vastly different spatial and temporal scales" (Strom). Strom goes on to quote desert nature writer Ellen Meloy, who spoke of a "'geography of infinite cycles, of stolid pulses of emergence and subsidence, which in terms geologic and human, is the story of the Earth.'" He adds in brackets "[and Mars]" (Strom).

133

Strom's "Earth and Mars" series thus calls to mind at least some of what Ray Bradbury evoked regarding the desert, for the desert is both Mars and Earth, as we can see when material ecocriticism reads such landscapes and sentient interactions with landscapes in both *The Martian Chronicles* and the film *It Came from Outer Space*. Both texts contain a kind of poetic more-than-sentient emplotment. With its implied extension of historicism to include physical processes we name cosmological, astronomical, geological and biological (and with its Marxist inflection due to this emphasis on matter itself), material ecocriticism is a rich lens through which to look at science fiction and science fantasy, especially Ray Bradbury's paeans to desert landscapes. These odes (and elegies) were clearly informed by his brief stay as a child in Tucson, surrounded by the Sonoran desert, a place that seemed strange and exciting to young Midwestern eyes; actual physical encounters with the landscape of aridity surely helped to create the represented actuality in Bradbury's various desert texts. As we will see, this actuality is part and parcel of the reveries needed for survival, at least according to what these two texts seem to claim, and according to the French philosopher Gaston Bachelard, whose approach to reverie prefigures and complements material ecocriticism.

Jonathan Eller and William Touponce argue that *The Martian Chronicles* is "nothing less than a critique of all life-destroying modes of 'emploting' ... history" (136–137). This critique includes "any kind of historical thinking that takes us away from the living present of this world" (137). Without intending such, Eller and Touponce are offering a quasi-materialist ecocritical valuation of *The Martian Chronicles*. However, in their claim that, because the book is "deeply carnivalized," there is "no final perspective on events," Eller and Touponce veer from their nascent ecocritical insight (138). In fact, the final perspective is the perspective of non-sentient nature, a cosmic frame, which is also the widest possible terrain for reverie itself. And reverie, as we will see, means something particular in the Bachelardian sense.

As for material ecocriticism, Dana Phillips and Heather I. Sullivan claim "it insists that human beings are 'actors' operating within material processes that include multitudes of other 'actors,' the majority of which are not human or, for that matter, conscious" (446). This is a literary-ecological extension, then, of such terms and categories as the poet Robinson Jeffers's "transhumanism" or prose writer David Abrams's "more-than-human" world. What seem like possible (and anti-textual) platitudes — "we will always be material beings living in a material world of one kind and/or another" and "we live in multiple worlds" (447) at varying scales, from the internal microbial environments of our bodies to the possible multiverse — are actually a form of ground-truthing textuality, representation and ideology in *the physicality that makes such activities possible.* Or, as geographer Yi-Fu Tuan puts it, "As for our identity, it is anchored in common objects and experiences to a degree we seldom acknowledge" (12). This quotidian fact is not to be underestimated. These objects and experiences include landscapes and animals, even those known of but not seen frequently or even at all. In fiction set on other worlds, of course, we are able to approach this materiality via defamiliarization.

In looking at representations of the Martian desert in *The Martian Chronicles*," focusing on the crucial story "And the Moon Be Still as Bright," then on visual and conversational evocations of the Mojave in *It Came from Outer Space*, I aim to show how Bradbury is enacting the kind of materiality that Phillips and Sullivan speak of: the struggle for right agency that is connected to and by necessity grows out of the physical and temporal sublime in a more-than-human world. Before unpacking the textual signifiers of matter in both these texts, I will connect material ecocriticism to my reading of reverie-as-survival via Gaston Bachelard's *The Poetics of Reverie*. I will also gesture toward Mikhail Bakhtin's concept of the "chronotope," which is another way of approaching materiality with an ecocritical inflection. Finally, and all-too-briefly, we will note that Ray Bradbury's engagements with and celebrations of desert landscapes also form a bridge between science fiction and nature writing; as it happens, Bradbury's attitudes are quite similar to those of desert nature writer Joseph Wood Krutch, who moved to Tucson in the 1950s. This is a necessary bridge because, modifying James Gunn's frequent claims that SF is *the* literature of change and of ideas, nature writing is also a genre that engages change and ideas — though one might argue that at their most staid, nature writers mostly produce a discourse of self-defeating stasis. That, however, is another exploration for later.

Material ecocritical approaches in concert with Bachelardian reverie offer nuances of interrelationships among sentience and non-sentience at varied scales. At the scale of the biped in a land mostly bereft of water, we might see most crucially an interplay between physical survival and psychic reverie. So this essay is also an implicit defense of the sense of wonder in Bradbury, but one that does not, I trust, stop there. While Darko Suvin, Joyce Carol Oates (see her "Against Nature") and others have criticized wonder or "AWE," as Oates puts it so sarcastically, as limiting praxis and emotional range, a Bachelardian material ecocriticism shows wonder or reverie as grandly more complicated, a catalyst for praxis and a foundational feeling-tone that allows for other emotional registers to come forth from a place (literally and ideally) of well-being. Ideally, for in the case of "And the Moon Be Still as Bright" we see starkly that reverie with a gun leads to violent praxis and a false consciousness of alleged well-being. That said, we might begin to see that reverie can function as a non-violent ethical foundation arising out of connection to materiality of the land. Various characters make this clear in the classic film *It Came from Outer Space*. Thus is setting — place itself— an argument for learning humility. This is a baseline ecocritical and political stance. After all, Cheryll Glotfelty has said that ecocriticism, "simply put ... is the study of the relationship between literature and the physical environment" (xviii). She goes on:

> All ecological criticism shares the fundamental premise that human culture is connected to the physical world, affecting it and affected by it. Ecocriticism takes as its subject the interconnections between nature and culture, specifically the cultural artifacts of language and literature.... As a theoretical discourse, it negotiates between the human and the nonhuman [xix].

Or as designer Charles Eames famously repeated, "Eventually, everything connects."

Ultimately, I want to show the value of material ecocriticism (or, if one prefers, "just" ecocriticism) as applied to these seminal texts of Ray Bradbury; to demonstrate the importance of Martian and terrestrial deserts as more-than-human foundations for sentient ethos and praxis; and to witness how crucial the role of Bachelardian reverie can be, seeing both how it falls short in "And the Moon Be Still as Bright" and how it does not in *It Came from Outer Space*, even as both texts gesture toward ways to healthful sentient materiality and reverie. Both Bradbury and Bachelard seem to be suggesting that without reverie we are unable to function as integrated sentient beings in relation to all that is around us. Reverie, like water, is a crucial component for survival. And in an arid landscape both water and reverie gain relevance. The protagonists of our two texts, archeologist Jeff Spender on Mars and writer/ stargazer John Putnam in Arizona, are both engaged in forms of Bachelardian reverie in relation to the land and the cosmos, a mode that separates them from many other actors in these texts, though not from all. Captain Wilder in "And the Moon Be Still as Bright" understands Spender's reveries even as he cannot abide the violence of Spender's praxis, and John Putnam's fiancé, as well as the telephone linemen in *It Came from Outer Space*, speak eloquently on behalf of the Mojave in ways that suggest not only a recognition of the more-than-human world but a respect for and even celebration of this one particular, very dry long result of time: the desert.

Bachelardian Reverie

Reverie, as Gaston Bachelard describes it, is an important feeling-tone. It is a "consciousness of well-being," among other things. (178) Something of a review is in order, to understand in Bachelard's own lyrical language, what he means by reverie so that we do not misunderstand it to be a dreamy form of sleep, a wistful sort of daydream. Here are a few crucial observations from Bachelard's masterwork, *The Poetics of Reverie*.

The reader's encounter with new images generates an innocent "wonderment [that] is completely natural" (4). Additionally, it focuses, as do eastern philosophies, on "awareness in the present" (4). Bachelard critiques the usual sense of reverie as a kind of "inattention" with the argument that "any awareness is an increment to consciousness, an added light, a reinforcement of psychic coherence" (5). He quips, "It is a poor reverie which invites a nap?" (10).

So Bachelardian reverie is a form of attention that is, as I understand it, swept up into what Freud called the oceanic — the sense or, rather, the *recognition* that we are offspring of and kin to larger forces in the universe. For some, these forces may be noncorporeal (almost in the sense of Henri Bergson's élan vital), and Bachelard and even, alas, occasional ecocritics seem to be in that camp sometimes. Be that as it may, empiricism and matter can be sparks toward connective reveries in which the self happily allows for knowing and feeling the more-than-human world: a way out of the myth of monadic unity. Bachelard focuses on how poetry can create the new images that spark reverie, reverie which then returns to the text to understand it in a new way, and, while this is so (and useful), my concern is to take Bachelardian reverie from the text of the page to the text of the world *and* to see how texts that invoke the world can provoke reveries — or, let us say mundanely, insights — regarding one's place in local and cosmic physicality. Finding one's place is more than a spiritual journey of individual awakening. Finding one's place is also, if not more so, an ecstatic slotting into the network of matter and energy, a trophic compassing. Reverie — attention, opening to grace, call it what you will — can be, should be, an ecological process.

Bachelard seems to agree with this in his way. He says: "Poetic reverie gives us the world of worlds. Poetic reverie is a cosmic reverie. It is an opening to a beautiful world, to beautiful worlds. It gives the I a non-I which belongs to the I: my non-I" (13). Further: "The cosmic reverie possesses a sort of stability or tranquility. It helps us escape time. It is a *state*. Let us get to the bottom of its essence: it is a state of mind" (14). It can be physical: "To bite into the world with no other 'care' than the happiness of biting, isn't that entering the world? What a grasp of the world is a bite. Then the world is the direct object of the verb 'I eat.'...what harmony, what unity of the total being!" (178). And this: "With reveries of cosmos, the dreamer knows reverie without responsibility, reverie which does not ask for proof. At the end, imagining a cosmos is the most natural destiny of reverie" (23). Bachelard says that reverie is a movement beyond "'preoccupations'" and "worry" (174). Any practitioner of mindfulness recognizes this fact.

But reverie is more than a recognition of the I-thou relationship between self and world. It *is* a sweeping clear of preoccupation and worry *that allows for* one to act skillfully on behalf of the world. Here we might say that while reverie might be free of responsibility — in the moment of its experience — it is a poor reverie that does not cultivate responsibility. So if, as Bachelard claims, "reverie is consciousness of well-being" (177–178), then that well-being can be maintained outside of reverie while in the world of doing. In fact, Bachelard speaks of "*working reverie* ... which prepares works" (182). He amplifies this proposition by saying that "harmonious reverie has returned us to a harmonious existence. Ah! the gentle fluency of the reverie which helps us pour ourselves into the world, into the well-being of a world" (193). How Jeff Spender and John Putnam pour themselves into the world of their respective deserts we shall see shortly.

For William Touponce, Bachelard is describing a strategy well-suited to reading the work of Ray Bradbury. While Darko Suvin suggests that Bradbury's work, in Touponce's words, has no "cognitive claims on the reader," because it isn't properly science fiction, Bachelard, on the other hand, not only venerates reverie, he can be used to posit landscape as a kind of heroic character in science fiction (xii, xviii). Reverie may seem soft-headed to Suvin, but it is not. Bachelard asks us to "perform a dreaming on the text" — his oneiric criticism — by taking the "images initiated by the text back in the text again with the help of the specific ambience created by reverie" (Touponce xxi). This is highly individualistic but seems full of material ecocritical agency. We go back with this ambience not only to the text but to the physicality text is grounded in. Reverie is a kind of reader-response theory, clearly, and Touponce articulates these multiple movements:

> This experience of intimacy at the heart of matter was for Bachelard always linked to the body, our childhood bodies, where the image is an act of the hand, a magical gesture working with valorized substances. Man in reverie is "man made dynamic by his work." In Bachelardian reverie therefore is none of that dreamy passiveness usually associated with the word reverie. Reverie is the exploration of a world.... Thus reverie satisfies our recessive desires to know and linger in a fantastic world and at the same time provides the possibility for *a critique of the real* [12–13, emphasis added].

Crucially, Touponce cites Herbert Marcuse's point that, as Touponce summarizes it from *Eros and Civilization,* "the cognitive value of reverie lies in its preservation of *a non-alienated relation to nature*" (18, emphasis added). Touponce is anticipating a material ecocriticism in his study of Bachelard and

Bradbury, when he also argues that "a typical object reverie involves a fathoming of the object in its material intimacy which then offers us a world" (21).

Contrary to Suvin, who, as Touponce puts it, dismisses *The Martian Chronicles* because the book "does not evince the narrative dominance of a fictional novum validated by cognitive logic," we may find that this text illustrates reverie (and induces it) so that, again in Touponce's words, "we nourish ourselves on the world" (58, 63).

This nourishment is not mindless gluttony at the trough but a sustenance necessary to establish right and balanced relation. We nourish ourselves on the world directly, of course, and via representations of the world. One form of representation worth noting in this context — though we do not have time to explore it great detail — is Mikhail Bakhtin's "chronotope," which Bakhtin defines as "'the intrinsic connectedness of temporal and spatial relationships that are artistically expressed in language ... it expresses the inseparability of space and time'" (qtd. in McDowell, 376). Michael McDowell goes on to claim that "Bakhtin's idea of the chronotope encourages us to recover the representation of place in even works of 'essential noninterest in the land.' The chronotope binds together these elements of literature, which are rooted in place" (378). McDowell notes that Bakhtin discusses several chronotopes, which we might also understand as akin to archetypal images; among Bakhtin's chronotopes are roads and public squares (378). It would be interesting to study chronotopes in Bradbury's work in particular to see how they might function as sites of Bachalardian reverie and, therefore, as loci for ecological relation-building. In the close readings to follow, we can only briefly note them.

McDowell also notes important definitions of landscape types in John Brinckerhoff Jackson's *Discovering the Vernacular Landscape*, in which there is, as McDowell puts it, "a folk landscape, attuned to the contours of the land and serving local needs" and "the official landscape, imposed upon the land without concern for local differences" (381). The gap between those two is a space in which both "And the Moon Be Still as Bright" and *It Came from Outer Space* emerge. Reverie seems well-suited to such a liminal space, as we will see, a hovering ecotone, as it were, that fosters reverie in the folk landscape and cultivates a critique of the official landscape.

"And the Moon Be Still as Bright": Reverie Toward Survival and the Failures of Jeff Spender

Published in 1950, *The Martian Chronicles* soon gained a major mainstream reputation and launched Ray Bradbury to decades of publishing success. Praised by such figures as Aldous Huxley and Christopher Isherwood, the book is a series of linked stories that tell of the first abortive attempts at human colonization of Mars, a project that succeeds only when terrestrial pathogens destroy most Martians. The book pivots toward depictions of callous human settlement of Mars, prompted by a looming nuclear war on Earth, settlement that concludes when, paradoxically, nearly all humans return to the post-war Earth: another clean slate, albeit more radioactive. Less a book of traditional science fiction and more a book of interplanetary magical realism using the tragedy of the conquest of the American West as its controlling metaphor, *The Martian Chronicles* takes a largely gloomy view of human survival, given our species's inability to experience reverie. This is never more clear than in "And the Moon Be Still as Bright," a story that comes early in the collection but that is, nonetheless, its philosophical core. Archeologist Jeff Spender delivers a crucial speech in this story and undertakes to resist the coming human occupation of Mars. He takes a material ecocritical view of nature and culture on Mars — prompted and sustained by reverie — but is unable to translate this stance into anything other than violent praxis. He fails and he dies.

In this story, the first expedition to survive on Mars takes place because chicken pox has killed virtually all the Martian population, a fact established on a foray into cities near the landing site. The stir-crazy crew, having "kicked a hole in space" (67), is interested more in drunken revelry than respectful contemplation of the meaning of their journey and of the dead civilization humans have accidently overthrown. It is Spender who wants the crew to stay quiet and think. It is Spender who punches his loud-mouth, vomitous nemesis Biggs. It is Spender, who, after a solo journey into the dead cities, takes up arms against his former compatriots, murdering several while planning a one-man Maginot Line against future human incursions against Mars's glorious past and its empty present. In the climatic scenes, when the expedition's Captain — the thoughtful though duty-bound Wilder — pursues and talks to Spender, we are treated to Spender's discourse on how to survive and how to revere a place, a speech about the natural outgrowth of a culture attuned to place. It could have been spoken years later by desert denizen Ed Abbey.

The role of the material world or environment in this book needs some attention before we hear from Spender. Both Carl Abbott and Kim Stanley Robinson argue for a SF as a historical genre, as a projection into the future of the past and of present concerns (Abbott, *Frontiers* 5). In this way, we can see in both "And the Moon Be Still as Bright" and *It Came from Outer Space* a concern with fitting human beings and cultures to the demands of the environment. The conquest of the American West is, in no small measure, an ecological story — to take but one example, note how the Anglo near-extinction of the bison catalyzed the fall of Plains Indian cultures. And, as Thomas Clareson points out, in *The Martian Chronicles*, Bradbury "transformed" this history "into a future American conquest of Mars. By doing this, he found a fresh basis for his metaphors" (50–51).

David Mogen makes the book's environmental foundation even clearer when he writes, "Like must Western fiction, *The Martian Chronicles* is ultimately about the relationship of alien intruders to the land" (90). He goes on to say that "though the physical environment of Mars changes from story to story the nature of the planet itself, with all the ambivalence and mystery that surrounds it, is the central subject of the book" (93). Drawing on Eric Rabkin, Mogen also writes that Mars is "the ambivalent promise of Edenic New Worlds in a space age future ... [a] new frontier ... deeply identified with lyricism itself, with fairyland images that refract back the heart's desire and secret fears of the pioneers" (82) It is "a metaphorical comment on the American Dream" (83). The book may point the way to "a more integrated new culture [that] may appear from the destruction of the frontier process" (85).

That dream of integration, alas, falls short in "And the Moon Be Still as Bright," even though the story makes clear that survival on the Martian desert requires forms of reverie. "Mars usually appears as a pastel desert planet, rather like Arizona lined with ancient canals," Mogen notes, the one exception being the "Johnny Appleseed" story of Benjamin Driscoll in the distinctly Midwestern atmosphere of "The Green Morning" (86). The ability to see the Martian desert *on its own terms* is a form of clear, ecological seeing but one with the feeling-tone of reverie, a capacity that Spender and Pops in "Night Meeting" both have (87). Crucially, Jeff Spender "is the only character who cares deeply about the future of the planet" (Eller and Touponce 152). Spender becomes a locus of time, bringing the past into the present as he fears a lost future. Spender is a kind of walking chronotope among the chronotopes Martian roads and squares. A representation/embodiment of place and time as one, the chronotope unites two aspects of the material ecocritical approach — its emphasis on pre-textual facticity and the changing passages of events as measured by what we call time. Spender's solo journey away from his loathsome crew-mates gives him a chance to discover the fusion of place and time so integral to Martian culture; he then embodies this and offers it back to Captain Wilder when the latter has caught up with Spender (who, by now, has killed several expedition members).

Spender's defense of Mars and attack on human values is primarily rhetorical and philosophical, but, early on in the conversation with Wilder, Spender asks, "How would you feel if a Martian vomited stale liquor on the

White House floor?" (Bradbury 88). This deft image reminds the reader of Biggs, who had vomited the tiles of a Martian ruin. Spender critiques the human — and American — propensity to distrust, diminish and destroy the other. He does this even as he admits his guilt in murdering his fellows: "I got sick. When you want to do a thing badly enough you lie to yourself" (Bradbury 87). The irony is that this very act of othering is what human culture has done and will do to the colonized, whether Native Americans in the 19th century or Martians in the 21st.

The crux of Spender's defense arises from his experience alone in the Martian cities, and we share his point of view until the hunt to kill him, at which point the story switches to Wilder's interiority. Thus, we are placed in a position of, in a sense, being Spender. To be Spender is to believe in synthesis, to praise what E.O. Wilson has called consilience, even if we are appalled at Spender's disassociative capacity to kill with no real deep remorse.

"They knew how to blend art into their living," Spender tells the Captain of the Martians. "It's always been a thing apart for Americans. Art was something you kept in the crazy son's room upstairs. Art was something you took in doses, mixed with religion, perhaps. Well, these Martians have art and religion and everything" (Bradbury 87–88). He deplores the fear of "anything's that strange" and notes that if colonization proceeds, humans — Americans in this case — will haul with them atomic research plans, plans for resource extraction and tourism (Bradbury 88). In sum, everything that's gone wrong in the deserts and mountains of the American West will go wrong on Mars. Nothing will have been learned. Spender, noting that "a good report" from Wilder will "hasten the whole invasion of Mars," plans to murder any future expeditions for as long as he can (Bradbury 89). Crucial to note is that Mars is now essentially depopulated, so Spender is planning to fight an invasion against the land itself, against the past.

"They knew," Spender says of the now-dead Martians, "how to live with nature and get along with nature. They didn't try too hard to be all men and no animal" (Bradbury 90). Our failure was to let science — symbolized by Darwin, Huxley and Freud — destroy religious or spiritual faith, Spender explains to Wilder. The implication here is that science can only go so far in giving us a rationale for life, a rationale that life itself gives via animal nature and sentient faith. The Martians "knew how to combine science and religion so the two worked side by side," Spender says, just as he implies culture and nature for the Martians also formed a holistic synthesis (Bradbury 91).

To illustrate, Spender shows Wilder an image from this utopia:

> Spender led him over into a little Martian village built all of cool perfect marble. There were great friezes of beautiful animals, white-limbed cat things and

yellow-limbed sun symbols, and statues of bull-like creatures and statues of men and women and huge fine-featured dogs.

"There's your answer, Captain."

"I don't see."

"The Martians discovered the secret of life among animals. The animal does not question life. It lives. Its very reason for living *is* life; it enjoys and relishes life..." [Bradbury 91].

Wilder is skeptical, calling the Martian culture "pagan," to which Spender replies, "On the contrary, those are God symbols, symbols of life. Man had become too much man and not enough animal on Mars too. And the men of Mars realized that in order to survive they would have to forego asking that one question any longer: *Why live?* Life was its own answer" (Bradbury 91).

For Spender, then, the ideal culture not only arises from or is tied to nature: It *is* nature. On Mars, it is the synthesis of deserts, mountains, and organic life/civilization that is culture. Such a synthesis cannot come about through only one activity — science, say — but through a reverential attitude in all activities. Through reverie. Martian reverie allowed that culture to survive and thrive. For Spender, this is life-affirming, and in his critique of the real culture of humans and Americans, there can be no quarter. Spender does not want to kill but feels he must to defend lost Martian ideals and the environment of Mars itself— and, selfishly, allow himself the space for reveries — and if, as he thinks, human culture is given over to compartmentalization, then that is a form of death. What can be wrong with killing individuals bound up in what Edmund Husserl has called the death-world? Spender is an eco-terrorist, justified in the eyes of some, less so in the eyes of others. However dangerous or misguided, he clearly occupies Husserl's life-world, which is the material world that Husserl, Bachelard and ecocritics posit as the locus for praxis (Nye 228).

Importantly, Spender tells Wilder about the things they both could do if only Wilder would join him in his defense of Mars: "There's a little patio down here with a reel of Martian music in it at least fifty thousand years old. It still plays. Music you'll never hear in your life. You could hear it. There are books. I've gotten on well in reading them already. You could sit and read" (Bradbury 92–92). Wilder demurs. Spender continues: "I have something to fight for and live for; that makes me a better killer. I've got what amounts to religion, now. It's learning to breathe all over again" (93). Thus faith and breathing are synonyms for Spender, the complex sense of trust in the universe coming forth from the simple act of breathing: a material, an animal, process. Spender's hopes of convincing Wilder to join him are, of course, in vain, though it suggests he is seeking some kind of alternative to violence. In any case, he foresees a life that will lead to further reveries and epiphanies: "And how to lie in the sun getting a tan, letting the sun work into you. And how to hear music and how to read a book. What does your civilization offer?" (Bradbury 93). The Captain doesn't answer the question; instead, he apologizes.

Lauren Weiner has recently argued that Spender's speech "is an example of impossibly learned philosophical arguments," one that "does not lend his character much believability" (88). Why, I wonder? Weiner correctly points out that while Bradbury offers ecological defenses of Mars he also promoted the idea of space travel because we are using up resources here on Earth. No less a perceptive nature writer than Kim Stafford has been dumbstruck by this; he cites Bradbury telling a reporter that "'we shall not be long of this Earth'" (25). By saying "of" instead of "on," Bradbury is, according to Stafford, promulgating the view that "the Earth is our campsite only," a temporary way station (Stafford 25). One might rebut Weiner by noting that Spender discusses a visit to Mexico City in which he was appalled at his parents' bigotry and the destruction of the indigenous desert culture by the Spanish (Bradbury 88). (One suspects that this has a root in Bradbury's own childhood; it seems likely he too visited Mexico while a child in Tucson).

While critics have naturally paid a great deal of attention to Spender's central speech, we can see in his other words, actions and in the story's imagery, further connotations of the yin and yang of survival and reverie. A few examples might suffice.

Spender criticizes the colonial project of imposed, non–placed-based naming: "We'll call the canal Rockefeller Canal and the mountain King George Mountain and the sea DuPont Sea, and there'll be Roosevelt and Lincoln and Coolidge cities and it won't ever be right, when there are *proper* names for these places" (74). This passage, of course, anticipates the bridge chapter, "The Naming of Names," and, in "And the Moon Be Still as Bright," foreshadows Spender's recognition of Martian culture as attuned to its desert environment. Eller and Touponce note that "we confiscate things by linguistic means, result[ing] in the erection of a second illusory world alongside the first world of pure power relationships" (149). This is the imposition of the official landscape onto the folk landscape, another scrim against reverie's "consciousness of well-being." David Mogen writes, "To the Martians, as to the Indian tribes, the land is sacred and magical. Names pay tribute to the spirit of the place. To the American invaders, however, the land is property" (91).

A powerful image of the complexities of reverie and survival in this story occurs when the entire crew sets out for the first time to explore a Martian city. As they do, the reflected light of Phobos and Deimos (a scientific impossibility) casts "double shadows" for each person, connoting the various binary natures within us, including peaceful/violent and reverential/hostile. Biggs, the partying bully of the crew, shouts, wanting the dead Martians to show up. Meanwhile, Bradbury renders Spender's reverie-toward-praxis, another double shadow of the present Spender dreaming back into being the past Martians, filling Spender with a glimpse to the wholeness humans have lost. It is the vital moment in Spender's journey to come and a powerful memento mori:

> Spender filled the streets with his eyes and his mind. People moved like blue vapor lights on the cobbled avenues, and there were faint murmurs of sound, and odd animals scurrying across the gray-red sands. Each window was given a person who leaned from it and waved slowly, as if under timeless water, at some moving form in the fathoms of space below the moon-silvered towers. Music was played on some inner ear, and Spender imagined the shape of such instruments to evoke such music. The land was haunted [77].

Though Spender is new to Mars — and let us recall he was trapped in a rocket for months before arriving — he violates Yi Fu Tuan's claim that "the importance of place depends notably on how long we have lived or worked in it" (16). He is in reverie. He is dreaming clarity. He goes native, coming home to the desert civilization of Mars, during which time — away from the crew — he will read 10,000-year-old philosophy and swim (Bradbury 84–85). The idyll does not last, as the crew hunts him down, culminating in that long discussion between Spender and Wilder, after which Wilder knows he must kill Spender (no one else should bear that burden) and after which Wilder must do his best to control his crew and, thus, temper the human invasion to come. Wilder's efforts will succeed no more than Spender's, leaving readers to wonder what can defend this reverie-inducing land and culture since both violence and bureaucracy fail.

In one of the powerful closing images of the story, Spender is laid to rest inside a Martian "sarcophagus," the corpse of a human inside the corpse of an entire culture, one that survived desert harshness and social troubles by rooting in the land and revering the cosmos — until the germs came, until the ecological imperialism of chicken pox. Wilder tells the crew that they should remember Spender, and when one crewman is vandalizing a Martian city, Wilder punches him (Bradbury 98–99).

Spender is an agent of history who refuses the history he has been trapped in. He moves expansively, carefully, among the Martian ruins, finding the strands of their stories, their lifeways, a rhizome he can move into. He has been hailed by the Martian past, an alien ideology that connects to human embeddedness in the material world of the non-human, a site of reverie and of contestation. Though Gilles Deleuze and Felix Guattari claim "a rhizome has no beginning or end" (522), Spender fears the end of the Martian rhizome because he understands the violence inherent in the colonial project. His reverie in the face of Martian land/culture is his survival and the catalyst for violent praxis to protect Martian cultural survival as he embodies it. Thus, Spender becomes a kind of nomad, a part of the human Nomadology come to Mars to escape/impose human history. He is liminal, between history and Nomadology. He hovers between two planets, even as he tries to psychically ground himself on Mars. In this middle place, Spender must move quickly, less to save his life from his angry ex-crew members and more to save the Martian rhizome of land/culture from human agents of history, the colonizers who, with few exceptions, must carry out the project of conquest via the othering of the Mars-to-be-conquered, whether alive/sentient or written/recorded/formerly sentient or the face of the Red Planet itself in its geological enormity. (The Red Planet has its name from its ruddy appearance in terrestrial skies yet one cannot fail to hear the ironic sound of this in the context of a tale of desert conquest that so mimics the subjugation of the American West with its "red men.")

The only other character to have the deep reverence for/reverie from Mars that Spender characterizes is Pop in "Night Meeting," who says to Tomáz Gomez that "we've got to forget Earth and how things were. We've got to look at what we're in here, and how different it is" (108). But this difference is the origin for othering in Pop's mind; it is the origin of learning to be in a new world that will become one's own not by way of property but, to invoke Bachelard again, by way of consciousness of well-being. "I'm just looking," he tells Gomez. "I'm just experiencing. If you can't take Mars for what she is, you might as well go back to Earth" (109).

Recall that Touponce says that "the cognitive value of reverie lies in its preservation of *a non-alienated relation to nature*" (18, emphasis added). This the Martians developed over time. Perhaps it was too much to expect an empathetic newcomer like Spender to quickly find such a relationship in a way that would have led him to some kind of effective form of resistance to the terrible colonial project about to visited on the dry Red Planet. Recall too what Bachelard says: "To bite into the world with no other 'care' than the happiness of biting, isn't that entering the world? What a grasp of the world is a bite. Then the world is the direct object of the verb 'I eat' ... what harmony, what unity of the total being!" (178). Spender's bite in the world of Mars already had in it his fear and his desire to assume responsibility. He thus violated the healthful sequence of Bachelardian reverie, which begins with careless tasting of the world, reverie itself, emergence into the world more capable of responsibility and then action. Perhaps Jeff Spender's rush to praxis must fail because his reveries are polluted with fear and loathing.

It Came from Outer Space *and Desert Reveries as Effective Ethos*

A mining town surrounded by Joshua trees of the Mojave Desert, the town of Sand Rock, Arizona, is set in a valley, and we first see it in an aerial over-cliff shot in *It Came from Outer Space*, a shot that subtly connotes a kind of crater, a visual suggestion that the residents here are themselves like the visitors we'll soon meet in an actual crater: aliens. Noteworthy is the fact that protagonist John Putnam lives outside of town; he doesn't like cities, and the suggestion here is that he is more closely connected to the desert, to its rhythms of survival and its possibilities of beauty. Putnam, a writer and amateur astronomer, and his fiancé Ellen Fields, a school teacher and former love interest of the sheriff, witness a fireball descend on the desert around Sand Rock one evening. With the help of a helicopter pilot, they visit the site of the impact, a massive crater that Putnam alone descends into and in which he finds not a rock from space but a space ship with aliens. "Oh, it's beautiful," Ellen says when she says the crater formed by the impact in the desert. She expresses no such sentiment concerning Sand Rock. This is the first indication that love of natural beauty will form a kind of ethical foundation for the actions of some of the characters, including John Putnam, who will save the aliens from human hatred.

In Ray Bradbury's screen treatment, the aliens are called Xenomorphs; so I will use that term throughout. The Xenomorphs, as comes clear, have landed accidently, mean no harm and want to repair their ship; in order to do so, they must assume the forms of humans in Sand Rock in order to procure supplies for the necessary repairs. Naturally, this raises the suspicions of Putnam; no one yet believes his claims that the meteorite is a space ship. Gradually, however, even the hostile sheriff comes to accept Putnam's story about aliens even as only Putnam is convinced of their benevolent motives. It is up to Putnam in the film's climax to dynamite the entrance to a mine — the only access to the buried ship — in order to give the Xenomorphs time to launch their ship toward home. In the meantime, Putnam has saved the actual humans whose forms the Xenomorphs were mimicking, including the lovely Ellen. The aliens are grotesque in appearance, and the human propensity toward violence against the frightening is a key moralistic element of the story. The aliens cannot show their true forms to the mob that seeks revenge at their crash site. But Putnam's acceptance of the desert — which seems so threatening to some — prepares him for the acceptance of the Xenomorphs — whose appearance would appall others in the story.

Bill Warren points out that *It Came from Outer Space* was pioneering in several ways: one of the first shot in 3-D, the first SF film by Jack Arnold, the first starring Richard Carlson and the first using the southwestern U.S. as an important locale, among other things (121). Filmed in California, the film is fictionally set in western Arizona, on the edge of the Mojave desert. Famously, though the screenplay credit goes to Harry Essex, Warren demonstrates convincingly that the story and script is essentially Ray Bradbury's, drawn from the writer's treatments for the film (122–125). These treatments were published in 2004.

Despite some changes in dialogue made by Essex, the essential lyricism of Bradbury is there and most of it has to do with the desert itself, such that setting becomes place, and place becomes locus for reverie. And reverie — again — is foundational for well-being. Unlike the murderous rampages of Jeff Spender, John Putnam is able to avoid most violence as he develops an ethical solution to the problems of saving the Sand Rock residents temporarily held by the aliens and letting the Xenomorphs escape the bigotry of a frightened posse.

"It's alive," Putnam tells Ellen early in the film. "And yet it looks so dead out there." He is speaking of the desert. Survival mechanisms that have evolved in the desert — such as slow growth and wide spacing to allow for successful utilization of sporadic and annually sparse moisture; thorns for protection against herbivores and for dissipation of heat; and diurnal burrowing followed by nocturnal foraging on the part of many animal species — give the impression of waste, of stasis and death. Putnam knows better: "But it's all alive and waiting for you.... And ready to kill you if you go too far. The sun will get you or the cold at night ... a thousand ways the desert can kill" (qtd. in Warren 123). Significantly, Putnam sees through the appearance of deadness — connoting an ecological understanding of place, thus complicating his outsider status. The people of Sand Rock may distrust the former urbanite but his knowledge of the world (astronomy to desert natural history) shows him to be a more rooted character than any of the other residents. Not only is the desert "alive," Putnam says, it is "waiting for you." He never specifies what it is waiting for — it's not only to kill — but given Putnam's connection to the sky and the land and given his coming sympathy for the aliens-as-outsiders, the suggestion here is that the desert is waiting for proper human recognition. It kills only when we fail to grant its due.

Reverie or clear-seeing, respect, well-being, connectedness, ambience, and non-alienation matters as the basis for survival, as telephone linemen Frank Daylon shows us. It is Daylon who expresses the essential beauty and strangeness of the desert in a scene that is partly autobiographical: As Warren and others have noted, Bradbury's father was a lineman. And surely Bradbury's Tucson years inform Daylon's lovely speech, one that Warren says reflects "poetic paranoia," but one that, I would emphatically argue, gives the desert proper recognition, thus placing humans in the wider context of plants and animals (125). This is not so much paranoia as it is humility, which is a precondition to reverie. From his perch on a phone pole, Daylon says:

> There's that sun in the sky, and the heat, and look at the roads, full of mirages. And the sand out there, full of rivers and lakes that are fifty, a hundred miles away.... And sometimes you get to thinking maybe some nights, or some noons like this noon, the sun burns on the wires and gets in the wires and listens and hums and talks like this talk you're hearing. And sometimes you think the wind gets in the wires and blows and that's what you hear now. And sometimes you wonder if some of the snakes and coyotes and the tumbleweeds don't climb the poles at noon, far off where you can't see them, and listen in on us human beings [qtd. in Warren, 125].

Daylon's anaphora is a kind of quiet chant; repetition can induce reverie, and vice-versa. The rest of the world takes notice of us, and the roads we build are not emblems of progress but sites of illusions: They are mirages. We are not so advanced, then, after all, this speech suggests. This is a world in which the sun might come to Earth and possess the elements of human technology, where the creatures of the desert itself are some larger ear, waiting to hear what we have to say and to decide if it's worth hearing. In the end, the Xenomorphs themselves decide what we have to say isn't worth pursuing, not yet, not until we have become better able to look past our bias against grotesque appearances. Daylon's soliloquy is perhaps the high point of the film, a moving testament to the power of desert lands.

Warren writes that "the desert provides a sense of isolation. Flat country covered with strange plants, which extends in all directions, seems almost like another world, far removed from the activities of men" (128). Vivian Sobchack writes in *Screening Space* about the power of the desert landscape, and while she does not specifically address it as a locus for reverie, it clearly is. What John Putnam does with that reverie is quite different from what Jeff Spender does with his. Sobchack rightly argues that in *It Came from Outer Space*, as in several other films set in the American deserts, the aliens "become virtually subordinate in their ability to evoke awe and wonder [relative] to the impressive visual power of the terrain itself." She says further that seeing the unshadowed and limitless stretches of desert punctuated by the stiff and inhuman form of an occasional cactus or the frantic scurrying of some tiny and vulnerable rodent, the spectator is forced to a recognition, however unconscious it may remain, of Man's precarious and puny stability, his vulnerability to the void "right here" as well as "out there," his total isolation, the fragile quality of his body and his works, the terrifying blankness in the eyes of what he thought was Mother Nature [112].

Driving "on a highway winding through the desert ... [becomes] a journey through an infinite and hostile void" in which we learn that "*the Earth is not part of us*, it does not even recognize us" (113, emphasis added). Sobchack reads the desert as, one might say, an Easterner would: a place of fear and alienation. Certainly she is correct when she says that "these films with their abundance of long shots in which human figures move like insects, their insistence on a fathomless landscape, we are forced to a pessimistic view of the worth of technological progress and of man's ability to control his destiny" (113). Just so. She goes on:

We are shown human beings set uncomfortably against the vastness and agelessness of the desert and sea, are reminded by the contrast that land and water were here long before us and our cities and towns and will be here long after we and artifacts are gone. We see ourselves — normal, human, incredibly mortal — against an unblinking and bare landscape that refutes any anthropomorphic sweetness with which we strive to endow it [114].

Granted, but rather than see this a negative commentary on humanity's smallness, one might read such visuals in *It Came from Outer Space* and other such films as a recontextualizing of our place in the cosmos, a truer perspective, as it were, and, as such, a more honest terrain to develop the kinds of reveries that lineman Daylon expresses. That is, the relationship of human to nonhuman, of human to desert, need not be uncomfortable. Daylon is not afraid of the desert. He respects it. So too does Putnam, who makes it clear he values the environment for its beauty and for its stripping bare of human hubris. His reaction to how others disbelieve him is not just the anger of someone called a liar but of an outsider who, in most ways, actually knows the place better than the locals, those residents who ignore the desert or bend it to the usual human uses, such as mining. (Sheriff Matt Warren criticizes Putnam for "poking around in the desert and squinting up at the stars" [qtd. in Lucanio 31].)

But Sobchack insists on an agoraphobic reading of the Daylon's speech, saying that "the camera scans a desert sky in which a row of telephone poles and the men working on the wires appear ineffectual breaking up the endless wasteland and the empty sky. The men doing their jobs, trying to impose limits on an expressionless and terrifying expanse of space." They "seem to unconsciously recognize the futility of their attempt to make an impression on the desert. One of them voices the uncertainty and discomfort we already feel from the images on the screen" (114). (Jerry Yamamoto has argued the phone poles may register as images of the cross, tying into his reading of the film as a morality tale of overcoming othering and of resurrection [101].) My point is: This is not terrifying. It's simply a *natural context*.

As I have indicated earlier, by noting desert-plant adaptations, such a region seems barren only if you approach with other ecosystem lenses, none of which apply here. The desert is a wasteland only if you fail to pay attention. Putnam, Ellen and Daylon are spokespeople for a more nuanced view of the desert. Carl Abbott notes that "science fiction extends that openness to infinity, from cold desert surfaces of the Moon or Mars to the wide-open spaces of entire galaxies. The western plains and desert are thus made boundless and their possibilities and dangers are extended to the ends of the imagination" (257). I appreciate that "possibilities" occurs before "dangers."

Importantly, the desert is a site for reverie not only for Putnam, Ellen and Daylon but for the Xenomorphs themselves. Daylon's co-worker George (once he's been taken over by a Xenomorph) stares unblinking at the sun and pronounces it "beautiful." In their original form, the Xenomorphs trail glitter — suggestive of a kind of magic, a fairy dust, a way toward enchantment — and, crucially, they see the desert through a gelatinous membrane. The subjective camera shots from the Xenomorph point of view are like *looking through water*. Further, when viewers witness the aliens directly, we seem them in a kind of fog or watery haze, and the primary impression is the largeness of the single eye. Intended or not, the visual connotations are that this monocular eye is big enough to see things we cannot. These Xenomorphs are watery creatures come to an arid land with eyes that see more than we can. Water is life. Seeing is life.

Says Bachelard: "And in the universe, still water is a mass of tranquility, a mass of immobility. In the still waters, the world rests. Before still water, the dreamer *adheres* to the repose of the world" (196). Though the Xenomorphic liquidity is not quite still, the point seems germane and, as he goes on to say, "melting into the basic element is a necessary human suicide for whoever wants to experience an emergence into a new cosmos" (203).

Of course, humans are mostly water as well, but our sense of self, of skin-tight boundaries between self and world, inculcates an illusion of separation. In their rather more gooey manner, Jack Arnold's cinematic aliens here show a breaking down of boundaries; there is a kind of fluidic transfer at work here, whereby the other — feared by us as death-giving — in fact should be embraced by us as more alive and more capable of higher feeling and intelligence. Putnam and Ellen realize this. If water is rather more ambiguous in its connotations in *The Martian Chronicles* (a discussion for another time), then in *It Came from Outer Space*, water imagery is the imagery of life, of survival and of the prospect of understanding.

Unlike Jeff Spender, the astronomer/writer Putnam is making a home in the desert, mingling survival and reverie. Perhaps it is Putnam who best fits the definition of a best possible self, as offered by Yi-Fu Tuan: "Rootedness is not the answer if only because it sets the self into a mold too soon. Mobility carried to excess, on the other hand, makes it difficult, if not impossible, for a strong sense of self to jell. A self that is coherent and firm, yet capable of growth, would seem to call for an alternation of stillness and motion, stability and change, place and space, the duration of each being calibrated by culture and individual temperament" (4). Interestingly, Yi-Fu Tuan speaks of the desert as his new-found home. Having arrived at Death Valley at night, he woke to moonlight or "lunar beauty," and dawn gave him "a phantasmagoria of shimmering mauves, purples and golds. Extraterrestrial, too, were the saline flats on the Valley floor, immaculately white, and stark sculptural reliefs unsoiled by life" (18–19). For him, as for Bradbury and several of his characters, the desert is "the objective correlative" of his personality. More than this, it is home not only to the body but to a sense of more-than-human survival, reverie and ethical action. Putnam's reverential relation with the land is the effective ethos of his wanting to bridge differences with the Xenomorphs. Reverie-of-land prepares responsibility-in-cosmos.

I read Bradbury's deserts on Mars and in the Mojave from my own desert home in Tucson, not far from the places he explored as a child. The search for self is, in no small measure, a search for self-as-selflessness in a wider world. This is the material ecocritical and Bachelardian project.

Conclusion

In his celebrated volume of living in Tucson's surrounding Sonoran desert, *The Desert Year*, the critic-cum-nature-writer Joseph Wood Krutch writes in a vein Ray Bradbury would have approved of: "To think of [animals and plants] in merely mechanical terms is to come ultimately to think of ourselves in the same terms — and that is precisely what the so-called educated man has been coming more and more to do" (28). This is ultimately an anti-scientific attitude that relies on scientific insight up to the point that Krutch's (or Bradbury's) psyche fears too much information, too much empiricism, too much threat to mystery. This is a stance that Jeff Spender clearly embodies, though not, it would seem, John Putnam. It happens to be a stance I find ultimately appalling, but Krutch believes that an overly scientific perspective threatens "the richness of our own experience by thinking of it merely as some process of mechanical adaptation"—which, of course, *it is* (28). It's the word "merely" that sticks in the craw, as though science cannot enrich our experience, as though learning is at some vague point for a Krutch, for a Bradbury, a form of impoverishment. There is a kind of stasis in much nature writing and, in some respects, Bradbury's work reproduces such a stasis—a refusal to accept that reverie will arrive no matter how much (in fact, because of how much) "data" we have gathered. Recall that Spender says of the Martians, "They never let science crush the aesthetic and the beautiful" (Bradbury 92). In any case, here is a contact point between two giants of their respective genres—Krutch, in nature writing, and Bradbury, in science fiction. Further, this contact point is contested by other writers in both fields who take very different approaches to the notion that science and the richness of human experience must be set against each other.

Though this matter is worth further study, it is enough here to note the fact of this contact between two only superficially dissimilar genres. We can conclude by appreciating that Krutch and Bradbury both arrive at this distrust of too much science, too much of a mechanistic view of life, in the spare landscape of the desert. Krutch and Bradbury both appreciate the desert for its strangeness and its aridity-enforced elbow room. Both find reverie in desert settings, a feeling-tone that makes life worth living. In writing about a sunset viewed from an Arizona mountain, presumably in the Santa Catalinas, a dramatic range that looms above Tucson, Krutch claims that "if the light was not beautiful, the light was not there; and if the light was not there, then neither was I" (135). Bradbury, in the persona of Spender, says, "Faith had always given us answers to all things. But it all went down the drain with Freud and Darwin. We were and still are a lost people" but the Martians "knew how to combine science and religion so the two worked side by side, neither denying the other, each enriching the other" (90–91). Spender even speaks about the qualities of light, parroting the notion of typical humans: "'A scientist can prove that color is only the way the cells are placed in a certain material to reflect light. Therefore, color is not really an actual part of things I happen to see.' A Martian, far cleverer, would say: 'This is a fine picture. It came from the hand and the mind of a man inspired. Its idea and its color are from life. This thing is good'" (92).

And in the concluding scenes of *It Came from Outer Space*, John and Ellen stand with a crowd that watches the crater, a crowd that assumes, along with the sheriff, that the alien Xenomorphs are dead. One writer has pointed out that when Putnam blows up the entrance to the mining shaft, he gives the gathered townspeople "a chance at introspection"—not quite reverie but a step toward it, perhaps (Lucanio 44). Jack Arnold's well-composed shot shows a background star in the upper-left of the frame and the reaching arms of a tree in the upper-right background. Then the spaceship launches from Earth. In the light of the take-off, the star in the background disappears, and the camera zooms slowly on to Putnam's worshipful face when he says, "It wasn't the right time for us to meet. But there'll be other nights, other stars for us to watch. They'll be back." The last scene stitches sky and fiery spaceship and desert together, as the vessel arcs above the low mountains and jagged Joshua trees, trees with an aspect of uplift, albeit painful uplift, all to be followed by long waiting for human reveries to construct peace and responsibility in a challenging land on a broken planet. The scene is *beautiful*: a spark to reverie that overcomes the disappointment of the wait-to-come.

Beauty is like water in the desert—a fundamental necessity—whether on Mars or Earth. From the desert, reveries can come, reveries that last a lifetime and nourish the self. In doing so, the selves so fortified may move into the world to act as skillfully as they know how—toward a wholeness, a consciousness of well-being.

Works Cited

Abbott, Carl. *Frontiers Past and Future: Science Fiction and the American West.* Lawrence: University of Kansas Press, 2006. Print.
_____. "Homesteading on the Extraterrestrial Frontier." *Science Fiction Studies* 32.2 (July 2005): 240–264. Print.
Bachelard, Gaston. *The Poetics of Reverie.* Trans. Daniel Russell. New York: The Orion Press, 1969. Print.
Bradbury, Ray. *The Martian Chronicles.* New York: William Morrow, 1997. Print.
Clareson, Thomas D. *Understanding Contemporary American Science Fiction: The Formative Period, 1926–1970.* Columbia: University of South Carolina Press, 1992. Print.
Deleuze, Gilles, and Felix Guattari. "A Thousand Plateaus." In *Literary Theory: An Anthology.* Eds. Julie Rivkin and Michael Ryan. Malden, MA: Blackwell, 1998. 514–523. Print.
Eller, Jonathan, and William F. Touponce. *Ray Bradbury: The Life of Fiction.* Kent, OH: Kent State University Press, 2004. Print.
It Came from Outer Space. Dir. Jack Arnold. Perf. Richard Carlson, Barbara Rush, Charles Drake, Russell Johnson, Kathleen Hughes, and Joe Sawyer. Universal. 1953. 1981. DVD.
Krutch, Joseph Wood. *The Desert Year.* Iowa City: University of Iowa Press, 2010. Print.
Lucanio, Patrick. *Them or Us: Archetypal Interpretations of Fifties Alien Invasion Films.* Bloomington: Indiana University Press, 1987. Print.
McDowell, Michael J. "The Bakhtinian Road to Ecological Insight." In *The Ecocriticism Reader.* Eds. Cheryll Glotfelty and Harold Fromm. Athens: University of Georgia Press, 1996. 371–391. Print.
Mogen, David. *Ray Bradbury.* Boston: Twayne, 1986. Print.

Nye, David. E. *American Technological Sublime*. Cambridge: MIT Press, 1994. Print.

Phillips, Dana, and Heather Sullivan. "Material Ecocriticism: Dirt, Waste, Bodies, Food, and Other Matter." *ISLE: Interdisciplinary Studies in Literature and Environment* 19.3 (Summer 2012): 445–447. Print.

Sobchack, Vivian. *Screening Space: The American Science Fiction Film*. New York: Ungar, 1987. Print.

Stafford, Kim. "Out of This World with Chaucer and the Astronauts." In *Having Everything Right: Essays of Place*. 15–27. Seattle: Sasquatch Books, 1997. Print.

Strom, Stephen. "Earth and Mars." *Stephen Strom — Fine Art Photography*. 2000. 13 Dec. 2012. Web.

Touponce, William F. *Ray Bradbury and the Poetics of Reverie: Fantasy, Science Fiction, and the Reader*. Ann Arbor: UMI Research Press, 1984. Print.

Tuan, Yi-Fu. *Place, Art, and Self*. Santa Fe: Center for American Places, 2004. Print.

Warren, Bill. *Keep Watching the Skies!: American Science Fiction Movies of the Fifties*. Jefferson, NC: McFarland, 1997. Print.

Weiner, Lauren. "The Dark and Starry Eyes of Ray Bradbury." *The New Atlantis* (Summer 2012): 79–91. Print.

Yamamoto, Jerry. "In Them We Trust? Fear, Faith, and *It Came from Outer Space*." In *Science Fiction America: Essays on SF Cinema*. Ed. David J. Hogen. Jefferson, NC: McFarland, 2006. Print.

Why Does Mars Beckon Us?

ARI ESPINOZA

We know that it is a desolate, dry world. No, there is nothing like descriptions of the Red Planet emerging from the fecund imaginations of writers. A desert planet that is absolutely unforgiving, where without the benefit of a protective spacesuit, you would freeze from your feet to your knees, burn from above the knees to your midsection, and freeze again top of your head.

And still, Mars beckons us.

For the Greeks — whose language is all across Mars in the form of Greco-Latinized place names — the god of war, Ares, was motivated by one thing: blood lust. For Ares, killing for the sake of it was as good a reason as any. While the gods could be capricious and indifferent to humanity, they were often capable of having pity, seeking redress for the wronged and promising justice in the face of the evil schemes of men. Yet for Ares, it was an easy thing, then, to associate the red color of Mars with a god described as "overwhelming, insatiable in battle, destructive, and man-slaughtering" (Burkert 69). How interesting then, that we can call Mars a hostile world, impervious to the dreams of men and talk of future colonization. We cannot change the nature — if we can say that — of the fourth planet from the Sun: cold, desolate, devoid of life but still harboring secrets of a past we can only barely imagine.

Even on Earth, deserts can be mysterious, foreboding, and deadly places. Get yourself lost in one, and you could die from heat stroke or dehydration during the day, but also freeze at night. As on Mars above, so it is on Earth below, so to speak. But maybe it is how we perceive the desert that also fuels our imaginations. Our first civilizations were carved in desert regions, of course. In one of the greatest of them, Egypt, civilization carved itself in the forms of the pyramids and the Sphinx, which stands as a testament to the will of men to control their environment, to defy the stillness and hostility of the

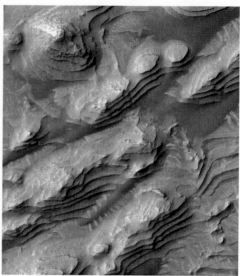

Left: Planetary Science Institute astronomer and artist William K. Hartmann's painting of Mars as it would have looked to approaching space probes, according to Percival Lowell's now-obsolete sightings on Mars and *Martian-Chronicles*–era concept (courtesy William K. Hartmann). *Right:* Layered sediments in Danielson Crater. The sediments have various thicknesses, so they indicate possible Martian climate change over long periods of time (courtesy NASA/JPL/University of Arizona).

desert and to proclaim, "I was here." (Never mind the countless souls who labored to make this all possible.) This image of a portion in Danielson Crater is almost Sphinx-like in how it teases us: layered rock sculpted by — by *what*? Wind, water or both, and for how long? The blue that we see isn't real, of course, it is red, but the color tells us the sand is basaltic in origin, forces long extinct leaving us a naturally carved landscape clothed in silence. On a more sublime level, Moses has his famous first encounter in the quietness of the desert; Jesus is tempted over the course of forty days there, and Mohammed is commanded to recite in the stillness of a cave, far from the city.

Even on Mars, where more probes have failed to land than those which have succeeded, humans leave their marks as tracks in the Martian sand with rovers like Opportunity, Spirit, and now Curiosity, slowly moving across the surface. Hardly the grandeur of what the Egyptians call Abu Hol (the Sphinx), but these recent marks will remain for an exceedingly long time. We humans take it for granted that we will get to Mars someday, but what if we don't? What if those tracks, leading to the mechanical servants that will at some point cease to move, are all that remains of man's attempt to claim triumph over another desert, another hostile landscape and say, "We were here!" Perhaps a different set of eyes might spy those tracks and those frozen robots in the Martian sand, attempting to divine their original purpose and the people who made them.

It is the austerity of the desert that brings me to my favorite vignette in Ray Bradbury's *The Martian Chronicles*, a chapter titled "Night Meeting." In it, Tómas Gomez is on his way to a new settlement, is gassing up his truck and talking to the station proprietor who remarks, "If you can't take Mars for what she is, then you might as well go back to Earth" (79). The old man goes on further to note how different everything feels on Mars, including the observation that "even time is crazy up here." Those words set the tone for an extraordinary meeting as Tómas trundles off, letting the old man's words sink in and bringing up his own feelings of experiencing Mars:

> Mars was always quiet, but quieter tonight than any other. The desert and empty seas swung by him, and the mountains against the stars. There was a smell of Time in the air tonight. He smiled and turned the fancy in his mind. There was a thought. What did Time smell like?... And going further, what did Time look like?... And tonight — Tómas shoved a hand into the wind outside the truck — tonight you could almost touch time [80].

Back to reality for a moment. Time *is* different on Mars, if for no other reason than a typical Martian year is almost twice that of Earth. While a Martian day is close to ours, while there are seasons on the Red Planet, and even snow, time itself is going to be different for Earth's first travelers. Right now it's a dry fact that Mars takes longer to revolve around Sol than our planet. Like Tómas Gomez however, a human presence on Mars is going to start experiencing time much differently.

Yet the feeling of time being a tangible thing is only the beginning of Tómas' curious meeting, for within moments of pondering the ancient ruins of a Martian city does he encounter a Martian himself. Both are startled at the presence of the other; both try to address one another but cannot grasp the other's language. It is only when the Martian runs his hand — literally — through Tómas' head and picks up English does their conversation begin.

The Martian insists that he is on his way to a night celebration, much to the confusion of Tómas, who can't possibly understand how his new acquaintance cannot see the dead city behind him: "Why, that city's been dead thousands of years." The Martian is equally confounded: "Dead? I slept there yesterday!" Through some more back and forth conversing, both uneasily decide that one is in the past, the other in the future. But who? The Earthling insists he the future while the Martian cannot fathom why the strange creature he's met on the highway insists the oceans no longer exist, that he's come from some unknown star and that the canals are dry: "The canals are full of lavender wine!" is his response, but to no avail. Both are disquieted, disconcerted, and absolutely certain, though, of their own reality, their own perception is being the correct one. They soon part, trying to convince themselves that they've just experienced a peculiar dream.

Anyone who has spent any time in the desert, especially in Arizona, understands that particular silence Tómas encounters during his drive. At midday, far from the road or the sounds of other people, you can just marvel at the silence. It's not the same as being in a quiet room. You are surrounded by living things — insects, plants, animals — but the quiet is remarkable. You can spy the roads and the houses — yes, those markers of civilization — from a distance but there is no noise. Think for a moment: mankind makes a thousand plans, but in the solitude of a desert setting, man is not the master. Nature carries on, oblivious to the scurrying of humans who build their cities, erect their signs and proclaim themselves victors over the landscape.

Still another theme that runs through Bradbury: the inevitability of human conquest, or as Tómas puts it, invasion. "Mars was a distant shore," Bradbury writes, "and men spread upon it in waves." We see Mars as a place for future colonization, at first under the guise of exploration, and some groups want to forsake the moon in order to get to the Red Planet sooner than later. Witness the words of wunderkind Elon Musk:

> Some money has to be spent on establishing a base on Mars. It's about getting the basic fundamentals in place. That was true of the English colonies [in the Americas]; it took a significant expense to get things started. But once there are regular Mars flights, you can get the cost down to half a million dollars for someone to move to Mars [Musk 2012].

Like Tómas, we look at Mars and see a dead planet, a place to be seeded, transformed. There may be things of interest to planetary science, but the true exploration of Mars begins with its colonization, the central subject of *The Martian Chronicles*. Of course, no one on Earth who waxes poetic about getting to Mars dares bring up the problems that humans will invariably bring with them, even with the conceit these failings have all been left behind. We leave it up to Bradbury to comment about that:

> Timothy looked at the deep ocean sky, trying to see Earth and the war and ruined cities and the men killing each other since the day he was born. But he saw nothing. The war was as removed and far off as two flies battling to the death in the arch of a great high and silent cathedral. And just as senseless [173].

In order to get to Mars, we must have the stars in our eyes and talk about the survival of the human species. And that also means seeing Mars as a resource to be exploited, a literal tabula rasa or more to the point, an interstellar manifest destiny. It's the same impulse that drove men west, establishing townships and claiming territory, renaming places that were already known to the natives, as when a character says, "I never saw any yet, but I hear they're around (79). Again, like Tómas and the other settlers of *The Martian Chronicles*, we may steal a few moments of superficial contemplation, but we must get to the building of colonies, transporting Oregon lumber and women for those lonely first men, because *that* is destiny of humanity.

We have tamed deserts before, and the desert world of Mars will be the largest, perhaps longest, taming we will undertake. We have constructed cities in the desert where there should be none; moved millions of cubic feet of dirt to make dams and

Nili Fossae has some of the best exposures of ancient bedrock on Mars — a good candidate spot for a future lander. The region itself is well known for clay (courtesy NASA/JPL/University of Arizona).

artificial lakes that power our hungry, growing cities. There are no waterways on Mars to commandeer, but we will be like Xerxes who lashed the waters of the Hellespont when it dared to prevent his crossing. Again, as Tómas notes, Mars will be invaded.

The public will grow tired, or worse, indifferent to Mars. There is only so much appetite for sending probes to Mars that can scratch several centimeters beneath the surface or analyze material to figure out if life may have existed on the Red Planet. It's a dead world, and we will never resurrect any of those vanished oceans or canals of lavender wine. Yet again, there is that notion of time that Bradbury writes about. What Tómas sees are broken, weathered pillars, abandoned homes, and a highway that is sixteen centuries old but still useful. He is right in one aspect: what we see of Mars today is a monument to an extremely distant past. A living fossil, if you will. There are lava fields that have contorted the landscape, looking impossibly like frozen seas. Impact craters that have slowly been filled with dust over millions of years, and fresher ones that have been around for millennia. We know that there is water on Mars in the form of carbon dioxide ice, but its abundance is only beginning to be understood. There are extinct volcanoes, lava tubes, and silent mountains: it's all incredibly Earth-like were it not for the utter sterility and the impossible silence. While there is no one picture that can capture the essence of Mars, this image of a section of the Nili Fossae sums up the experience of both Tómas and the Martian: layered bedrock practically says, "Decipher me." We see what Tómas does: old, long-gone. Indeed, for most of us (and like many other characters in *The Martian Chronicles*, it could barely merit attention. We see it, it's there, we move on. Dead and uninteresting. But that bedrock — so much easier to see in a desert environment — reminds us of a history that the Martian insists is reality. What was Mars like so long ago? What story is in that bedrock?

Oh yes, there is sound on Mars, thanks to a thin, mostly carbon-dioxide membrane of an atmosphere, but it's not the same as on Earth. We know of the wind and dust devils that trace their fingers across the landscape, exposing dark subsurface into amazing patterns. Those global dust storms? Seemingly terrifying, although none of them could knock you over. Imagine if you can, Martian wind whistling past you, then stillness. If you are in the right place at the right time in the polar regions, you might hear the crack of subsurface material exploding as the Sun changes it immediately from a solid to a gaseous state, darkening the surrounding terrain so that it looks like a pockmarked battle field. Or, creating formations that look like spiders. Or, knocking material off a clip and creating bilious avalanche cloud. Then again, silence.

This is the world that we see, much as Tómas sees: ruined, old, devastated. It is an ancient past; we look to a future of manned Mars expeditions, of building colonies, of terraforming a dead world into another habitat for humanity. At that point, as Bradbury notes in his closing, we will be the Martians. Our vocabulary will change so that we no longer describe Africa as the birthplace of humanity, but Earth as the birthplace of humanity. Yet for now, as the old gas station owner tells Tómas, "Well, that's Mars. Enjoy it. Don't ask it to be nothing else but what it is."

Ambiguity. That may be the future of our relationship with Mars, in a similar way that the Greeks developed an ambiguous attitude about Ares. Homer dedicated an a hymn to the god of war: "Shed down a kindly ray from above upon my life, and strength of war, that I may be able to drive away bitter cowardice from my head and crush down the deceitful impulses of my soul" (Cook 8). Hardly the words of someone who considers one of the sons of Zeus to be beyond the pale. By a similar measure, the Orphic Hymn to declares, "Magnanimous, unconquered, boisterous Ares..." (Taylor 65). It could very well be that the old man has developed his own relationship to Mars and accepted it. He doesn't want to transform it or conquer it. He merely wants to be, living at peace with it. Once real humans have started traipsing around Mars, maybe they will change their thinking about the planet being a hostile world and start to think of it as home. And again, this is the final point of *The Martian Chronicles*, with a human family staring into a canal and the Martians staring back up at them. Who is the past and who is the future?

It's just as the old man said. "Even time is crazy up here."

Works Cited

Bradbury, Ray. *The Martian Chronicles*. New York: Bantam, 1979. Print.
Burkert, Walter. *Greek Religion*. Malden, MA: Blackwell, 1985. Print.
The Homeric Hymns. Ed. Erwin Cook. Baltimore: Johns Hopkins University Press, 2004. Print.
The Hymns of Orpheus. Trans. Thomas Taylor. London, 1792.
Musk, Elon. "Royal Aeronautical Society Presentation." Royal Aeronautical Society, London. 16 Nov. 2012. Keynote Address. Web.

The Exploration of Mars
An Unintentional Invasion?

DAVID M. ACKLAM

Sadly, only a few months before the passing of Ray Bradbury, I first learned of his childhood stays in Tucson, Arizona. This geographic connection means that his Southwest experience may have been embedded in *The Martian Chronicles*. As I gathered my personal recollections of *The Martian Chronicles*, I realized that I had actually read, or attempted to read, this book three times over the past forty-some years. Now I am seeking to recall a few traces that may relate to his formative Tucson and Southwest time. Besides recalling my experience with that famous novel, I want to discuss what kind of an influence Bradbury was as I decided to become an aerospace engineer.

Let me spend some time over the years of my personal life and share some of the places where my interest in space and science happened to cross paths with Ray Bradbury's *Martian Chronicles*. A baby boomer, born at the end of 1946, I grew up in the Midwest. Even though the collection of short stories which make up *The Martian Chronicles* where published in various magazines over the next four years, I certainly do not recall reading or even hearing about any of them. Obviously I was just too young at the time. However, I do remember in the early 1950s, a year or two before Sputnik, how my older brother Jess, my uncle Darrell, and I often talked and played games about space. I remember our watching the *Buck Rogers* serial at the Saturday morning movie matinée and we also often watched a television show called *Space Patrol*. I can remember playing as space explorers, believing in our young, innocent minds, that someday real explorers would live on space stations, visit the Moon and Mars, and travel throughout the solar system in our life time. I still recall watching Werner von Braun on television in the mid 1950s. He was working with Walt Disney, animating and illustrating how mankind could go into space.

About this same time, Hollywood released a science fiction film called *Forbidden Planet*. This film put space travel in a whole different perspective, envisioning future Earth space explorers traveling in a flying saucer to a planet in another solar system some 16 light years away. The concept of the long-dead Krell civilization, sustained in substance by a gigantic thermonuclear powered super-computer embedded in an ancient underground complex, was simply fascinating. Robby the Robot was the best robot we had ever seen. The invisible monster was a type of threat we had not thought about before and made us wonder how we could ever defend ourselves if something like that ever landed on Earth.

Turning from science fiction, I remember my brother and uncle telling me how the planet Venus was shrouded in clouds that totally obscured seeing the surface. We often wondered what existed on the planet's surface. Were there swamps and jungles? Maybe there were still dinosaurs roaming this cloud-covered sister planet of ours. On the other hand, they explained to me that Mars was a planet on which astronomers could actually see surface features with their powerful telescopes. Around this time, I heard about Percival Lowell and the Martian canals he saw on the planet's surface. Even amateur astronomers could see the polar caps and light and dark features on the surface that seemed to change with the seasons. Now this was a planet that mankind surely must explore in our lifetime, I concluded.

I clearly remember my uncle and brother telling me about the plans President Eisenhower announced regarding putting a small satellite in orbit as part of the International Geophysical Year. I had no clue at the time what a satellite was and remember how they laughed so hard when I asked if it were some kind of special light that was installed on a fancy horse saddle. Space satellites and rockets now really caught our attention and we knew it would not be long before real space exploration would happen. We certainly were caught by surprise when we learned that the Soviet Union launched Sputnik before the United States. The subsequent failure of the Vanguard launch was also a real disappointment to us. Space exploration had begun but our nation was not leading it.

Not long after Sputnik went into orbit, finally followed by the successful launch and orbiting of the Explorer 1, I began experimenting with amateur rocketry. Along with several of my friends, we built and launched many home-made rockets. Our earliest rockets used a simple hobby rocket motor called Jet-X, not very powerful, but good enough to allow are rockets to get off the ground. We first made our little model rockets to look like the V-2 and the WAC, but found them to be too heavy for our Jet-X motor to power. They could barely lift off the launcher. We ended up making a stick and frame design from balsa wood that looked like a small four legged stool that could get off the launcher and climb to maybe 20 to 30 feet.

Months later we discovered and used another, much more powerful commercially made model rocket kit and motor. This was the model of the Aerobee missile that was manufactured and sold by the Estes Corporation. These types of rocket kits and motors are still available today, and are used by many amateur rocket enthusiasts.

About a year after Sputnik, another science fiction film made a deep impression on my 12-year-old mind, a film about an alien life form arriving on Earth in a meteorite. *The Blob* caused me to consider the danger of unintentional visitors from space. *The Blob*'s scenario was much different than the usual alien creatures that Hollywood typically had arriving in flying saucers. Meteorites were real and regular visitors to our home (Yeaworth).

Over time we eventually graduated to learning how to make our own rocket motors. The public library provided us with much information on rocket engines and a mail order houses provided us with the materials and chemical propellants to assemble our own rocket motor. Our improved version was a seven-inch long, ¾-inch diameter, motor that we mounted in a two-foot-long, three-finned rocket airframe. Like our earlier rockets, we launched this much larger and more powerful rocket from my parents' suburban backyard. I can still see our rocket roaring off the launcher, filling our backyard with smoke and leaving a beautiful trail of exhaust and fire as it climbed into the clear blue sky, heading south and coming back down a couple of blocks away. Cheering and grinning, we hopped on our bikes, rode over to where we thought it had landed, and were met by a grown-up carefully examining our rocket. I remember his stern look as he politely explained that our rocket had bounced off his roof harmlessly. However, in a very serious tone, he said that it was high time for us to find a new launch site.

My rocket motor building days waned and I became more interested in the science, physics, and mathematics related to rockets. I spent a good amount of my spare time trying to design and build an inertially-guided rocket with a preprogrammed, integrated flight control system. The rocket airframe had a three-inch diameter, was over three feet long, and was to be powered by a cluster of three of our seven-inch motors. I had not yet learned about gyroscopes and accelerometers, so I tried using mercury switches to detect deviations from vertical and a two channel punched paper tape system to generate my steering commands. I also designed and built very primitive electromagnetically-controlled actuators that were supposed to move the control surfaces. These control surfaces were intended to move in response to deviations from vertical detected by the mercury switches and from commands provided by the preprogrammed punched tape system. The concept actually worked in a static, unpowered flight environment, but my electromagnetic actuators were simply too weak and could not overcome the aerodynamic loads of flight. Also, the mercury switches provided only an on or off command and were not fast enough to effectively respond to deviations from vertical. My prototype system never flew but was a good trial and error learning experience. The prototype remained in my hobby collection for years to come.

By the early 1960s, cosmonauts and astronauts were a reality, the Moon race was well under way, and a future human mission to Mars was a real possibility. My interests became scattered between graduating from high school, assessing my college chances, playing in a local rock and roll band, keeping up with the NASA and Soviet space programs, the growing Viet Nam War, and dealing with the draft when I graduated.

Returning to Ray Bradbury, I first stumbled onto his *Martian Chronicles* in my senior year high school English class. Because of my interest in space, I checked this Mars book out from the school library as just one of several books. I was not specifically assigned to read *The Martian Chronicles* or any of the other books I checked out. We just had to read some books of our choice and write book reports on them. I vaguely remember trying to read this book about Mars but never really digested it. I think I just skimmed through it, reading the first few chapters and the end chapter and then skimming and essentially guessing what might be in the middle to simply complete another required book report. At the time, it was simply not the kind of Mars book that I could wrap my mind around. In the end, I did manage to pass my English class, completed high school, and was not drafted before I joined the Air Force.

The Air Force provided me with the opportunity to attend a technical training course to become a ballistic missile analyst technician and then work with the Titan II weapon system at Vandenberg Air Force Base in California. The Titan II was the same rocket that was being used in the NASA Gemini space program, the forerunner of the Apollo moon mission. This Air Force missile training provided me with my initial education and skills in inertial guidance systems, rocket engine technology and electronics. The training also explained in detail where I had gone wrong in my first attempt to design and build my amateur rocket inertial guidance system. The Air Force encouraged my participation in continuing education and I enrolled in several correspondence courses and attended after duty hours college courses which eventually lead to my making a career in the military. My military career turned out to be our gateway to the West, allowing my wife and family to travel and live in several Southwestern states and communities, including Tucson.

Until joining the Air Force, the only impressions I had of the southwest were essentially influenced by what I saw in feature films, watched on black and white television, read about in magazines and saw in some of those 35-mm photographic slide shows my grandfather would show us after his visit with distant relatives in southern California. Now my family and I were traveling to live there.

In 1972, while stationed in Nevada, I enrolled in an on-base undergraduate evening class in philosophy. By this time, NASA's Apollo program was already landing astronauts on the moon. During this same period of space exploration, the Mars Viking mission was underway with plans to have two robotic spacecraft set foot on the surface of Mars by the mid–1970s. I, like many other space enthusiasts, were even more convinced that we would be landing astronauts on Mars by the early 1980s.

An interesting aspect of this philosophy class was that my professor and her husband were both also participating in a NASA-sponsored study. They, along with several other renowned philosophers, were asked by NASA to essentially think outside of the box about alien life and the possible consequences the Viking Landers might inadvertently cause when they landed on Mars. This raised a serious question. Could the exploration of Mars be an unintentional human invasion?

I believe this NASA study was probably instigated, in part, by the results of a returned television camera that was recovered from a moon robotic probe, Surveyor 3, during the Apollo 12 mission. Streptococcus mitis, unintentionally left on this hardware during assembly, was found on the camera and had survived after being left on the moon for over two years. This contamination was a problem that took many scientists by surprise and demanded additional decontamination processes be applied to space hardware. As early as 1967, international agreements required participating countries to avoid harmful contamination of the moon or other celestial bodies. Today, NASA and other participating countries still follow these earlier agreements. NASA has the Office of Planetary Protection which generally follows the policy of the Committee on Space Research, which is part of the International Council of Science.

As a part of this philosophy course, our professor invited our class to share our thoughts regarding this NASA study. To assist in our discussions, we were required to read Ray Bradbury's *Martian Chronicles*. This was my second opportunity to read this novel, but unfortunately, like my high school experience, I struggled to read the entire book and digest much of its contents. I remember my military work schedule and growing family responsibilities really impacted much of my reading time. However, I do recall our classroom discussions being very enlightening and providing me with a much deeper insight to some of the philosophical aspects of the book.

Our classroom discussions mainly concentrated on the perception of life. How could NASA recognize life forms that may be unlike anything that has ever been considered? What if there is some type of life existing in a different dimension? Could there be life that exists but is shifted in time from our time frame? Could there be something outside the range of our instrumentation detection capabilities? Could there be life that possessed mental capabilities far different than ours? Could there be something like the Martian life described by Bradbury? We tried visualizing the Viking Lander approaching the surface of Mars, its rocket engines blasting away, the landing pads about to touch the surface of the planet. The Landers had been cleaned and sterilized to preclude what had occurred on the Surveyor 3 Moon Lander. However, what if there were some type of life that was too small to detect with our existing technology in the landing zone? What possible destruction could the Lander cause to this unknown life? Would the rocket engines literally fry this unknown life? Could the landing pads simply crush this life? Could this life even be an alien Martian civilization?

By this time, NASA had begun to collect many more photographs of the surface of Mars, strongly indicating that the planet was quite desolate and even moon-like, probably lacking any form of life typically presented in science-fiction texts and films. We could see no ancient Martian cities, no canals, no seasonally changing regions of Martian vegetation presumed to be fed by the melting polar caps. In short, Mars was a planet with a very thin atmosphere, mainly made of carbon dioxide. As for the questions we raised and debated in our Philosophy class, I simply don't know if any of them actually filtered their way back through the NASA study.

Prior to actual landings on Mars, the Viking orbiters sent back images used to verify the selected landing sites, confirming that the Martian dust storms had subsided, and signaling that it was safe to proceed with the landing. The two Viking missions both successfully landed on the surface of Mars in 1976. The Landers dug shallow trenches into the surface of Mars; instruments analyzed the soil and came up with some mixed and questionable potential biological results. The Landers unfortunately found nothing totally conclusive regarding the existence of Martian life. In fact, the ultraviolet and solar radiation on the surface of the planet probably did a better job of sterilizing the Lander than NASA was able to do on Earth. If there were any life as we knew it to be found, it would not survive on the surface. However, additional photographic observations from the orbiters presented the intriguing face on Mars and the ancient Martian pyramids of the Cydonia region. These were only artifacts in the low resolution imaging but raised some public speculations about possible ancient Martian civilizations.

In the early 1980s, I was stationed with the Air Force Plant Representative Office at the Martin Marietta plant in Colorado. One day I had the opportunity to see one of the full-sized models of the Viking Lander in storage at the plant. To my surprise, the Lander was much larger than what I had envisioned. It looked almost alien. Later, I the opportunity to pick up a copy of a Martin Marietta publication about the Viking program and remembered first seeing the orbiter photo of the face on Mars. The photo was a raw image with several obvious data drop outs and low resolution artifacts and the caption did not identify it as the face on Mars, but just a surface feature, over a mile in length, where the shadows look something like a human face. I have to admit, to me, it really looked like a face resembling something from our ancient Egyptians. The mysterious geographical feature did raise the question that, perhaps, like Bradbury's Martian civilization, was there once was an actual, ancient Martian civilization?

In my military assignment prior to being assigned to the Martin Marietta plant, I worked with a test program at the Yuma Proving Ground in southwest Arizona. I can recall wondering about whether or not there could be an alien probe similar to the Viking Lander. What if that probe landed on a remote part of the test range? What could it have assessed, and how long would it sit there before anyone stumbled upon it? There are ancient petroglyphs, some estimated to be over 9,500 years old, on and near some of the more remote portions of the proving ground. The Viking Lander, with its cameras, could have easily assessed these as evidence of civilized life, but not determine their age. Just imagine the excitement if the one of the Viking Landers had captured an image of a petroglyph on the Martian surface. I have to wonder if Bradbury was aware of these ancient rock drawings when he lived in Tucson.

In the 1990s, I was retired from my Air Force career and working as an engineer in the defense industry. I remember reading a book about the face on Mars and the author's efforts to encourage NASA to revisit the face and the Cydonia Mesa region of Mars. The author presented some very interesting theories that actually raised my interest in wanting NASA to get a closer look at these Martian surface features. The Mars Observer spacecraft was the next NASA mission to Mars and the orbiter had a camera with much better resolution than the cameras on the two Viking orbiters. Photos from this mission could provide the details of an ancient Martian civilization or simply put an end to all the speculations the author presented in his book. Unfortunately, in 1993 the spacecraft was lost just a few days before insertion into orbit around Mars. In 1996 the Mars Global Surveyor was the next NASA mission to Mars and, this time, it was successfully placed in orbit around the red planet. This orbiter's high resolution camera photographed the Cydonia Mesa region and finally put the face of Mars to rest in 1998 by showing it to be simply an eroded hill. Like the face, the pyramids were also shown to be simply terrain features.

I retired from industry in 2002, and in my retirement I rediscovered reading for pleasure. In 2004, for the third time, I again read Bradbury's *Martian Chronicles*, finally having the time to read for pleasure and digest the contents. I also purchased and enjoyed the DVD of the 1980 televised miniseries of *The Martian Chronicles*. The video was enjoyable but as usual, not nearly as good as the book. For an in-depth analysis of the cost-benefit ratio between text and TV miniseries, see Paul Cote's essay in this collection. Now, eight years later, as I began preparing my for the draft of this essay, I read the book for the fourth time. I can now better perceive the subtle hints of Bradbury's relationship with our southwestern deserts. I can see parallels of our early settlers moving west and their impact on our Native Americans. In particular, I note Bradbury's oblique depiction of the disastrous consequences of small pox and other infectious European diseases alien to the New World.

I can remember when my family and I were stationed in Tucson back in the early 1970s and how so many of the older neighborhoods looked to us like they were simply transplanted from the Midwest. At that time, water in the desert valley didn't seem to be much of a concern, landscapes were lush with green lawns, non-native plants, and trees that were common in the more verdant parts of the country. Even today, in the older parts of Tucson there are still remnants of this era. I suspect that much of Tucson looked the same when Bradbury lived here and I have to wonder if this may have influenced his creation of the Martian telepathic presentation of the second and third expedition's Midwest home towns.

The chapter in *The Martian Chronicles* called "November 2005: The Off Season" describes the hot dog stand at the crossroads of the ancient and empty Martian highway, where the owner, with high expectations of success and wealth from his lifetime investment, is waiting for all of the new business traffic to finally arrive. This reminds me of my early travels in my military days along old Route 66. I can recall how the various businesses, so dependent upon the tourist and commercial traffic, were slowly dying off because of the new interstate system that was being built and slowly bypassing them. Over the years, more and more of Route 66 was bypassed and occasionally, as we traveled back to visit family in the Midwest, we could see the remnants of some of these old businesses, killed by the interstate transportation system.

There they stood, like Bradbury's ancient Martian ghost towns, along the now barren old Highway 66.

As I think back about the ancient petroglyphs in the Yuma Proving Ground area that I discussed earlier, I can recall how careless people were, and probably still are, with their off-road vehicles and dirt bikes. The Bureau of Land Management was erecting fences to protect many of these ancient artifacts from the ever-increasing and thoughtless intrusions by the public. There was thoughtless graffiti constantly showing up on both public and private property along with the senseless vandalism. Today we still have to deal with the public's thoughtless intrusions on the ancient civilization sites here in Tucson. Tumamoc hill is a favorite walking place for many, but I wonder how many of them actually realize or even care where they are trespassing when they diverge off the designated walking paths.

We have since returned many times to Mars and have successfully landed several spacecraft and rovers on its surface. There have also been several failures, leaving impact scars and hardware debris and rocket thruster propellants on the surface of Mars. In 2007 and 2008, I had the privilege to volunteer with the Education and Public Outreach team during the Phoenix Mars Lander mission operated by the University of Arizona.

During our daily public presentation we would project on a large screen, the latest images taken by the Lander operating on the surface of Mars. Some of these images were stereographic, so while wearing the simple red and blue 3D glasses, everyone could experience what it would be like standing on the surface of Mars, gazing around and out to the distant horizon. To me and most everyone else, the Martian landscape looked very much of the deserts of the Southwest. So similar, I could jokingly point out that just to the left and at the horizon was Yuma, and over to the right of center was Quartzite. In the foreground, the Martian surface features and rocks looked very similar to our Arizona deserts with the exception of the total lack of vegetation.

In mid-summer of 2012, I had the opportunity to again share the Phoenix Mars Lander mission at two Science Downtown events in Tucson. The full-scale model of the Lander was being displayed at both of these events and I worked the exhibit and shared my education and public outreach experience on the project with the public. Dr. Peter Smith, the Phoenix Mars Lander Principal Investigator (PI), and a keynote speaker at the events, came by the exhibit on several occasions to brief the public on the details of the mission and the Lander. During one of his visits, I was able to confirm a long suspected internal rumor. Peter is quite tall, much taller than I, and while he was standing by the Lander's mast-mounted stereo camera assembly, I could clearly see this camera was at the same height as his eyes. Conclusion, all of those beautiful images taken from the Phoenix Mars Lander were as seen from the PI's viewpoint.

Besides Mars, mankind has also sent space probes to Venus, some which have landed on the planet's surface. The planet Mercury has been visited by spacecraft and currently has one craft working in orbit. We have also sent spacecraft to Jupiter, with one probe parachuting into the upper atmosphere and finally being crushed by Jupiter's heavy and denser, lower atmosphere. At the completion of the Galileo orbiter mission, the spacecraft was intentionally sent into the planet to avoid an unintentional collision and possible contamination of one of Jupiter's many moons. Europa, a large ice moon with a liquid ocean below its surface, is one of those moons that could have suffered from such an unintentional collision with the Galileo orbiter. Another spacecraft called Juno is currently en route to Jupiter. This spacecraft will be positioned in a polar orbit that will avoid Jupiter's extreme radiation belt thus allowing its instrumentation to explore deep into the gas planet's internal structure.

The Cassini spacecraft is currently in orbit around the planet Saturn. The Huygens probe, carried by the spacecraft, was successfully landed on the surface of Saturn's largest moon, Titan. As this probe penetrated the moon's dense and hazy nitrogen-rich atmosphere and floated down to the surface, suspended from a parachute, the probe's cameras captured an almost Earth-like landscape. Images captured on the surface looked both Earth-like and Mars-like. At nearly minus 300 degrees Fahrenheit at the surface, the image showed a plain covered with small pebbles and rocks. Further analysis determined them to be primarily made of frozen water.

The dwarf planet Pluto, with its five moons, has a space probe on its way to make a fly-by and then head out into galactic space. This probe was preceded decades earlier by the Pioneer and Voyager spacecraft.

Today, NASA has successfully landed another space probe on the surface of Mars. This is the Mars Science Laboratory (MSL), affectionately called "Curiosity." The probe is the largest rover to date that mankind has sent to the planet. This is a six-wheeled robotic vehicle, powered by a radioactive thermal isotope power plant, loaded with an array of specialized science instruments, communication equipment, including a high-powered laser that can vaporize rocks. Such a machine, from a Hollywood science fiction standpoint, could easily pass as an invader from Earth. I was pleased to hear that the landing site was officially named Bradbury Landing. I hope that he would have been pleased with this naming. However, I was recently reminded that in *The Martian Chronicles*, Bradbury describes with apathy and disapproval of the renaming of the Martian cities, towns, lakes, mountains and other features after Earth people and places. In chapter called "June 2001: And the Moon Be Still as Bright," the character Spender tells Captain Wilder, "No matter how we touch Mars, we'll never touch it... (54).

I also recently read a news story in *Space*, an online aerospace engineering magazine, about some Mars Science Laboratory project developers deciding not to send a set of drill bits (the bits that are mounted on the exterior of the rover) through a final cleaning step. These bits will be used by the drill installed on the robotic arm of the rover. Apparently the deviation was not communicated in time to the NASA planetary protection officer to be corrected (David par. 5). Management considered the risk to be very low since the rover will not be drilling anywhere near any potential life-harboring ice. I read through the NASA Planetary Protection web site information and learned more about the required sterilization that a planetary probe is required to undergo. There are several categories of sterilization that depending on the purpose of the mission. Contamination is limited but not totally eliminated. A certain level of biological loads is allowed when the spacecraft leaves Earth and travels to Mars. Additional sterilization occurs naturally by the harsh space environment during its long journey to Mars. Additional sterilization also naturally occurs once on the surface of Mars.

Tests have been accomplished in laboratories here on Earth to better quantify these natural sterilization processes but it still remains an open question to what may have survived on the Landers and rovers we now have on Mars. The undersides of the landing pads or wheels could have pushed biological material into the Martian surface. Maybe the underside of the Landers and rovers' structures, including their solar panel assemblies, could have provided enough protection from the ultraviolet and cosmic radiation to allow some of the remaining biological load to survive. Could our rovers be distributing biological material from Earth everywhere they have been and continue to explore? I do not know but still wonder what consideration, if any, has been given by the NASA scientists on any of these planetary and deep space missions related to the questions addressed by those philosophers back in the 1970s NASA study and by Ray Bradbury's philosophical dialogues between astronauts and Martians. Could our exploration of Mars be an unintentional invasion?

Works Cited

The Blob. Dir. Irvin S. Yeaworth, Jr. Perf. Steve McQueen. Irvin Yeaworth Productions, 1958. DVD.
Bradbury, Ray. *The Martian Chronicles.* New York: Bantam, 1970. Print.

Daronco, Darren. "Area Petroglyphs Offer Glimpse into the Past." *The Yuma Sun*. 10 July 2011. 10 Jan. 2013. Web.

David, Leonard. "NASA's Mars Rover Curiosity Had Planetary Protection Slip-Up." *Space*. 30 Nov. 2011. 20 Jan. 2013. Web.

Forbidden Planet. Dir. Fred M. Wilcox. Perfs. Walter Pidgeon, Anne Francis, Leslie Nielson. MGM, 1956. DVD.

The Martian Chronicles. Dir. Michael Anderson. Perf. Rock Hudson. Stonehenge Productions, 1980. DVD.

A Martian Chronicle

CHARLES L. DUGAN, JR.

"We'll only continue as long as everyone is quiet." The teacher's warning was absolutely unnecessary; it was a waste of words. Every mouth was closed, and every ear was focused, transfixed on each syllable the teacher read. It was 1965, and I was in Miss Youngblood's fourth grade class. (In "those days," we always said "Miss" or "Mrs." It was never, ever, "Ms.")

Back then, we still had actual books, you know, with real paper. *Time Magazine* had instituted an educational reading program called the "Time Reading Program" (spiffy title). Every day, during our rest period right after lunch, our teacher would read to the class a section from one of the "re-released" titles on *Time*'s recommended list. This one was *The Martian Chronicles*, my first memory of "science fiction," though at the time I was sure that it was prophesy.

My classmates and I were captivated as we heard of the adventure of space travel — and the danger. Bradbury's earliest Earth-ships would visit the Red Planet, and more often than not, they were never to be heard from again. In retrospect, that is so eerily similar even to our present-day experience with Martian probes. *The Martian Chronicles* told of apparitions and superhuman powers detailed and yet still mysterious and misunderstood. In "The Earth Men," we are shown that Martians have the ability to change their shapes at will. A woman is described as she "stood changing. First she was embedded in a crystal pillar, then she melted into a golden status, finally a staff of polished cedar and back to a woman" (Bradbury 26). It is possible that we, as young students, could understand these passages better than the adults who through "maturity" had already crystallized their thoughts and perceptions.

And, of course, *The Martian Chronicles* had Martians ... actual Martians! These however, were not the weapon-wielding invaders of H.G. Wells *War of the Worlds*; they were not the monsters that caused panic in the streets when

Orson Welles reported the invasion on radio. No, these were aliens that could woo the Earthling. They were soft and appealing — and they were familiar and comforting when they chose to be, tapping our human memories and adapting their appearance to calm us, to make us unaware, unsuspecting. Years later, as an adult re-reading the chapters, I recognized the portrayal that is often not grasped as a younger reader — or listener. In the chapter "Ylla" Ray Bradbury describes them as "fair, with the brownish skin of the true Martian, the yellow coin eyes, the soft musical voices" (Bradbury 2). Disarming indeed!

Of course, even we fourth graders knew that *The Martian Chronicles* was science fiction, but we found that, apparently, even adults were sucked in by the allure of space, of humans traveling to Mars, the possibility of finding native inhabitants of Mars. After all, it was our teacher that chose the book! To a fourth grader though, in the middle of the "space race," this was a book and a subject that didn't just get your attention, it demanded it and it grabbed your mind. What red-blooded fourth grader *wouldn't* be attracted to such a tale? I could tell from the "pin-dropping silence" that all the students felt the same way. Every morning was torture; it was excruciating just having to wait for that reading period ... I had to find out what happened next. Surely, this author was providing me a glimpse of our future — of my future.

At that stage of my life, I was unaware of where my future would again cross paths with the writings of Mr. Bradbury. As it turns out, I have lived in Tucson, Arizona, for the last 40 years, in the same area where Ray Bradbury spent a portion of his youth as well. It is here that I have come to appreciate some of the parallels of his writings about Mars, and how they compare to the desert southwest. The Sonoran Desert is surely a strange land, and in the days when *The Martian Chronicles* was coming to be, it was thought to be nearly as foreboding as the climate of Mars! The challenging environment of the southwestern desert is very apparent in Bradbury's writing. We read of Martian vistas rolling out to empty fossil seas, crystal clear Martian air, and blinding sand storms. Then there is the passage from "Night Meeting" where Mr. Gomez (an obvious reference to the strong Hispanic heritage of the Sonoran Desert) tells his son,

> We've got to look at what we've got here, and how *different* it is. I get a hell of a lot of fun out of the weather here. It's *Martian* weather. Hot as hell daytimes. Cold as hell nights. I get a big kick out of the different flowers and different rain. I came here to retire and I wanted to retire to a place where everything is different [Bradbury 79].

The same feelings are echoed across Arizona, a haven for retirees who wish to witness the monsoons and the desert wildlife, and they experience the extremes in day and night temperatures — "It's *Tucson* weather!"

Venus Transit by David A. Harvey (courtesy NASA and David A. Harvey).

On June 5, 2012, when Ray Bradbury passed away; it was the exact same day that the planet Venus passed across the face of the Sun — an event that will not come again until the year 2117. The image shows the planet Venus can be seen crossing over the solar face during the last transit on June 5, 2012, the day of Ray Bradbury's passing. Events such as this one are about as rare as Bradbury's talent. On this occasion, the spectacle can be seen with the Kitt Peak National Observatory as the backdrop — a rare occurrence indeed. Even without the stunning visuals, the next Venus transit isn't scheduled until the year 2117.

I am a program specialist in the Education and Public Outreach department at the National Observatory in Tucson, and Ray Bradbury is one of the reasons that I "do what I do." It was only in retrospect, after hearing of his passing, days later, that I became aware of the eerie coincidence that a writer of such rare talent, one who brought space, space travel, and astronomy to so many people, would leave us during one of the rarest of astronomical occurrences — a Venus transit.

I recognize that my past, my present, and my future were at least tangentially influenced by my early childhood exposure to the writing of Mr. Bradbury, but there was yet another future connection to come. At the end of June 2012 an email from the Jet Propulsion Lab of all places caused me to

Left to right: Opportunity, Sojourner, and Curiosity science platforms (courtesy NASA/JPL).

reminisce one more time of the passing of this prolific science-fiction writer. A "temporal intersection" of sorts, one that is coincidental not just in timing but also in subject, was scheduled in just over a month.

On Sunday August 5, 2012 at 10:31 P.M. PDT, exactly two months after Ray Bradbury's passing, "humans" would once again set foot on Mars — the destination and subject so prominent in his stories. As in all previous missions, the visitor would be a robotic emissary, christened "Curiosity," that's been sent to do our bidding. Formally assigned the rather mundane moniker Mars Science Laboratory (MSL) it would be an obviously unintended but perfect tribute to the life of Ray Bradbury. In the photograph of the three Mars science platforms, we have a visual comparison of Opportunity, Sojourner, and Curiosity (from left to right). Obviously, the size, scale, and scientific and experimental armada of the Curiosity rover make all previous stations, orbiters, and rovers appear almost primitive. In fact, at 10 feet in length, it weighs in at nearly a ton (1,984 pounds).

Now, when it comes to Mars, just as in Bradbury's very prophetic tales, "dangerous" is still an unfortunately accurate description, and "innovative" is not exactly an adjective that we want associated with our plans ... we have lost nearly 50 percent of the missions we've sent there. And, while Curiosity's mass required nuclear power, something we do have experience with from the Viking landers of over 40 years ago, the landing of this behemoth required something quite unique. In fact, when we view the NASA video "Seven Minutes of Terror," it looks suspiciously like this plan must have been developed by a science fiction writer — someone not tethered to reality ... and yet, it worked.

With the Mars Science Laboratory safely in place in Gale Crater, it was now time to turn from the "fiction" of Ray Bradbury's *Chronicle*, and get down to the actual "science" of the mission. Here is where we find another oddity — we come full circle with the truth of Mars and the strange prophecy of *The Martian Chronicles*. You see, we as humans have always been enamored of the possibility of life on the Red Planet; for instance, Percival Lowell went to the grave believing in Mars' ancient civilizations. But, by the time of Ray Bradbury, every scientist, and even the dreaming youngsters knew that Mars was an arid and lifeless place. Mr. Bradbury knew the current science too, and yet he wrote of the ancient ones, and their long forgotten, but maybe not quite gone civilizations.

I have come to realize that the "reality" of a situation is, more often than any other characteristic, a function of "time." We see this too in Bradbury's writing. Which reality is "real?" What we consider "history" or "future" is written and rewritten with more study, more analysis, and more time. Now, with the latest science, we find that Mars may not have always been the dead world it so long appeared to be. We once again believe that there may have been oceans and seas, and if that is true, might there not also have been life?

Bradbury's fiction becomes more like current science with each passing day. In fact, one of the main Mars Science Lab goals will be the search for evidence of past or present life on Mars. With Curiosity's advanced scientific and experimental payload, we seek to answer the question of whether there *is* or *has been* life on the Red Planet, to finally resolve the frustratingly ambiguous results from past missions. Yet, even if we fail to answer this one question, we will still be laying the ground work for what may be actual human landings on the surface of Mars in the near future. In any case, Ray Bradbury will ultimately be vindicated — it is now nearly obvious to everyone, adults, scientists, and fourth graders alike, that either there *are* now, *were* at one time, or *will be* "Martians" on Mars. Curiosity will help to determine which of these very Ray Bradbury–like scenarios is true.

Works Cited

Bradbury, Ray. *The Martian Chronicles*. New York: Bantam, 1962. Print.
Wells, H. G. *The War of the Worlds*. New York: Fawcett, 1978. Print.

The Naming of Names

CHRISTOPHER P. MCKAY *and*
CAROL STOKER

The "Bradbury" Landing Site on Mars (Christopher P. McKay)

The Martian Chronicles by Ray Bradbury is arguably the most significant science fiction text about Mars. On the web today in 2013, more than 50 years after it was published, a search on science fiction books about Mars shows it to be the number one item on virtually every list. I recall the effect it had on me when I first became interested in Mars just after the Viking landers.

I was part of the generation that lived in the shadow of the first space missions to the Red Planet. Soon after Viking landed on Mars, several graduate students at the University of Colorado formed a group known as the Mars Study Project. We organized a self-taught, one-credit seminar class on Mars. We grew radishes under Mars-like pressures and enlisted the microbiology department in a set of experiments related to microbial nitrogen fixation at Martian partial pressures of N_2. In 1981, we organized a conference entitled "The Case for Mars" which brought together scientists, engineers, students and members of the public for three days to contemplate human missions to Mars. The proceedings of this conference were edited by Penelope J. Boston and several more "Case for Mars" conferences were held on three years intervals. In those days, before the Internet, U.S. mail was still the way to keep in contact with colleagues in distant institutions. Thus, after the success of the first "Case for Mars" we started a newsletter. Of course, we called it *The Martian Chronicles Newsletter*. We published maybe half a dozen issues before the pressures of being in graduate school reasserted themselves. Naming our publication *The Martian Chronicles Newsletter* was more than just a nod to Ray Bradbury, it was a statement of the immediate identification of what we were doing with a vision of Mars exploration that Bradbury captured in his stories in *Chronicles*. I had read Bradbury's *Chronicles* then and I re-read it recently to see why it inspired us.

Many of the essays in this book discuss *The Martian Chronicles*, and much of Bradbury's other writing, as commentary or satire about social issues in the American Southwest. The Martians are the natives and the Earth people represent the American cultural displacement of that native heritage. In this way of reading *The Martian Chronicles*— Mars is just the stage and the book is no more about Mars than *Animal Farm* is about animals and farms. But this interpretation of *The Martian Chronicles* is incomplete even if were to be correct. Bradbury's own recounting of the history of *The Martian Chronicles* as indicates that it is science fiction, not social commentary. If it also acts as social commentary, that is another example of the power of the text. The text can speak in many ways to many readers.

To us as young students interested in life on Mars, *The Martian Chronicles* spoke of the human desire to explore, to see, to name, and to make homes. It also spoke of the inevitable loss, the possibility of mistake, and the very human nature of everything we do. *The Martian Chronicles* is not a book about rockets and how they work or how Mars operates as a planet. To us, students interested in Mars, it was about how humans explore and how Mars beckons us to explore.

As I re-read *The Martian Chronicles* recently in 2013, I saw there are at least three major themes in the book; invasion, armageddon, and the beauty of Mars. There is a forth aspect of the book, not really a theme, that strikes the modern reader and runs through the entire Chronicles; sexism. Female protagonists are conspicuous by their absence throughout the book.

The first theme is that of invasion. Humans arrive on Mars. The two members of the first expedition are killed by a jealous husband. The four members of the second expedition are killed by a psychiatrist who thinks they are terminally insane, the 16 members of the third expedition are killed by the Martians posing as the lost relatives of each crew member. The Martians are winning 0–3. But these were not invasions and there was no reason that the Martians needed to kill the crews. When the fourth expedition arrives the Martians have been wiped out by the chicken pox. While the pox obviously came from Earth, it is not clear that the Earth men (and they were only men) are to blame. Perhaps if the Martians had not murdered the members of the Third Expedition they would have learned from the same Earth men from which they ultimately caught the pox how to vaccinate against it. The invasion of Mars is not analogous to the Spanish in Mexico or the American Indian Wars. There is no battle. After the Fourth Expedition the American settlers move into the vacuum left by Martian extinction. The invasion story of *The Martian Chronicles* is entertaining to read but was not of much inspiration to me then and it is not very interesting now.

The second theme that runs through *The Chronicles* is the atomic war that destroys civilization on Earth. Some of the most poignant stories in *Chronicles* deal with aspects of this war, its effects on Earth, and its effects on Mars. When the atomic war begins all the human colonists on Mars rush to return to Earth. A few are left behind and are the focus of interesting stories. The classic story "There will come soft rains" documents the devastation on Earth in an eerie way from the perspective of an empty house. Fortunately Earth did not suffer a nuclear holocaust during the Cold War and looking back from 2013, this possibility seems only of historical interest. The atomic war aspect of *The Martian Chronicles* was not too interesting even in the late 1970s and early 1980s when nuclear winter scenarios were discussed and Ronald Reagan was saber rattling with the so-called Star Wars program.

The third theme of *The Martian Chronicles* is that of Mars itself as a land of indescribable beauty. It is with this geological theme that we near the topic of naming names on Mars. Both Martians and Earth settlers name the features of the planet, often re-naming what had already been named, in fact. Bradbury's Martian landscape consists of long canals through vast dried sand seas, with purple mountains in the background and lights making a "sky filled with flame." A small side note to the novel's theme of beautiful Mars is the story of "The Green Morning." In this story, trees from Earth are planted on Mars. This planting seems like the only addition to Mars that the Earth people bring that fits, the gift from Earth is the trees, not the cities, or the cars, or the hot dog stand.

Early in the space exploration era when it became clear that there was no ancient civilization on Mars. Bradbury famously re-named humanity when he said, "We are the Martians." That moment of Bradbury's re-naming humanity was recalled by Jon Eller, the Bradbury biographer, in an email interview:

> There was this festive feeling, like a surprise party, at the Caltech Planetarium the night the Viking ship landed. Carl Sagan and I and a lot of others stayed up all night. Suddenly, the first photographs of Mars started coming back on the giant screen. We were all exhilarated — dancing, laughing and singing. Around nine in the morning, [a television network reporter] came by and held this microphone in front of my face. He said, "Mr. Bradbury, you've been writing about Mars and its civilizations and cities for all these years. Now that we're there and we see that there's no life, how does it feel?" I took a deep breath —

I'm so proud I said this out loud to him — and replied: "You idiot! You fool! There is life on Mars — look at us! Look at us! We are the Martians!"

And in one of the best known scenes in *Chronicles*, a father takes his children to the canal to see Martians (Bradbury 180–181). They look in the water and the Martians were there reflected in the water. The real Mars is a planet as a beautiful and mysterious as Bradbury portrayed it and indeed as he predicted, we are the Martians.

The Martian Chronicles runs from the "Rocket Summer" of 1999 to 2026. Bradbury seemed to like rockets. One of his best known books is *R Is for Rocket*. Bradbury also has a keen sense of what it means to name a place. How some names were natural and some were ignorant, even arrogant. It seems appropriate then that NASA named the landing site of the Curiosity Rover after Ray Bradbury. The Bradbury Landing Site is on Mars at 4.5° S, 137.4° inside Gale Crater. The dark areas are the scour marks created by the landing rocket engines as they blew away the smaller light colored dust. The Curiosity Rover and its tracks are seen as well. The image is about 100 m across. The Bradbury landing site is in a rather flat non-descript area and is made interesting and worthy of a name because of the scour created by the rocket engines as the Curiosity Rover was lowered to the surface. I think Bradbury would have appreciated the eponymous rocket pad, perhaps more than having a mountain, a crater, or a valley named after him.

Carol Stoker has other insights into the process of naming the Martian landscape and what it means to name places the first time.

Naming of Names (Carol Stoker)

The reality of exploring Mars has only a few connections with the way Bradbury envisioned the events of space exploration and settlement. As a novelist, Bradbury could skate over the

Mars "Bradbury" landing site (courtesy NASA). details of setting up a high stakes scientific mission, but with a tight production schedule, there are many planetary science facets to cover. Yet the goal is the same for both Bradbury's fiction and NASA's fact: explore Mars, look for aids to habitation and signs of life.

We can summarize the unifying goal of our real life Mars Exploration program, laid out in the 2004–2006 roadmap of NASA's Mars Exploration Payload Analysis Group (MEPAG), as being the search for life on Mars, published in 2004 and by David W. Beaty, et al., in 2006. However, experience from the Viking Landers clearly shows that this goal is difficult to achieve without characterizing the physical and chemical environment of Mars and thus the approach recommended is first to identify habitable environments prior to conducting a mission to search for life. The Phoenix mission was the first NASA Mars Scout mission, led by a principal investigator (Peter Smith), and competitively selected through peer review. It was also the first mission launched with the specific objective of assessing the habitability of the current Martian environment. The mission was designed to land in Mars' far northern hemisphere where near surface ground ice had been identified by W.V. Boynton and co-authors based on data from orbiting neutron detectors on the Gamma Ray Spectrometer (GRS) carried by Mars Odyssey. The area was considered important for study because of the possible periodic presence of liquid water as orbital dynamics change the regional climate. Peter Smith and his co-researchers in 2008 summarized that the two primary mission objectives to be achieved at the landing site were (1) study the history of water in all its phases, and (2) search for habitable zones. A habitable zone, by definition, is capable of supporting living organisms with capabilities similar to terrestrial microbes. One of the major requirements for life is the presence of liquid water and the northern region of Mars, with its water ice cap and shallow subsurface ice, promised to provide the greatest likelihood for achieving both of the primary mission objectives.

The Phoenix mission launched on 4 August 2007 and landed on 25 May 2009 at the northern polar location of 68.22°N, 234.25°E (areocentric) and elevation of -4.1 km (referenced to Mars Orbiter Laser Altimeter topography). The entire regional area where the spacecraft landed was covered with patterned ground, a common feature of periglacial terrain. Michael T. Mellon's group determined in 2009 that around the landing site this manifests as small-scale polygon features only a few meters in typical size. Fortuitously, both a polygon center and trough areas separating polygons could be accessed with the robotic arm (Figure 1a).

The process for selecting the landing site is reviewed in Raymond E. Arvidson et al.'s 2008 report. A driving consideration was to find a location where water ice could be accessed within the digging depth capability of the robotic arm, a maximum of 50 cm. Detailed consideration of the GRS data from the N. Polar region, images from the High Resolution Imaging Science Experiment (HiRISE) on Mars Reconnaissance Orbiter (MRO), as well as other studies, identified a landing site with the desired characteristics of near surface ground ice and low rock abundance. The average dry soil abundance over the icy surface was predicted by Arvidson's 2008 modeling study using the Odyssey GRS data for the landing site area to be 10 gm/cc (5cm soil depth). The observed ice table depth at the landing site was in good agreement with this prediction.

Prior to landing on the planet Mars, a naming convention was adopted by the Phoenix team that allowed features to be named for fairy tale characters only. This was a naming convention that Ray Bradbury could have approved, considering his early interest in fairy tales and *The Wizard of Oz* stories. Naming of features was important because this allowed each feature to have a unique and unambiguous identifier that was used by the mission planning software to plan operations. Immediately upon landing, features were named that were within the reach of the robotic arm (1.5 m from the lander deck). The first series of arm operations were planned that were to yield 3 samples, a surface, an intermediate, and an ice table interface sample.

The arm work area and locations of the main trenches is shown in Figure 1a. Figure 1b shows the topography of the arm work area including a polygon and the surrounding trough. The trench at the far left of the work area was called Goldilocks and was dug in a topographically low area sloping to the southwest along the edge of a polygon and grading into a trough between polygons (Figure 1b). A hard bright layer was encountered at 3 cm. depth. The trench at the far right of the work area was called Snow White and was

Opposite: Figure 1a. Diagram of the work area accessible by the Phoenix lander's arm (blue outline) superimposed on an image mosaic acquired by the SSI camera. The boxed areas are sites where trenches were dug for sample collection and exploration of subsurface material. Arrows point to locations where samples were acquired that were analyzed by either WCL (cells 0,1,2) denoted as W0-W2 or TEGA (ovens designated T0-T7). The arm's maximum reach is approximately 1.5m. *Figure 1b.* Visualization of the arm work area displayed as a color-coded elevation model. A graphic model of the lander is at the bottom left. Radial grid lines spaced 20 cm apart are centered on the robotic arm shoulder rotation axis. The color scale is shown at left. Dark blue represents the lowest regions which are 120 cm below the lander deck. The highest regions (pink) are 35cm higher. White dotted lines illustrate approximate polygon boundaries. Dashed lines demark the position of troughs. White boxes show the two trenches Goldilocks and Snow White (courtesy NASA).

dug in the center of a polygon in a higher flat-lying area. The hard layer at the trench bottom was soil colored. The first (surface) sample came from the Goldilocks trench. Deeper trenching revealed pure ice at the trench bottom but this was not sampled. The rest of the samples came from the Snow White trench and were either loose soil or were scraped from

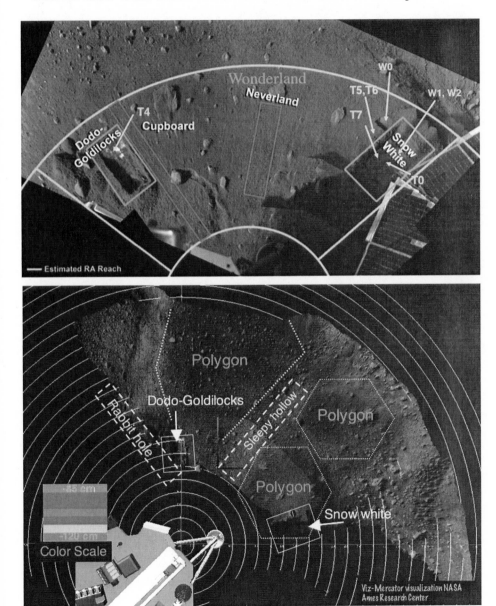

Figure 2 left. SSI camera image of the Goldilocks trench showing the white material in the trench floor. The boxed area contains the bright chunks that broke off during digging that subsequently disappeared completely in 3 sols. *Figure 2 right.* SSI image of the Snow White trench after excavation. The trench bottom was hard, presumably due to the presence of ice-cemented ground, but the material was spectrally identical to soil (courtesy NASA).

the soil-ice interface. Figure 2 shows the Goldilocks (left) and the Snow White (right) trenches.

The target of the first sample was named "Goldilocks" with the idea that three samples would be acquired there (surface, middle, ice interface) , and named for Goldilocks and the three bears. However, after the surface sample was acquired, further digging exposed a white substance at 3 cm depth. Chunks of the white material were initially seen in the scoop and trench (Figure 2a) but disappeared over time There was initially disagreement amongst the Phoenix science team about the nature of the white material; although some thought that this white material was ice or snow, not all agreed. Furthermore, some were concerned that the Goldilocks location was "anomalous" and not the best place to obtain the rest of the samples. A vigorous discussion was held about sampling at this location for the other two planned samples, with the result that it was decided to obtain other samples at a different location that had already been named "Snow White." The Snow White area was preferred because some members of the science team thought it was more typical of the region. It was, in fact, at a polygon center whereas the Goldilocks site appeared to be in a trough, or gap between polygons. However, some members of the team (including the authors of this paper) wanted to sample the white material because the trough was exactly where ice would be expected to occur in a polygon formation mechanism called "ice wedging." The ice wedges form as a result of freeze-thaw processes, and we reasoned that this white material was pure ice segregated into the trough.

In the end, after much discussion, all the remaining samples were collected at the Snow White location. Digging at Snow White revealed that a hard layer was encountered at 5 cm depth, but this hard layer was visually and spectrally indistinguishable from soil. The white material in Goldilocks contained the spectral signature of water ice, and only 5 percent admixture of soil would have masked that spectral feature. In short, the Goldilocks site had a subsurface composed of nearly pure ice, while the Snow White feature was composed of a frozen soil that contained ice. This latter was determined by scraping and rasping the soil colored hard layer to acquire samples, and measuring them with the TEGA instrument which could detect water molecules directly. Thus samples from Snow White contained a mixture of soil and ice. The exact ratio of soil and ice could not be determined from the measurements. The pure ice in Goldilocks was never measured.

Why Was the Pure Ice Not Sampled?

Often things do not run as smoothly as a well-edited scientific documentary. Bradbury knew this and showed the disagreements and differing priorities among the first landing parties on Mars. While no debates so exciting as whether to settle Mars or leave it alone and untouched (as in the story "And the Moon Be Still as Bright" in *The Martian Chronicles*) occurred in the months of discovery by the Phoenix Mars Lander, many of the science team, of the NASA managers, of the external science community, and of the public, thought that it was important to sample the pure ice. And in this arena, debates as to where and what to dig were bound to heat up, as is inevitable with any high stakes space mission.

The Phoenix science team members responsible for the Habitability assessment (Stoker et al.) thought that the pure ice was the most likely place to find evidence of organic molecules associated with life since a plausible process for emplacing the ice required liquid water. The NASA managers thought it should be sampled because the mission objective was to "sample the ice." The public thought it was exciting that Phoenix had encountered "white stuff" and assumed it would be sampled. However there were several reasons that weighed against sampling it. First, because Goldilocks was in a trench, it was actually sloped slightly towards the southwest. The robotic arm team argued that this made it more difficult to access with the robotic arm. However, the robotic arm had no difficulty digging to the ice to begin with, and later excavated more white material adjacent to it. Second, it was found that icy material collected with the rasp into the scoop from Snow White stuck to the scoop and could not be poured into the instruments. Some argued that the white ice would stick to the scoop even more and not pour out. A third argument against sampling it came from scientists on the Wet Chemistry Laboratory instrument team. That instrument mixed soil samples with water to measure ions in the soil. If the samples were primarily ice already, the chemistry might be too diluted to measure. In the end, sampling the white ice was not rejected outright, but was given a low priority to be accomplished after other objectives were met. In the end, the mission ran out of power and ended before this sampling was accomplished.

In post mission summaries of the Phoenix findings, the discovery of the white ice is often given top billing. Very few people outside of the Phoenix mission realized that this ice was never sampled but the rather unfortunate and accidental assignment of names may have contributed to the confusion. The place that was sampled heavily was called "Snow White," although it was not white at all. The place that the white ice occurred was called "Goldilocks." As both names were assigned prior to digging, this was an accident.

In Ray Bradbury's story "Naming of Names," the people come to Mars as settlers and bring with them their Earthly names, renaming all the Martian features after things on Earth. But in the end, the environment of Mars causes the humans to evolve and change. They become, in effect, new Martians, and in the process of this evolution, they stop using the Earthly names for things and use the Martian names instead. The naming of names on the Phoenix mission added to the confusion with the outcome that important samples were not acquired. The scientists from Earth called the thing that contained snow "Gold" and the thing that contained soil "Snow." As things progressed, and our understanding of Mars improved, the importance of the snow was recognized and our names for the sites should have changed, but all this took too long for the very fast paced Phoenix mission to change its plan. It remains for a future mission to sample the white snow-like ice at the Phoenix landing site and determine whether or not it holds a record of life on Mars. Ray Bradbury's story shows that Mars will change our way of thinking about it to become more Martian in the long run.

Works Cited

Arvidson Raymond E., et al. "Mars Exploration Program 2007 Phoenix Landing Site Selection and Characteristics." *Journal of Geophysical Research* 113 (2008). Web.

Beaty, David W., et al. "Findings of the Mars Special Regions Science Analysis Group." *Astrobiology* 6 (2006): 677–732. Web.

Boston, Penelope J. "Life in the Extremes: An Interview with Dr. Penelope Boston." *Astrobiology: The Living Universe*. Oracle ThinkQuest. 2000. Web.

_____, ed. *The Case for Mars: Proceedings of a Conference Held April 29–May 2, 1981 at University of Colorado, Boulder, Colorado*. San Diego: The American Astronautical Society and Univelt, 1984. Print.

Boynton, William V., et al. "Distribution of Hydrogen in the Near-Surface of Mars: Evidence for Sub-Surface Ice Deposits." *Science* 297 (2002): 81–85. Web.

Bradbury, Ray. *The Martian Chronicles*. New York: Bantam, 1970. Print.

Eller, John. "Re: Martians." Email to Gloria McMillan. 19 Feb. 2013. Web.

Mellon, Michael T., et al. "Ground Ice at the Phoenix Landing Site: Stability State and Origin." *Journal of Geophysical Research* 114.53 (2009). Web.

Smith, Peter E., et al. "Water at the Phoenix Landing Site." *Science* 325 (2009): 58–61. Web.

Stoker, Carol R., et al. "The Habitability of the Phoenix Landing Site." *Journal of Geophysical Research* 155.6 (16 Jun 2010). Web.

Taylor, G. J., ed. (MEPAG:) *Scientific Goals, Objectives, Investigations, and Priorities: 2003*. NASA 2004. Web.

De-Alienating the Alien
The Limits of Empathy in NBC's The Martian Chronicles *Miniseries*

PAUL COTE

NBC's 1980 miniseries *Ray Bradbury's The Martian Chronicles* rarely receives serious consideration as an important literary adaptation. Bradbury famously called the film "boooooooring" at the time of its release, and critics generally dismissed the film for its languid pacing, questionable visual effects, and perceived "unfaithfulness" to the original novel (Landry 3). By and large, these criticisms have stuck, and NBC's *The Martian Chronicles* has more or less become a forgotten curio, rarely regarded with serious critical consideration. Yet the miniseries makes a compelling case study, for it offers illumination on both the subtler qualities of Bradbury's original novel and on questions involving cinematic adaptation studies in general. This is not due to any particularly outstanding quality in the film itself, for the adaptation is indeed problematic, both on a storytelling and production level. But many of the film's problems are precisely what make it compelling. Bradbury's novel is, at heart, a critical rereading of the Conquest of the West, an attempt at giving a voice to the conquered people who Western literature so frequently frames as fundamentally "Other." The miniseries seems, on the surface, to be an attempt at conveying the same message, echoing many of the same story beats and capturing the same Conquest narrative. But because the film is so steeped in a Hollywood tropes designed to render every non-white/non–American personage inhuman and frightening, the miniseries version of *The Martian Chronicles* ultimately undermines the very humanistic message it wants to convey. The film in the process offers a strong reflection on the subtlety that makes Bradbury's work so effective, and it offers a reminder for

193

why a comparative model in adaptation studies actually does have productive value.

Before I begin, however, I must emphasize that my intent is not simply to lambast the miniseries for some imagined lack of "fidelity" to Bradbury's novel. As current scholars in adaptation studies such as Robert Stam and Thomas Leitch have noted, filmed adaptations of great literary works have long been plagued with critical attitudes that favor fidelity to the original text above everything else. As Stam explains in his introduction to *Literature and Film*, the "conventional language of adaptation criticism has often been profoundly moralistic, rich in terms that imply that the cinema has somehow done a disservice to literature. Terms like "infidelity," "betrayal," "deformation," "violation," "bastardization," "vulgarization," and "desecration" proliferate in adaptation discourse, each word carrying its specific charge of opprobrium" (3). Something inherent in adaptation studies tends to send otherwise reasonable critics into an unproductive pejorative mode, citing textual transformations as "deviations," rather than artistic decisions in their own right. Thomas Leitch affirms this trend in *Adaptation and Its Discontents*, noting that the field of adaptation studies has "continued to organize itself so largely around ... the position that novels are texts, movies are intertexts, and in any competition between the two, the book is better" (6). In Leitch's view, this prejudice comes from what he calls a "humanist" bias in literary studies, "a triumph of an evaluative impulse to insist that originals are always touchstones of value for their adaptations" (5–6). The prevalence of fidelity, both Stam and Leitch suggest, limits the productive analysis that might emerge if we approached film adaptations as unique texts in their own right, rather than subordinate intertexts. As Stam explains, "standard rhetoric has often deployed an elegiac discourse of loss, lamenting what has been 'lost' in the transition from novel to film, while ignoring what has been gained" (3). In other words, by focusing incessantly on fidelity as a key critical touchstone, we end up ignoring the uniquely cinematic audio-visual presentation that the film adaptation contributes to the novel.

In principle, I agree with Stam and Leitch's general objections to these trends in adaptation studies — trends that too frequently limit productive analysis by evaluating films exclusively on how "faithful" they remain to its source text. This may seem surprising, given that in the article that follows, it may often seem like I am simply finding different ways in which *The Martian Chronicles* miniseries fails because it changes some aspect of the original novel. This, however, is not my purpose. I am less interested in judging the changes made to the text so much as I am in interrogating the impact that those changes have on the film's governing ideology. This is of particular significance between the film seems, on the surface, to be on the same progressive ideological page as the novel. Bradbury's book is, at heart, a critique on the Conquest of the American West and its indigenous populations. Using Mars as a stand-in for the West and the Martians as stand-ins for its Native American tribes, Bradbury's novel offers an alternative history to Manifest Destiny, one that recognizes the personhood of its conquered peoples. The miniseries, to all appearances, is genuinely trying to maintain fidelity to its novel's core thematic material — it remains a story about the colonization of Mars, with the parallels to Westward Expansion largely left intact. But the film undercuts the heart of this message because it remains steeped in audio-visual devices that encourage sympathy for the conqueror and fear of the conquered. Where Bradbury's Martians are paradoxically the novel's most human characters, the film constantly renders the Martians as Others, inhuman beings who are incapable of inviting the audience's empathy. With that in mind, a comparative approach between the novel and miniseries is crucial, because it enables an understanding of the way Hollywood's central practices are so rooted and regressive Othering that they sabotage even progressive-minded films.

Bradbury's book is of course about many things in addition to Westward expansion. The bulk of *The Martian Chronicles* consists of previous published short stories originating from various pulp magazines, and they consequently cover a wide range of themes — from the growing threat of nuclear annihilation ("November 2005: The Off Season"), to a growing cultural ambivalence towards literacy ("April 2002: Usher II"), and to the increasingly dangerous automatization of daily life ("August 2026: There Will Come Soft Rains"). Yet Bradbury revises and rearranges this material so that the stories all form pieces of a larger narrative, turning what might have seemed like a loosely-themed collection of stories into a miniature epic that traces the rise and fall of two entire civilizations. Collectively, the stories form a counter-history of the European conquest of the American West and its indigenous tribes. "I decided first of all that there would be certain elements of similarity between the invasion of Mars and the invasion of the Wild West" (qtd. in Weller 155), Bradbury noted in an unpublished essay, and the finished work bears out an at-times painstakingly specific allegory for the decimation of the Native American tribes under the European settlers. *The Martian Chronicles* does more than simply retell the story of the West, however — it makes a concentrated effort to give a voice to the displaced peoples, and capture the subjective experience of the conquered alongside the conquerors. Bradbury paints an evocative portrait of the Martian culture, one steeped with its own traditions, customs, history, and architecture. Yet he also does not sentimentalize the Martians, or treat them as noble victims. Though nominally members of a different species, his Martians are fundamentally human, with the same desires, flaws, fears, and ambitions. They are capable of profound compassion, but also capable of marital jealously, familial longing, and crimes of passion. Moreover, Bradbury gives us their perspective at multiple points in the novel, giving us a third-person omniscient perspective that explicitly displays the Martians' thoughts and desires. In the process, the novel eliminates the distance between the reader and the Martian, compelling the audience's identification with multiple parties. In this regard, Bradbury makes overtures towards a post-colonial perspective of the conquest of the American West — using Martians as stand-ins for all conquered peoples, he removes the "Otherness" that plagues so many representations of non-white male subjects in 20th century popular fiction.

Unfortunately, that Otherness is often intrinsic to much of the American film industry. In using Martians as stand-ins for Native Americans, the novel evokes two figures that, by the time the miniseries enters production in the late '70s, will become synonymous with the Other in Hollywood — The Indian and the alien from outer space. In the decades preceding the miniseries, countless Hollywood Westerns have cemented the popular conception of the former as what Jose Prats refers to in *Invisible Natives* as "the visual and immediate presence of the Other" (5). The Indian might come in the form of a violent and bloodthirsty savage (as in *Stagecoach*) or as a noble savage who functions to impart wisdom on his white conquerors and then quietly disappear from history (as in *Broken Arrow*). Yet whether presented as violent or sentimental, by 1980 the Hollywood Indian has become firmly etched in the popular consciousness as what Prats refers to as an "Other whose destruction is not only assured but justified" (2). As far as the mass majority of these films are concerned, the Indian is less a human than an obstacle to divine right of Westward expansion. Similarly, by 1980 the figure of the alien has solidified itself in the popular imagination through three decades of science fiction films and television shows. While these portraits range from menacing (*Invasion of the Body Snatchers*) to sympathetic (*The Day the Earth Stood Still*), the overall trend has been to define the alien through its inhumanness. Cinematic aliens might bear human likeness, but they are overwhelmingly cold, exotic, and fundamentally inhuman. Even 1960s television shows such as *The Twilight Zone* and *Star Trek*—shows that often used alien creatures to make progressive social statements — had an overwhelming tendency to rely on audio and visual tropes that emphasized their aliens' exotic otherworldliness. By 1980, both the alien and the Indian have become firm cinematic tropes, and they are part of a legacy that *The Martian Chronicles* miniseries inherits.

While the production team of *The Martian Chronicles* may not intentionally be evoking these tropes, the stereotypes guide the film's presentation of Bradbury's story. Throughout, the film presents the Martian characters as inaccessible foreign objects that stand in stark contrast to the human characters. As with the aliens in 1950s invasion films, The Martians speak and behave with steely reserve that displays little recognizable human emotion, and the score frequently accompanies them with dissonant music designed to render the Martians' presence frightening. In theory, there is no reason the film could not have favored strategies designed to invite audience identification with the Martians. A different version of this film might have allowed the actors playing the Martians to display just as much outward emotion as the human characters, or might have scored the Martians with music that communicates what the aliens themselves are feeling. But because the filmmakers are following in Hollywood's firmly established traditions of portraying both aliens and non-white conquered peoples, the film instead does everything in its power to keep the audience at an emotional remove from the aliens. This constant insistence on the Other's fundamental difference ultimately compromises any attempted message of tolerance that the film might otherwise have conveyed.

To illustrate this point, observe the differences between the novel's version of the "February 1999: Ylla" story and its cinematic equivalent in the miniseries. Set on the eve of humankind's first landing on Mars, the story shows us the impact that this human incursion has on a married Martian couple. The Martian wife, "Ylla," begins anticipating the human arrival with erotic dreams of the first astronauts. Her husband grows incensed when he learns of these dreams, so much so that he kills the first humans in a jealous rage when they finally do land on Mars. In the context of Bradbury's larger novel/anthology, "Ylla" serves as a painful reminder of how much petty human insecurities can compromise even the most seemingly momentous occasions. What should have been the historic first meeting of man and Martian turns violent due entirely to a husband's fear of emasculating cuckoldry. But the story quietly makes an even more dramatic point by presenting this scene of domestic drama from a Martian perspective. These characters are aliens of another species, aliens who will soon be decimated by the invading human colonists. Yet the book does not allow the reader to regard these aliens as Others, as non-human entities incapable of subjectivity. Bradbury describes the couple in predominantly human terms, practically ensuring that we will identify with Ylla and forget any difference between the aliens and ourselves.

Bradbury achieves this effect in part by describing the couple's interactions with the most emotionally expressive language possible. When the couple interacts, they rarely just "say" things. The husband "cries" when interrogating his wife on her dreams, and when his jealousy rises to a pitch he "almost screams" his questions at his wife (21). Bradbury likewise gives detailed descriptions of their body language, noting the way the husband responds to the dream by "turning away violently, his jaw working" (21), or the way Ylla "holds her breath" waiting for her human fantasy figure to arrive (24). Grinding teeth out of rage and holding breath in anticipation are both ways that humans express their emotions through body language, gestures that the reader intuitively recognizes. This is the way a human couple registers marital strife — remove the setting, and this couple could easily be any American couple from the suburbs.

Bradbury does not rest at making Ylla and her husband seem human to us, however — he also compels us to identify with Ylla by giving us access to her internal thoughts and emotions. At times, this means shifting into free-indirect discourse, as when Ylla waits for her human visitor:

> It was like those days when you heard a thunderstorm coming and there was the waiting silence and then the faintest pressure of the atmosphere as the climate blew over the land in shifts and shadows and vapors. And the change pressed at your ears and you were suspended in the waiting time of the coming storm. You began to tremble [24].

Here, Bradbury's narrator seamless shifts into Ylla's point of view, practically giving her an internal monologue. Yet it is an internal monologue that invites the reader's identification as well, for Ylla's sensory description uses second person to address the audience directly: "*You* heard a thunderstorm," "*You* began to tremble," she says. These "you"s allows Ylla to simultaneously look within and appeal to the reader's own memories of those pressure changes that anticipate a storm. The reader's subjective experience and Ylla's subjective experience blur together in the process. There is no separation, no distancing effect that might allow us to view Ylla or her unhappy marriage with detachment — whatever her nominal species, she is as fundamentally human as the reader.

When the miniseries adapts this scene, the core narrative stays the same. While the action has now been condensed into a single evening, the central premise of a jealous Martian husband who murders the invading humans of his wife's dreams remains intact. Yet in its presentation of this sequence, the film eliminates every device that emphasizes the Martian couple's essential humanness. Though "faithful" to the novel's narrative, the miniseries presents the story with an overwhelmingly exotic audio-visual presentation that thwarts any viewer identification. This happens for a wide variety of reasons, some of which are actually born of a good-faith effort at fidelity to the novel. The film stays true, for example to Bradbury's description of the Martians' "fair, brownish skin," and "yellow coin eyes" (14). But because Bradbury is working with prose, he can easily draw our attention away from this exotic appearance once has established it. When describing the way Ylla's husband "flung her hand away stiffly" or "kissed her cheek mechanically," the emphasis is not on the alien appearance of the hand, or the orange color of the cheek — it is simply on the expressive action. This ensures that even though we consciously realize the couple is alien, we are not necessarily thinking about this when we watch their interactions. In film, however, there is no way of avoiding the couple's alien appearance. We are constantly faced with their unnervingly smooth orange skin, and their cat-like glowing orange eyes. This may be the way Bradbury initially described the Martians, but in presenting us with a constant reminder of their visual difference, the images provide a constant reminder that the Martians look inhuman. Simply by moving into a visual medium, the Martians verge into Otherness.

Yet that sensation is not entirely due to the newfound prominence of the novel's imagery. The filmmakers of *The Martian Chronicles* also make very specific decisions that direct our attention away from the human drama and onto the alien strangeness of the couple. Nowhere is this more prevalent than in the otherworldly performances given by actors Maggie Wright and James Faulkner. Again, the novel makes great pains to describe Ylla and her husband's complex expressions of emotion, from the husband's angry outbursts to Ylla's anguished screams. The actors who play the Martians in the mini-series, however, display little clear external emotion. The husband (here named "Mr. K.") does not "cry" or "almost scream" at his wife at his wife when he interrogates her on her dreams. When he confronts her, he simply says, "I heard every word you spoke in your sleep," with a borderline-monotone voice and a blank expression that hides all but the subtlest traces of recognizable human emotion. He does not move about violently as she describes the dream, nor does he grind his jaw — he stays perfectly still, as a mannequin. Throughout the scene, both parties speak and move with painstakingly slow and deliberate precision, effectively disguising any pained jealousy or frustrated sexuality that might be implied by the dialogue itself. These are performances designed to keep us from recognizing any clear human emotions in the Martians, designed to remind us instead that we are witnessing the interactions of an alien species.

What little change the film does make to the narrative from the book only emphasizes Mr. K's emotional detachment. In the novel, the husband leaves to kill the humans on some pretext of going to meet a friend, leaving little doubt that the murder is an act of raw jealous rage. In the film, however, he announces his intentions as though taking part in some ancient ceremony. He refers to his wife's dream as "a sign," as he dons a ceremonial mask and a triangular weapon. This is a narrative shift towards mystical "signs" creates the impression that Mr. K's is acting out some exotic ritual, rather than killing through basic human jealously. While it is true that later in the film another Martian explains that K was acting out of jealous anger, the fact that we need this explained to us only emphasizes how unclear K's emotions are in the sequence itself. Moreover, the use of these ceremonial objects, coupled with Mr. K and Ylla's inability to express recognizable human emotion, make the Martians seem like strange creatures engaged in some ancient ritual, rather than an unhappily married couple dealing with sexual frustrations.

One might argue, of course, that the film is at a disadvantage in portraying the characters' emotions because it cannot delve directly into their internal feelings the way that prose can. For example, it would be very difficult to recreate Ylla's intense internal monologue in a film without resorting to a potentially awkward voiceover. But film has less direct means of expressing a character's internal thoughts and feelings that this version of *The Martian Chronicles* never utilizes — chiefly music. Faced with the problem of conveying feelings that cannot be expressed visually, many films turn to non-diegetic musical underscore can often emphasize characters' hidden emotions. For example, when speaking of his experiences scoring Francois Truffaut's adaptation of Bradbury's *Fahrenheit 451*, composer Bernard Herrmann notes that because the characters in the film are "politically oppressed from displaying any emotion or compassion, I felt that the music score should mirror the innermost thoughts and feelings of the leading character" (Herrmann). Though more abstract than prose, Herrmann's turbulent and romantic score gives the audience just as visceral an experience of the characters' emotions as Bradbury's writing does in the novel. Music in "Ylla" scene from *The Martian Chronicles*, however, only further obstructs any chance of seeing the humanity in the film's Martian characters. Throughout the sequence, Stanley Meyers scores the couples' exchange with grating dissonance that is devoid of any accessible melody. When Ylla dreams of her human fantasy, we do not hear any romantic music that might make us understand the character's sexual yearning. We instead hear atonal choral music, cacophonous moaning that evokes a sense of horrific strangeness. This also holds for her interactions with her husband — discordant string music most commonly associated with horror films underscores Ylla and Mr. K.'s conversation, making the audience ill at ease for every moment of the confrontation. Any personal drama inherent in this scene goes entirely unnoticed by the music — instead, Meyers fixates on creating a general tone of disorienting terror, as though our only reaction to this couple should be one of total fear of the unknown. By the time this sequence has concluded, the film has left its audience with the opposite impression of its Martians than the book has. Rather than a typical married couple with the same vulnerability to domestic strife as your average human couple, the Martians come across as members of some bizarre species that we can only observe with uneasy detachment.

Again, these are not devices the film invents for the specific purpose of undermining the novel's intentions. Rather, the filmmakers seem to be simply relying on the familiar devices that Hollywood has been using to depict aliens since the 1950s. Initially, the alien emerges as a response to a very specific set of cultural anxieties. For America in the 1950s, the threat of social conformity is a constant source of fear that emanates throughout the decade's popular culture. That threat might come from an external source, from the menacing Soviet Union that presumably wishes to brainwash the world into a hive-like mentality. Or it might come from within, from the suburban community's self-enforced adherence to the picture-perfect image of the American family. But in both (ironically ideologically opposed) cases, the alien serves as an ideal bogeyman, a creature that displays the what Mark Janovitch refers to as "lack of feelings and the absence of individual characteristics" (qtd. in Geraghty 20) that can be associated either with the Communists or with suburbia. The alien functions so well as an Other in part because it could act as an inkblot, allowing the viewer to project onto it his or her greatest fear. It is during this decade that many of the tropes now associated with the alien emerge: inexpressive faces (*Invaders from Mars*), unsettling avant-garde music (*Forbidden Planet*), and emotionless speaking patterns (*Earth Versus the Flying Saucers*). As the years move onward and society's fears drift elsewhere, we gradually see a shift away from the alien as a symbol sheer terror to one that is alternatively an object of exotic attraction (*Star Trek*), sympathy (*The Twilight Zone*), or even divine wisdom (*2001: A Space Odyssey*). Yet those foundational tropes that render the alien as an Other that stands in "in stark contrast to the human" (Geraghty 20) largely remain intact, regardless of the message. The result is that even by 1980, a film like *The Martian Chronicles* still presents its ostensibly sympathetic alien couple as strange and eerie members of an animal species.

And just as the film struggles to humanize its alien figures, it also seems reluctant to make any of its human characters explicitly unsympathetic. Where the book often offers an unforgiving critique of the jingoistic bigotry that fuels the conquest of indigenous peoples, the film constantly resists painting its American invaders in an overtly negative light. This is particularly true of the way it treats the "November 2005: Off Season" sequence. In the novel, this sequence functions as an eviscerating satire on the bigotry and false sense of entitlement that underlines the Myth of the Frontier. In this story, we see

American Sam Parkhill setting up a hotdog stand with materials he's scavenged and land he's appropriated on Mars. When a Martian appears and attempts to speak to Parkhill, the American lashes out, immediately suspecting that anybody different from him must be a threat. When the Martian assures him, "We mean you no harm," Parkhill barks back, "Well I mean you harm! I don't like strangers! I don't like Martians. I never seen one before. It ain't natural" (168). From the start, Parkhill reveals himself as an ignorant and xenophobic bully. Martians "ain't natural" because he has never seen one before — anything outside of Parkhill's limited sphere of knowledge is an inhuman Other that does not merit respect or decency.

He then grows jealous of the territory he has stolen, imagining that the Martian must want his appropriated land back. He preempts this demand by claiming, "Well, the old got to give way to the new. That's the law of give and take. I got a gun here" (168). Give and take in Parkhill's eyes apparently means that his gun entitles him to take everything he sees, regardless of who else might have prior claims to the land. In fact, that Martian is actually trying to give Parkhill a deed to half to half of the territory on Mars. When the Martian attempts to show Parkhill this land deed, however, Parkhill screams, "A gun!" and shoots the Martian dead. Though he convinces himself that he has killed the Martian because he mistook the creature's "bronze tube" for a gun, his action seems less a mistaken self-defense than a murder predicated on a willful misunderstanding. Parkhill sees a gun in the Martian's hand because he wants to see a gun — none of the Martian's peaceful protestations to the contrary can invalidate the American's preset prejudice. As Jose Prats explains when detailing the history of Native Americans in cinema, "The conqueror must produce an Other whose destruction is not only assured by justified" (2). The Martian is Parkhill's Other, a fiction he has created for himself in order to "vindicate ... the 'history' that transmutates might into right" (Prats 2). By the time the story is over, Parkhill has killed four other Martians and briefly even has turned his gun on his own wife. Only when he runs out of bullets are the Martians able to reveal that they only wish to grant him half of the planet. By this point, of course, it is too late. Earth, a planet filled with billions of angry Sam Parkhills, has erupted into nuclear war. There will be no customers to serve at the hot dog stand, and no more conquerors to help Parkhill colonize the new frontier.

Little of this satire makes it into the miniseries, which can never fully embrace the notion of white cowboys as antagonistic bullies and alien/Indians as fully humanized characters worthy of empathy. True, the miniseries does maintain the general narrative arc of Parkhill's episode — the American still attempts to set up a hotdog stand on Mars, still kills several peaceful Martians in an act of mistaken self-defense, still ultimately learns that the Martians have left him half of the planet, and still returns to his hotdog stand to see Earth destroyed by nuclear weapons. Yet the miniseries shifts the tone in the sequence considerably, rendering Parkhill more sympathetic and the Martians more menacing. As portrayed by actor Daren McGavin, the film's Sam Parkhill is less a vitriolic racist than a childlike clown, one too guileless for actual hatred. Dressed in what appears to be a Los Vegas entertainer's approximation of a cowboy and speaking with an affable "aw-shucks" Southern drawl, McGavin plays Parkhill like a well-meaning buffoon. The film echoes McGavin's portrayal by writing all of Parkhill's uglier qualities out of the story. This Parkhill never goes on a vitriolic rant against all Martian strangers, never turns his gun on his own wife in the midst of his killing frenzy, and never even raises his weapon in anger. While he is certainly still in the wrong when he kills the Martians, the film takes pains to make his mistake seem understandable, emerging less from prejudice than from innocent childlike panic.

We can see this change most vividly in the way screenwriter Richard Matheson has rewritten Parkhill's encounter with the first Martian. The script eliminates the heated exchange that precedes the murder; the Martian never states his peaceful intentions and Parkhill never declares his hatred of all things Martian and unnatural. Instead, the Martian simply appears abruptly behind Parkhill, says, "I have something for you," and extends a long cylindrical object. Without the set-up that the novel provided, the Martian's behavior here actually does appear menacing. Dressed in a triangular metallic mask that hides his facial features, he looks less like a humanoid creature than a machine, and he speaks with cold inflection that hardly sounds like a friendly overture. Even his single line of dialogue has been rewritten to sound more ominous. When he holds out the metal tube in the novel, he says, "Let me show you this" (168). This is a request, one that that could hardly be mistaken as a threat. Changing that line to "I have something for you" renders the Martian more ominous, as this is an expression that often does precede murder (especially in pulpy thrillers). Adding even more to this effect, dissonant piano scales on the soundtrack accompany the Martian's appearance, musically registering the creature as a monster from a horror movie. The creature comes across so menacingly that we can hardly fault Parkhill for screaming, "Hit the dirt!" and firing his pistol in a blind panic. After all, he is responding to the same horrifying Other that we see and hear. As a result, Sam's reaction comes across not as consciously motivated bigotry, but rather as a visceral response to the same audio-visual sign that is frightening the audience.

It is true that we do still learn of the Martian's peaceful intentions and of Sam's tragic mistake in killing them. But recognizing that the Martians are technically in the right is not the same thing as recognizing them as fellow subjects deserving of empathy. Even when they are ostensibly behaving benevolently, as when they give the Martian property to Sam, the film continues to present the Martians as cold, inhuman figures who thwart audience sympathy. Instead, the novel keeps our sympathies purely with Parkhill. This is particularly notable in the way it treats his reaction to his first murder. Unlike the novel, in which Sam justifies his mistake as "the circumstances of fate" (169), the film gives Sam space for genuine remorse. Upon killing the first Martian, he dejectedly slumps in his chair and reflects on the opportunity for inter-stellar interaction that he has destroyed. Thinking of all the occasions in which his peers dreamed of meeting and learning from the Martians, Parkhill mutters, "Me I finally see one and what do I do? I shoot him." McGavin delivers the dialogue with a level of world-wearied self-loathing, exhibiting self-awareness unseen by the novel's version of the character. In lingering for so long on the character's earnest lamentations, the film positions us to feel sorry for Parkhill, rather than the Martian he has killed. His is the only experience that seems to matter, for the film does not trust its audience to identify with anybody other than the white American cowboy. As a result, the scene becomes less an indictment on American bigotry than an opportunity for a benevolent conqueror to demonstrate remorse for people he has destroyed — people that the film has already registered as inhuman.

Yet even with all of these devices that render the Martians menacing and fundamentally Other, the film does at times make a good faith effort at presenting the Martians and their culture in a sympathetic light. This comes primarily through the film's treatment of the Martian ruins, the spare and serene monuments that stand out amidst the planet's desert. On multiple occasions throughout the miniseries, human characters pause to reflect on the beauty of these ruins, which come to stand as symbol for a benevolent culture that has been buried by humankind's frenzied colonization of the planet. When, for example, Colonel Wilder makes a pilgrimage to the ruins late in the film and gazes at the triangular and spherical structures, the film takes advantage of the medium's unique ability to communicate complex ideas through wordless audio-visual juxtaposition. Occupying Wilder's perspective, the camera gazes out at the spare angular beauty of the Martians' ancient city. Production designer Ashton Gorton turns the film's limited budget into an asset, favoring a minimalistic aesthetic based on simple geometric structures. The simple precision of these ruins under the bright desert light evokes the conquered indigenous peoples of the American Southwest without ever making the comparison explicit. Though it never evokes any specific group of people, the film incorporates general iconography associated with tribes of the American Southwest, subtly compelling the viewer to see the analogy between this planet's disappearing culture and the cultures that are in danger of disappearing on our own planet.

This extends into Stanley Meyers musical score, which treats the ruins as a rare occasion for tonal serenity. Breaking from the grating dissonance that so frequently accompanies the Martians, Meyers here leans towards a gentle merging of European impressionism and indigenous Native American music. As with Gorton's production design, Meyers uses icons commonly associated with the indigenous peoples of the Americas — in this case, through panpipes and other wood instruments. During this sequence, panpipes provide the music's lyrical and yearning melody, while strings and wordless choir provide impressionistic color. True, the music is not an "authentic" portrait of any particular tribe or culture, for Myer's melody and harmonic language is far more based in a Western Romantic/Impressionistic idiom than in any regional idiom of the American Southwest. But as with the production design, the wood instruments draw on the audience's more general associations with indigenous American music. Music becomes another method of drawing an unspoken connection between the lost culture represented by the Martian ruins and the endangered cultures in the United States' own conquered frontier. These moments emphasize a potential that the miniseries only occasionally realizes — they take Bradbury's critique on American expansionism, and they translate it through the purely visceral language of cinema.

Yet the nostalgic portraits of the Martian ruins are also deceptive. While these scenes seem at first to present a sympathetic portrait of the displaced Martian culture, it is significant that we always see the culture through the perspective of the conqueror. When, Colonel Wilder gazes out at the ruins near the end of the film, the emphasis is on his emotional experience as an American colonizer. The Martian point of view remains unavailable to us. Martians in this film never have the agency to look back and reflect, or to invite our identification — they are never subjects, only objects that are only relevant in terms of their relationship with the human conquerors. This means occupying a space of fear when the narrative requires them to frighten the human conquerors, and occupying the place of a noble victim when the narrative requires remorse and reflection from the human conquerors. In all cases, however, the emphasis is pointedly on the humans and their emotional experience.

In this case, that emotional experience belongs to Colonel Wilder, who has become the hero of the film. Wilder represents perhaps the most significant instance of the film reshaping the novel on a purely narrative level. Though

Bradbury's novel contains a broad story ark in its gradual depiction of Mars' colonization, it does not feature a standard linear narrative. Bradbury's *Martian Chronicles* takes advantage of the anthology format, one in which the reader gains insight into multiple characters, human and Martian, and encounters wide variety of experiences. The novel does not feature a single protagonist with a traditional hero's quest, but rather a fragmented series of characters who appear and fade while the larger forces of history press onward. Unfortunately, this format is the antithesis of the classic Hollywood narrative, which demands a consistent active protagonist who functions as an agent of change. To better fit *The Martian Chronicles* into this mold, screenwriter Richard Matheson restructures the story so that Colonel Wilder is constantly at the center of the action. Wilder becomes the story's protagonist, the constant figure who makes the story more closely resemble a Hollywood narrative.

The decision makes a certain degree of sense — Wilder is, after all, one of the novel's more decent characters. As the military commander who oversees the third expedition to Mars, Wilder is a colonist who harbors reservations about the potential destruction that colonization will bring to Mars. But the character only appears in a few of the novel's segments, and he rarely has any significant impact on events in the story. In the miniseries, Wilder becomes the focus throughout the larger duration of the narrative. He takes roles that belonged to other characters in the novel, such as that of the young man who meets a Martian ghost in "August 2002: Night Meeting" or the father who declares his family the new Martians in "October 2026: The Million-Year Picnic." And as the novel's disparate episodes gradually reshape themselves to emphasize Wilder's character arc, the fundamental nature of the story transforms. Instead of a disparate multiplicity of human and Martian experience, it becomes the story of one man's gradual transformation — from reluctant colonizer and voice of reason to noble steward of the new human–Martian way of life.

While this story development might seem at first like a necessary move to give the film more narrative unity, it is also one more factor in the film that emphasizes sympathy with the conqueror at the expense of the conquered. By giving us equal access to a wide variety of stories featuring both humans and Martians, Bradbury's novel has an equalizing effect. No single character seems more important than the others — instead, their collective experiences provide insight into the larger history of the planet's colonization. By re-writing Wilder as the story's hero — played by glamorous movie star Rock Hudson, for that matter — and structuring the movie around his path, the film elevates Wilder above all of the other characters. It becomes less about a collective experience and more a straightforward Hollywood film in which the white male hero's experience is the defining lens.

The film in this manner situates itself less as a rebuke to the standard cowboys-and-Indians conquest narrative, and more as a revisionist Western. Here, Wilder plays the role of the remorseful conqueror who yearns to learn from the same people whose destruction he has enabled. By 1980, the revisionist Western has become a relatively popular subgenre for filmmakers eager to atone for the negative Indian stereotypes of Hollywood's past. These films, such as *Little Big Man* and *A Man Called Horse*, typically involve a white hero who lives among Indians and gradually comes to sympathize with their ways and lament their inevitable destruction. The revisionist Western frames itself as a progressive alternative to Hollywood's past negative portrayals of the Indian "savage." But as Prats explains in *Invisible Natives*, these films are often only "Conquest's own lament over its consequences, a jeremiad for atonement's sake, rather than — or at least in addition to — an invective against Conquest or an elegy for the Indian" (133). In revisionist Western, the white protagonist is still the heroic figure, and still central to all experience. In many cases, this white hero was once an Indian fighter himself until he learned the "true" nature of the Indian. But in sympathizing with and mourning the passing of the Indians he and his kind have destroyed, the revisionist hero makes an "atonement" for conquest that ultimately absolves him of guilt. As Prats puts it, "only those who are enlightened about the real Indians could indulge such an exquisite lament upon their passing. Remorse is therefore wisdom, and eulogy absolves" (142). The model of absolution for Conquest serves as the framework for *The Martian Chronicles*. Wilder becomes the noble hero, once on the side of the Conquerors, who gradually learns the wisdom of the indigenous peoples his kind have destroyed — but only after, of course, those indigenous peoples have been eliminated.

Nowhere is this more pointed than in the film's re-appropriation of the novel's "August 2002: Night Meeting," which in the film immediate follows Wilder's pensive reflections in The Martian ruins. All throughout the film Wilder has been hoping to encounter and learn from a Martian. As he stands staring out, a phantom Martian from another time appears and engages Wilder in a conversation about the nature of time and experience. Eventually, he reveals to Wilder the secrets of the Martian philosophy, and teaches Wilder a better way of approaching life. To a certain degree, the sequence is similar to the novel's version of scene, particularly in the beginning where both parties mistake each other for a ghost. But the novel's version differs from that of the film in one crucial way — it favors neither character as a protagonist, and instead gives both Martian and human equal importance. Where the film casts the Martian as a peripheral character whose function is to aide Wilder on his journey, the novel grants them equal status as fully-developed subjects.

This contrast is partially due to the difference in narrative form between the film and the book. The scene in the novel is a standalone vignette, a story that stars two characters who will never feature again in the novel. The man and Martian who meet are both young men, off on their way to a night of carousing on the town before they run into each other. After engaging in some philosophical argument, both reach an understanding of one another, depart to enjoy the life waiting in front of them, and then vanish from the novel. Neither party is the "main" character; both share equal emphasis within the story. By changing the standalone nature of the sequence and instead making it the climax of Wilder's lifelong quest to meet a Martian, the film favors the experience of the white male hero over that of the Martian. The Martian becomes part of Wilder's story, rather than an equal player in a shared story.

The shift is particularly glaring because the "Night Meeting" section of the book is Bradbury's most explicit demonstration of the fundamental sameness between Martian and human. The segment provides us with both of their internal thoughts, and in doing so reveals how similar man and Martian are to each other. When the two realize that one is a phantom, Bradbury describes their mutual reaction simultaneously: "They pointed at each other, with starlight burning in their limbs like daggers and icicles and fireflies, and then fell to judging their limbs again, each finding himself intact, hot, excited, stunned, awed, and the other, ah yes, that other over there, unreal" (106). Both parties recognize their own experience as real, and the being in front of them as "unreal"— this is precisely how Othering begins. Yet by demonstrating that both human and Martian have this exact same experience, Bradbury reveals the arbitrary nature of the line that separates the self from the Other. He further emphasizes the point by revealing both characters as young men in similar stages in their lives. At the story's end, Tomas leaves thinking of "the rockets, the women, the raw whisky, the Virginia reels, the party," while the Martian anticipates "the festival, the canals, the boats, the women with golden eyes, and the songs" (110). Both are equally reckless young men looking forward to a night of carousing on the town. One doesn't function to teach the other a lesson, as the object of the other's subjective experience — they are both fully developed subjects.

The film, in fairness, cannot give access to either characters' inner thoughts, short of indulging in dueling internal monologues. But it constantly favors Wilder's perspective by turning the Martian into less an equal than a mystic sage who proffers advice on the meaning of life. Where the Martian in the novel was a young man eager to run off for a night of revelry, this Martian is a noble and wise figure who arrives at the film's climax in order to give Wilder his answer to the meaning of life. The Martian tells Wilder:

Life is its own answer. Accept it and enjoy it day by day. Live as well as possible. Expect no more. Destroy nothing. Humble nothing. Look for fault in nothing. Leave unsullied and untouched all that is beautiful. Hold that which lives in all reverence. For life is given by the sovereign of our universe.

These are not unwise words, and in fairness, parts of this monologue originate from Spender's thoughts about the Martian culture in the novel's "June 2001: And the Moon Be Still as Bright." But by placing this god-like wisdom in the mouth of a Martian who occupies less than ten minutes of screen time, the film reduces the Martian's role to that of a Noble Savage in a revisionist Western. Like the Noble Savage, this Martian exists less as a character in his own right than as a dispenser of ancient wisdom for the white hero's benefit. This Martian is easily the most sympathetic Martian that appears in the film, but he never emerges as a character who might invite viewer identification the way Wilder does. The Martian still speaks with a cold clipped speaking pattern and stares with the same blank expression that emphasizes his fundamental Otherness. He is just a different form of the Other — a noble, rather than a violent savage. His role is offer the Conqueror words of sentimental wisdom before vanishing quietly into history.

Once Wilder receives this knowledge, he takes his family out to the canals to declare them all the "new" Martians. Though this scene also takes place in the novel as "2026: The Million-Year Picnic," its meaning is significantly altered in this context. Instead of the story of a new set of characters attempting to pick up where others failed, the scene in the film becomes the culmination of the white hero's journey — after destroying the Other and then learning the Other's wise philosophy, Wilder and his family effectively replace the Other. Ironically, it seems that the only time the film is willing to allow empathy for the Martian is when the Martian is in fact the white human conqueror.

What thus emerges is a film that, for all of its noble intentions, turns Bradbury's critique of the Myth of Conquest that into a new iteration of the Myth of Conquest. It happens because Othering conventions are so central to Hollywood practice that nobody even thought to question their value. And until both the film industry and its audiences learn to question these modes of representation, they will continue to drive American cinema. *The Martian Chronicles* miniseries came out in 1980, but the tropes have carried over well into films from the following three decades — from Westerns like *Dances with Wolves*, to high-profile science fiction parables like *Avatar*. Again and again, we see conquered peoples relegated to the role Other, relevant only as reflections of their white conqueror's experience. By comparing Bradbury's novel to the film, however, we see all more clearly how those assumptions can be subverted — how subtle moves that do not seem at first like crucial decisions can mean the difference between recognizing the Other as a fellow subject and castigating the Other as the necessary casualty of colonization.

Works Cited

Bradbury, Ray. *The Martian Chronicles.* New York: Doubleday, 1958. Print.
Geraghty, Lincoln. *American Science Fiction Film and Television.* New York: Berg, 2009. Print.
Herrmann, Bernard. Liner Notes. *The Fantasy Film World of Bernard Herrmann.* Decca, 1974. Vinyl.
Landry, Christopher. Liner Notes. *The Martian Chronicles: Original Television Score.* Airstrip One AOD 003, 2002. CD.
Leitch, Thomas. *Film Adaptation and Its Discontents.* Baltimore: John Hopkins University Press, 2007. Print.
Prats, Armando Jose. *Invisible Natives: Myth & Identity in the American Western.* Ithaca: Cornell University Press, 2002. Print.
Ray Bradbury's The Martian Chronicles. Dir. Michael Anderson. MGM, 1980. DVD.
Stam, Robert. "Introduction: The Theory and Practice of Adaptation." *Literature and Film.* Ed. Robert Stam and Alessandra Raengo. Malden, MA: Blackwell, 2005. Print.
Weller, Sam. *The Bradbury Chronicles.* New York: HarperCollins, 2005. Print.

The Illustrated Man Illustrates Our Future

HOWARD ALLEN

In 1969, following a less-than-successful attempt at screenwriting on his own (*The Picasso Summer*), Ray Bradbury witnessed the Hollywood take on one of his story collections. He had sold the rights to *The Illustrated Man* to Warner Bros./Seven Arts and they made the film with their own writer and director's choices in the storytelling. Did it fare any better? In a strange way, the film succeeded beyond his wildest dreams.

In 1953–54, Bradbury wrote the screenplay for *Moby Dick* with director John Huston, to great success. Following this box office achievement, in 1966, the brilliant French filmmaker, Francois Truffaut, adapted and directed Bradbury's novel, *Farenheit 451*, to great critical success. So hopes were high for *The Illustrated Man*, a story collection that touched upon deep and almost obsessive themes from Bradbury's early life. For example, he had a lifelong fascination with magicians.

Ray Bradbury was moved to explore the true magic of the storyteller by actual magicians he met as a child. At age 11 (and later with his daughters), he famously got to meet Blackstone the Magician. As a 12-year-old boy, Bradbury joined his family on a move to the Tucson, Arizona. The landscape of his life changed. At age 12, Mr. Electrico tapped a sword on young Ray's shoulder and said, "Live forever." Bradbury said, "I started writing every day and I never stopped" (Weller 50, 56, 57). Those encounters and two more moves — back to Waukegan and then across the Southwest to Los Angeles — instilled in the boy an admiration for the magic of new worlds. He often compared going to Tucson from Waukegan to a trip into Oz. New landscapes become new worlds — of the science fiction and fantasy and horror varieties — in the mind of this writer.

Not surprisingly then, *The Illustrated Man* film's story begins in a remote location: low hills and hardy Earth-bound plant life, few trees, a small lake, a lonely crossroads, where a young hitchhiker, Willie, exits alone from a 1930s–era vehicle. It could be the Midwest or the Southwest but was probably filmed entirely in California. It could be happening in the mid 1940s or almost any time.

In his twenties, Ray Bradbury made an adventurous trip through the Southwest into Mexico in 1945. Though he did not drive and was legally blind without his glasses, he acted as "navigator" for his friend Grant Beach on a trip that took them through all kinds of Mexican terrain — from jungle to Mexico City. They witnessed the famous October event Dia de los Muertos (Day of the Dead) on the island of Janitzio in Lake Patzcuaro and saw the infamous mummies in Guanajuato before they even had a chance encounter with John Steinbeck at breakfast in Mexico City (Weller 127–128).

In the film, Willie's own cross-country adventure is interrupted by Carl, the illustrated man of the title. Carl's magical skin illustrations come to life with stories from the future — stories as frightening as anything Bradbury witnessed in Mexico. In the book version published in 1951, Carl and Willie's meeting is only a brief Prologue to the short story collection (Bradbury 1–7).

Neither man had a name in the Prologue because Bradbury's purpose was merely to give a creative way to introduce the following 18 stories, which corresponded to 18 illustrations on the homeless carnival freak's body. Hollywood had other ideas. More than half of the film focuses on Carl and Willie as well as flashbacks to the days many years before when Carl met the mysterious Felicia, who tempted him into a body full of her very special skin illustrations.

In producer-writer Howard Kreitsek's screenplay, Willie (played by actor Robert Drivas) is on his way to Fresno California where his sister may have a job waiting for him. Carl (played by Rod Steiger, a personal friend of Ray Bradbury) is "hobo-in" and searching for a house he's seen in *Liberty Magazine* that looks like the one where he met Felicia, another Kreitsek creation played by Claire Bloom, who was actually married to Steiger.

Carl tells Willie that Felicia's work comes alive and "she has created my own private hell." Later, struck by the images that Carl says are "everywhere on my body and I do mean ev-er-y where," Willie wants to know why he let himself be tattooed. Carl says, "I wasn't thinking about getting tattooed, I was thinking about getting laid. And for the last time — I told you they're skin illustrations" (Kreitsek, *The Illustrated Man*).

And so begins Kreitsek's approach, aided by director Jack Smight, who only the year before directed Steiger in the black comedy *No Way to Treat a Lady*. More important, just two years before he directed Paul Newman in one of the best detective stories on film, *Harper*. So Bradbury still had reason to hope for the best.

Kreitsek and Smight chose to illustrate Steiger's body top to bottom in a temporary process that took 20 hours to complete each time it had to be done. So imagine the actor even having to sleep in between and during applications, especially for the memorable scene when he is naked on a couch in Felicia's home. And for much of the filming, Steiger was naked to the waist. A promotional TV documentary about the film at the time shows Kreitsek, Smight, the principal actors and even a glimpse of Bradbury in the Warner Bros. documentary *Tatooed Steiger*, available online (Warner Bros.). The skin illustrations did represent all 18 stories, but the filmmakers chose to fully "illustrate" only three of Bradbury's stories from the collection: "The Veldt," "The Long Rain" and "The Last Night of the World."

In the film, Willie focuses on one tattoo first and it dissolves into a filmed version of "The Veldt," a story that was published originally as "The World the Children Made" in the September 23, 1950, issue of *The Saturday Evening Post*. After each story, the film version returns to Willie and Carl at the end of the day around a campfire, joined only by Carl's dog that he carries in a canvas bag. And after "The Last Night of the World" comes to life, the film returns to an Epilogue at the campsite where Willie fears for his life after watching the one blank portion of Carl's back. It is the "screen" where Carl has warned him he will see his own death.

In Bradbury's print text of *The Illustrated Man*, the tiny one-page Epilogue ends there (280). In the film, Kreitsek's melodramatic approach continues with Willie trying to kill Carl and a bloodied Carl "chasing" after Willie in a humorous Frankenstein-like walk. The film ends abruptly with the cast list. The stars of Kreitsek's prologue/epilogue "story" become major characters in the film and the actors play roles as well in the Bradbury's three stories chosen from the collection.

The melodrama by Kreitsek overwhelms the best of the sci-fi and fantasy and drama in the other stories. Bradbury actually wrote a story called "The Illustrated Man" that was not what he used in the framing device of the prologue/epilogue (Weller 170). Kreitsek's melodramatic tendencies distort the Bradbury stories as well. "The Last Night of the World" takes place in the year 4187 when families live in cheesy-looking white tents in the countryside like some kind of Midwest Bedouins instead of normal looking folks in the near future of Oct. 19, 1969. And Bradbury's version does not have one parent killing the children to "protect" them from the end of the world. A mistake as it turns out (not unlike the recent foolishness about the Mayan calendar "prediction" for Oct. 21, 2012).

In plot and story design, "The Long Rain" comes as close as any in the film to Bradbury's version in the short story collection. However, it too focuses on the melodrama of three men fighting each other rather than men trying simply to survive their rocket's crash, leaving them caught outside in a Venusian landscape of horrific and continuous rain. They are searching for man-made Sun Domes for their safety. Only one survives. Bradbury's version did have Venusian monsters that were cloudlike lightning dispensing aliens (78–96). Not so in the film. But then the filmmakers did not have the computer-generated-imagery or CGI effects available today.

This brings up the point that contemporary critics of the film often fall into the fallacy known as the Arrogance of Hindsight. Certainly a film today could make for astounding production design elements to create Venus. While this does not excuse the melodramatic dialogue in "The Long Rain," it should excuse what was a pretty good attempt at continuous rain. The real actors spent a lot of hours drenched continuously to make it work.

And the production design of "The Veldt" would have been improved by CGI when the tattoo transforms into a futuristic home that unfortunately looks like a 1970s white plastic and white-walled terrarium. What it does have is Bradbury's brilliant idea: the Nursery where the children play. The story begins with the parents disturbed about their young children using the virtual reality of the nursery to create a scary realistic version of the African veldt, complete with a pride of hungry lions.

In the book version, father George tries to comfort his wife Lydia and himself by reminding her the charging lions that made them run from the Nursery are all "dimensional superreactionary, super sensitive color film ... behind glass screens. It's all odorophonics and sonics" (Bradbury 12). He wants to reassure her that the technology is still in their control. Today the description may be funny but pretty good for sci-fi of the time: Bradbury's original "The World the Children Made" came out in the September 23, 1950, issue of *The Saturday Evening Post*.

Fortunately in the film version, Carl and Felicia (they keep the same names as the prologue/epilogue characters) don't engage in explaining how the Nursery works. Bradbury brilliantly focuses on the psychology of the family. The Nursery simply comes to life visually with a dissolve from a wall of interesting-looking electronic elements. In fact, it comes to life like the best video game ever made. In fact, the futurist in Ray Bradbury brilliantly imagined Augmented Reality inventions of today.

> What is Augmented Reality? The basic goal of an AR system is to enhance the user's perception of and interaction with the real world through supplementing the real world with 3D virtual objects that appear to coexist in the same space as

the real world ... we define AR systems to share the following properties: (1) Blends real and virtual, in a real environment (2) Real-time interactive (3) Registered in 3D; Registration refers to the accurate alignment of real and virtual objects [Azuma, Introduction].

In the Happy-life Home of the book and the film, technology does much of the work for the family. The parents call up the government psychologist assigned to their children on something that looks just like Skype of today. Played by Drivas (Willie) in the film, the psychologist responds to the father's fear the Nursery is making his children neurotic — not unlike parents today worrying about role-playing video games.

"No, it's supposed to help them work off their neuroses in a healthful way," says the counselor in the book (Bradbury 18).

Not surprisingly, Kreitsek finds a way in the film version to make "The Veldt" parents deal with their sex life (not in the Bradbury version). And this parallels the sexual intrigue of Felicia the skin illustrator and her subject, Carl. When he's frightened by the first batch of illustrations, he worries he won't even get laid.

"I'll be a freak," he says, and Felicia answers, "Pain is part of everything good. I will make you happier than you've ever been in your whole life." And she leads him to the bedroom (Kreitsek, *The Illustrated Man*).

Quite a journey away from both pieces as they appear in Bradbury's book. Some would say it's not surprising then that the film was a critical and box office failure. "After an early screening, as the audience left the theater, Ray noticed a teenage boy, a fan, staring at him. 'Mr. Bradbury, what happened?' Equally disappointed in the film, Ray ... could hardly reply. 'The script was bad and the film, as a result, wasn't any better,' Ray concluded years later (Weller 280).

In his review of the film at the time, Roger Ebert begins with this semi-famous quote from Claire Bloom's Felicia: "Each person who tries to see beyond his own time must face questions for which there are no absolute answers." A line that describes Ray Bradbury's life as a storyteller as well, of course.

When I was in high school, I was a science fiction fan of incurable proportions.... And I faithfully followed the s-f fan magazines, wherein raged heated philosophical battles over the difference between science fiction and fantasy. My side contended that science fiction was fantasy, but that fantasy was not science fiction (are you following this?). The crucial difference was that s-f pretended to realism, while in fantasy literally anything could happen and you never knew when a door knob might open a blue eye and wink at you. Of course, anything could happen in s-f, too, but you had to explain how [Ebert].

Ebert uses the classic definition of SF that requires unrealistic elements to have real logic in the supernatural, whereas fantasy makes fewer demands on the logic. He then comes back to the film genre, where he too struggles with the mix of melodrama, fantasy skin illustrators and sci-fi futuristic locations as performed by Kreitsek and director Smight. "What finally brings the film down is its inadequate attention to the expectations of the audience. It cheats in reverse. Instead of slipping goblins into nuclear reactors, it slips logic into an illogical universe." And later after describing the four stories in one film, he said, "And so the film finally doesn't work for the same reason that comic Westerns usually fail: Because it's risky to fool around with a genre unless you know what you're doing" (Ebert).

Without resorting to the Arrogance of Hindsight, times have changed about the mixing of fantasy and science fiction elements to some extent. However, the melodramatic fantasy story of the carny worker and the disappearing witch-like tattoo artist would still today match up very poorly with the magical speculations of Ray Bradbury's stories.

The often unrecognized genius of Ray Bradbury comes from his ability to take a sci-fi story idea, infuse it with great horror and suspense and still manage to pay off the human to human conflicts in masterful and insightful ways. Or put more simply: a futurist hiding inside human dramas.

"The Veldt" is genius in this way. While taking us into the future to see what video games might become, he also horrifies us with the dangers of augmented reality but his ultimate goal: showing us what it might do to our children — in a very human-oriented, character-oriented, masterful storyteller-oriented way. In a confrontation that still frightens us today, the young children, especially the boy, challenge their father and his dominion over "their" Nursery. The parents, the government psychologist, the book readers and the film viewers get a moment of horror to go with a futuristic sci-fi story.

Stephen King, another storyteller who can mash up genres, said, "Well of course without Ray Bradbury there is no Stephen King ... I never 'studied' him. I just absorbed what he was up to, mostly in the early small-town horror stories but also in the early science fiction stories" (Weller 153).

Storyteller Steven Spielberg said, "Ray Bradbury's most significant contribution to our culture is showing us that the imagination has no foreseeable boundaries" (Weller 11).

As Bradbury began to write what became *The Illustrated Man* stories in the late 1940s, he used "the loose framework of science fiction, or the weird tale, or even the occasional backdrop of noir crime, but he was writing about people rather than about science, or terror, or detection" It's a fundamental hallmark of his work (Eller 165).

Not surprisingly, a very successful producer and writer, Frank Darabont, of *The Shawshank Redemption* and *The Walking Dead* fame, has announced his intention with director/ producer Zack Snyder (*300* and *Watchmen* films) to take another run at *The Illustrated Man*. The hope is they will rely much, much more on Bradbury's writing. They might add one or two more stories from the book version and focus on his gift of infusing great horror and suspense into science fiction and pay off the great human to human conflicts as well.

Works Cited

Azuma, Ronald, et al. "Recent Advances in Augmented Reality." *Computers & Graphics*. Nov. 2001. 20 Dec. 2012. Web.

Bradbury, Ray. *The Illustrated Man*. New York: Simon & Schuster, 2012. Print.

Ebert, Roger. "The Illustrated Man." Review. *The Chicago Sun-Times*. 6 Aug. 1969. 20 Dec. 2012. Web.

Kreitsek, Howard. *The Illustrated Man*. Screenplay. Warner Bros./Sevens Art, 1969. Print.

Warner Bros. film short. *Tatooed Steiger*. 1969. [Re-titled as "*The Illustrated Man*: The Making of the Making-Up." 20 Dec. 2012. Web.

Weller, Sam. *The Bradbury Chronicles*. New York: Morrow, 2005. Print.

Silver Locusts on
the Silver Screen
Bradbury's Western Mars Confronts
1960s British Art-Cinema

Martin R. Hall

"[T]hat way of life proved itself wrong and strangled itself with its own hands. You're young. I'll tell you this again every day until it sinks in."—Bradbury, *The Martian Chronicles*/UK title *The Silver Locusts*, 180

Early editions of Ray Bradbury's collection of short stories were published in the UK under the title, *The Silver Locusts*. Interestingly, with a more explicit impact than *The Martian Chronicles*, the title *The Silver Locusts*, like the episode "The Locusts," vehemently suggests the more sinister aspects of the "invasion" of Mars by humans. The suggestively destructive nature, and the connotations of plague, inherently invoked by the idea of "locusts" reinforces the pervading theme of the threatening and damaging effects of colonization:

The rockets came like locusts, swarming and settling in blooms of rosy smoke. And from the rockets ran men with hammers in their hands to beat the strange world into a shape that was familiar to the eye, to bludgeon away the strangeness, their mouths fringed with nails so they resembled steel-toothed carnivores [Bradbury, *Martian*, 78].

Ray Bradbury's social commentary is one which explores the idea of the evolution of mankind beyond an outdated system and the subsequent rejection of a superannuated lifestyle; one which must be destroyed, and indeed is, by nuclear war. Bradbury's narrative, amidst the pervading scrutiny of colonization, questions humanity's cultural identity through his protagonist's introspection and consequent assimilation of a new and improved lifestyle. While this is an apt and accurate description of *The Martian Chronicles*, this encapsulation applies as fittingly to *Fahrenheit 451*. These two texts follow each other closely, converging on a number of themes, the most prominent occurring within the *Martian Chronicles* episode "Usher II."

Otherness plays an important role within both texts, while in *The Martian Chronicles* this otherness is manifested in the Martian civilization, *Fahrenheit 451* takes the theme of rebellion and nonconformity; while the former focuses on the "evolution" of humans into Martians, the latter examines Montag's process of becoming more "human," taking his wife's existence as a microcosm for society.

In 1980, the BBC and NBC released *The Martian Chronicles* as a TV miniseries to largely negative reviews. Interviewing Ray Bradbury for *The Guardian* newspaper, W.J. Wetherby observed, "British TV critics had been rough on the series" (Wetherby 10), to which Bradbury replied, "We had very mixed reviews in the States, too" (qtd. in Wetherby 10).

Reviewing the series, Clive James exclaimed simply that "this is the pits" (40), while Nancy Banks-Smith complained that the show "turns out to be like every old B-movie you ever made a point of missing" (9). Even the book itself took some harsh criticism from the British press. Writing in response to the publication of the two-volume *The Stories of Ray Bradbury*, David Hewison claimed,

> *The Martian Chronicles*, which have probably earned him more money than anything else he has written, are a blatant Western soap opera on the theme of colonization transferred, for no other reason than money, from Colorado to outer space [5].

Despite Banks-Smith's contention that "the plan is evidently to bore the invaders to death" (9), the miniseries was indeed a "faithful rendering of the Ray Bradbury book" (James 40). That is to say that the series, with regards to the material chosen from the book, is faithful, if not to the letter, in spirit. From the omission of the devastating ecological impact that the launching of the first rocket has on a wintry Ohio, recorded in "Rocket Summer" to the little attention paid to the transformation of Mars' surface through the plantation of trees and the erection of settlements, there were a number of omissions from the book. In support of the powerful thematic association of *The Mars Chronicles* with *Fahrenheit 451*, the most glaring excision of the series is that of the episode "Usher II." Perhaps it was by virtue of its utmost similitude to *Fahrenheit 451* that "Usher II" was omitted from the series?

"Usher II" tells the story of the reaction of one man, Stendahl's to the banning and burning of all books on Earth; his own grand collection confiscated and destroyed. Stendahl rebels against this controversial decision by Moral Climate Investigators and subsequently vacates the oppressive society in order to find another, more liberal civilization on Mars. Stendahl's actions closely echo Montag's, albeit manifested in a much more aggressive and revengeful manner; the inherent message of "Usher II" being the, "paying back of the antiseptic government for its literary terrors and conflagrations" (Bradbury, *Martian*, 110). Like *Fahrenheit 451*, "Usher II" hinges upon the "living" embodiment of books. Here, Stendahl, and his associate Pikes, reenact murders from the works of Edgar Allen Poe (interestingly, this is the book which François Truffaut's Montag "becomes" in his *Fahrenheit 451* adaptation). Stendahl, having strategically befriended all of the Moral Climate Investigators, invites them to a dinner party at which he shows robotic duplicates of each of them being murdered. The robots, however, turn out to be the ones who are watching, while the victims were in fact the genuine individuals. Garrett, the Investigator assigned to report on Stendahl, is taken to the cellar and walled into a cell, brick by brick, as in Poe's short story, "The Cask of Amontillado," while the house collapses and sinks into its foundations as in the "The Fall of the House of Usher," this episode's namesake.

While the narrative of *Fahrenheit 451* questions the role of individualism, free thought and rebellion in the face of injudicious totalitarian government control, "Usher II" concludes in surmising the danger of ignorance and anti-intellectualism, as Stendahl informs Garrett,

[Y]ou burned Mr. Poe's books without really reading them. You took other people's advice that they needed burning. Otherwise you'd have realized what I was going to do to you when we came down here a moment ago. Ignorance is fatal, Mr. Garrett [Bradbury, *Martian*, 117].

While the BBC/NBC, television miniseries thought to remove this episode from the narrative, the sentiment of opposition to injudicious totalitarian government control remains. The book's final episode, "The Million-Year Picnic," portrayed in the TV series by Rock Hudson's Colonel John Wilder and his family, delivers this message most succinctly. At a camp fire Colonel Wilder, burning government papers, tax forms, and other items tells his children he is, "burning what's behind us, burning a way of life. The same way of life burned on Earth." As *The Martian Chronicles* concludes, the message is that one must flee the oppressive and ineffective way of life, one that brings only destruction, and find a new civilization in which, "a new way of life" can be found and the new people can once again, "learn to live." Montag's escape to the commune of the "book people" in *Fahrenheit 451* reads similarly. Montag discovers that, to live effectually, one must abandon society as it now stands in a state of inexorable demise, and develop a new native culture in which to learn to live.

In his famous polemic against adaptation, François Truffaut himself considers the nature of literary adaptation into film through an extensive analysis of the work of two of French cinema's most prolific writers, Aurench and Bost. He wrote:

> They will tell me, "Let us admit that Aurench and Bost are unfaithful, but do you also deny the existence of their talent...?" Talent, to be sure, is not a function of fidelity, but I consider an adaptation of value only when written by a man of the cinema. Aurench and Bost are essentially literary men and I reproach them here for being contemptuous of the cinema by underestimating it [229].

For Truffaut, he saw that this type of cinema which he classified the "tradition of quality," directly works in opposition to notions of art in the cinema, he wrote, "I do not believe in the peaceful coexistence of the 'Tradition of Quality' and an 'auteur's cinema'" (229).

However, for some critics, adaptation is far from detrimental to artistic credibility or to auteurship. Supporting his strong statement against adaptation, Truffaut, himself a "man of the cinema," went on to adapt Ray Bradbury's 1953 *Fahrenheit 451* (Bradbury, 1953) in Britain in 1966. Francois Truffaut's adaptation of Ray Bradbury's *Fahrenheit 451* (1966) is a film which, along with Roman Polanski's *Repulsion* (1965) and *Cul-de-sac* (1966), Michelangelo Antonioni's *Blow-Up* (1966), Jean-Luc Godard's *Sympathy for the Devil* (1968) and, to an extent, Jerzy Skolimowski's *Deep End* (1970), marks a point in British cinema history which saw a previously unprecedented "invasion" by European cinematic masters. These films marked a period of a new art-cinema for Britain, coinciding with the 1966 publication of the famed *Time* magazine cover story attributed with coining the term "Swinging London." During this period, in an air of artistic and creative climax in British cinema, a number of European "masters" came to London to make films, as did Truffaut with *Fahrenheit 451.*

One of the more powerful, consequential and indeed predominant themes throughout Ray Bradbury's narrative is the idea that Television is used by the state as a means of thought control and as a tranquilizer. As the novel's Faber so acutely observed of society,

> Who has ever torn himself from the claw that encloses you when you drop a seed in a TV parlor? It grows you any shape it wishes! It is an environment as real as the world. It becomes and is the truth [*Fahrenheit* 92].

While it is an important aspect of Bradbury's narrative, Truffaut's film builds its impact upon the suggestion that television has an enormous negative influence upon society. It was indeed a bold move for a film to propose that a visual, mass media information delivery system should be subordinate to the more intellectual text; the book, the word. In fact, Ray Bradbury himself commented: "a man falling in love with books. That's a fantastic theme for a film! How dare they be so intellectual!" (qtd. in Atkins 99).

As an extension of what is seen in *The Martian Chronicles'* "Usher II" episode, Bradbury's novel is an anti-popular culture piece of satire attacking, in parable fashion, a futuristic society which is so anti-intellectual as to ban the reading of books; as Montag thoughtlessly regurgitates the political dictum, "Books disturb people, they make them anti-social" (Truffaut sc. 2). In a mocking nod towards both the prohibition of the written word and the over-proliferation of television in modern society, after credits that are spoken and not printed, the film opens with a montage of television aerials atop houses. In his 1964 book *Understanding Media*, Marshall McLuhan suggested that "as a cool medium TV has, some feel, introduced a kind of rigor mortis into the body politic" (330). As Penelope Houston acutely observed, "In the future posited by *Fahrenheit 451* (Rank) television is the master" (42). Building upon McLuhan's concept, Montag's brainwashed statement is just as easily applied to the effect of television, initiating this sense of the damaging influence of television which is an integral motif to Bradbury's narrative. Furthermore, Mrs. Montag's friends Mrs. Bowles and Mrs. Phelps discuss, in cold, utilitarian fashion, the impact of having children, two of which the former has had by Caesarian section, "no use going through all that agony for a baby" (104). This element of Bradbury's narrative is crucial in highlighting the anti-social mindset which this community holds. Mrs. Bowles talks of pacifying her children by use of the television, "you heave them into the "parlor" and turn the switch. It's like washing clothes" (104). This enormously impersonal approach to parenting, the classification of parental duty as tantamount to menial household chores akin to the emotional investment required in turning on the washing machine is symptomatic of a society in which mass media 'entertainment' no longer entertains but simply narcotizes.

Another of Bradbury's seething attacks upon television, beautifully treated by Truffaut's film, comes in the form of the TV coverage of Montag's staged death. As in the novel, television plays a large and important role in Truffaut's film, where the authorities, having lost the genuine Montag, stage his capture using a doppelgänger of sorts, filming his faux demise as a thrilling capture. Onscreen 'Montag' leaps over railings, evades the helicopter, dodges bullets and hurtles down steps and through the streets in an exciting and suspense-filled performance. He is of course outsmarted by the authorities who capture and eliminate him at the door of the fire station, that vivid red icon of the enormity of the stranglehold of power over the people. This sensationalized sequence functions as gladiatorial entertainment for the digital age. Granger, known in the film only as *The Journal of Henri Brulard*, indicates that "anybody will do to provide them with their climax" (Truffaut sc. 16), and so it is that innocent people are bodily sacrificed for the good of television and mass entertainment. What is most chillingly indicative of the importance afforded sufficiently exciting television for this society is the announcement made by the television voice-over declaring that "a crime against society has been avenged" (Truffaut sc. 16). It is evidently more important that the masses are adequately satiated by their media sources than that allegedly "dangerous" criminals be punished and brought to justice.

In Bradbury's written-word-free world, besides the comic-strip newspapers, television is the only form of media seen to present the populous with information. Thus by association these comic-strips too act similarly as a biting commentary upon the devastating impact that TV had. McLuhan suggests that TV hit the comic book world extremely hard, he posited that comics,

> being low in definition, are a highly participational form of expression, perfectly adapted to the mosaic form of the newspaper. They provide, also, a sense of continuity from one day to the next. The individual news item is very low in information, and requires completion or fill-in by the reader, as exactly does the TV image, or the wirephoto [McLuhan 177].

McLuhan championed this idea that the TV, in its moving-image mastery, so akin to that world of the comic book, in its aesthetic similitude, yet its more encompassing form, damaged the comic book industry. McLuhan suggested:

> From the three million dots per second on the TV, the viewer is able to accept, in an iconic grasp, only a few dozen, seventy or so, from which to shape an image. The image thus made is as crude as that of the comics [McLuhan 176].

Thus one reads Truffaut's inclusion of the comic-strip as the only form of print media within his *Fahrenheit 451* as an analogue for television, and its grossly damaging influence.

For *The Martian Chronicles*, identity anxiety is a powerful theme running throughout Bradbury's biting post-colonial narrative, as Jan Leeming observed, in commentary on the TV miniseries, that she had "never seen the case for colonialism better put" (7). Colonization and the questioning of one's own identity is the predominant thread pursued throughout the text, with Martians donning the guise of humans and the book culminating in the evolution of humans into Martians. In addition, Truffaut's adaptation reads also as a quest for identity as it is Montag's quest for self-discovery that punctuates this narrative. Within *Fahrenheit 451* it is the influence, once again, of television and the parasitic media that have caused these identity anxieties by normalizing society and by stripping the populous of individualism and therefore removing Montag's sense of identity; a wrong he strives to right through subversive intellectualism: "Intellectualism, of course, became the swear word it deserved to be" (65). Most interestingly, it is not until his perceived identity is entirely destroyed and consumed by his "becoming" *The Works of Edgar Allen Poe*, that his journey can find peace and closure. This *Monthly Film Bulletin* critic too noted that "Truffaut's Fireman is on a hunt for a real self, a hunt of which he only gradually becomes aware through his encounters with other people making similar, if sometimes less successful, journeys" (P.J.S. 3).

For Bradbury's *The Martian Chronicles* the theme of remaking oneself in a new world is key to the impact of the parable. Equally, in the film adaptation of Bradbury's *Fahrenheit 451*, remaking oneself becomes paramount in Montag's quest. The concept of both novels centers on one's desire to evolve beyond ineffectual systems and make cultural contact with new and more advanced worlds. For *The Martian Chronicles* this impetus comes from the desire to explore new frontiers and an inherent longing for colonizing the Martian West. In *Fahrenheit 451* however, this desire comes from provocation by a more learned individual. Here, Clarisse acts as the free thinking rebel, in league with the owner of a secret library, about which Beatty astonishingly says, "Only once before have I seen so many books in one place" (Truffaut sc. 10). It is Clarisse who introduces the idea of intellectual thought and indeed the radical idealism that fuels Montag's enlightening journey. Through the simple act of questioning in order to provoke thought, Clarisse asks why, and implants ideas in Montag's head by asking whether Montag reads the books he burns, questions his inherent belief in what he does, and poses the question, "Are you happy?" (Truffaut sc. 2) By questioning the foundations of his beliefs, she provokes within Montag the system of self-discovery and intellectual expansion that ignites his subsequent insurgent acts against propriety. Interestingly, Clarisse's home was the only house on the street that did not have a TV aerial and therefore the only home impervious to the penetrating influence of the mass media, thus Clarisse, whose attention is turned only towards literature and intellectual expansion, is a dangerous subversive. The semantic association is made here, between those individuals who refuse to conform by not giving themselves over to television and with independent thinking revolutionaries.

Interestingly, Penelope Houston noted that "Truffaut's film views the future not as some alien machine world, but as the present subjected to a slight case of dislocation" (Houston 42). In this sense, Truffaut's warning that there is very little distinction between the hardiest recusant and the most placid conformist can be read as a parable, strengthening the idea that the contemporary world of mass media, and television in particular, is in danger of turning the intellectual free thinker into nothing more than a media drugged conservative who longs only for more saturation and yet another TV wall-screen. Linda's captivation by these wall-screens is astounding. At the news of Montag's upcoming promotion and the prospect of a bigger house and a better standard of living, Linda replies, "I'd rather have a second wall-set put in. They say when you have your second wall-screen it's like having your family grow out all around you" (Truffaut sc. 3) This attitude of familial devotion to television, to the "family," and to one's "cousins," extends throughout the film, demonstrating television and its damaging effect to be Truffaut's perception of Bradbury's pervading motif. Even when Montag breaks through his own inhibitions, under the influence of Clarisse, to bring himself to read a book, "ironically, he reads by the light from the blank TV screen" (Houston 42).

Earth's destruction through civil war and nuclear holocaust is the prevalent thematic connection between both *The Martian Chronicles* and *Fahrenheit 451*. As Spender acutely observes, "We Earth Men have a talent for ruining big, beautiful things" (Bradbury, *Martian*, 54). Throughout *The Martian Chronicles*, the looming destruction of Earth is present until Sam Parkhill and his wife eventually witness its obliteration through their telescope. While it is not directly explicit within "Usher II," *Fahrenheit 451*'s closest thematic relation, its presence is readily detectable. Stendahl complains to Garret, the Moral Climate Investigator, of the strict censorship on Earth that they, "told your film producers that if they made anything at all they would have to make and remake Earnest Hemingway. My God, how many times I have seen *For Whom the Bell Tolls* done!" (Bradbury, *Martian*, 108). This of course is Hemingway's great study of the Spanish Civil War.

While the TV miniseries showed, explicitly, Earth's destruction, drawing from stock footage of genuine nuclear detonations, Truffaut's adaptation took another approach. Truffaut's ending moves away from the book in a number of subtle ways, including the appearance of a young boy whose sobriquet for the book people's commune is "Ray Bradbury's *The Martian Chronicles*." The ending however, controverts the book's message in two more distinctly significant ways. The first of these relies on the film's abstaining from the mention of 'war.' Bradbury's novel is set in a world which has "started and won two atomic wars since 1960" (81) and one in which war is once more declared and the city is devastated. The impact of this decision to forego the theme of war is of consequence, firstly, because Truffaut's film is set in a future that is only marginally dislocated from the present. By eliminating this alien principle of a world torn apart by war, Truffaut's interpretation of Bradbury's parable hits harder and indeed rings truer. The absence of war manifests itself most significantly within the film in that the city is not destroyed as it is within the novel. This altered ending performs an extremely gracious act in that it presents the audience with an element of hope. Despite assertions by some that "Truffaut's films are about loneliness, and *Fahrenheit* is, thematically the bleakest yet" (P.J.S. 3), this film pivots upon a conflict of binary oppositions, primarily between those of cultural desolation and hope of salvation. Just as the commune of book people function within the novel, these literary men and women make up the last hope for a culturally and intellectually informed future; a new native culture. That the city is not eliminated is a tool through which Truffaut provides encouraging hope of salvation for the rest of the community.

Moreover, contrary to the novel's impetus, for the film's ending Clarisse reappears, having escaped persecution by the authorities. We see Clarisse evading capture by hiding in her uncle's attic and reappearing as *The Memoirs of Saint-Simon*, once Montag too has found the book people. Observing this element of the adaptation process, David Robinson similarly observed:

> The ending in Truffaut's adaptation will be more cheerful, if not actually more optimistic than Bradbury's. Bradbury has Clarisse vanish for good within the first fifty pages of the book, and ends with Montag witnessing the atomic annihilation of the city from across the river. Truffaut, it appears, will spare both Clarisse and the city [Robinson 60].

Robinson contends here that "Truffaut's adaptation will be more cheerful, if not actually more optimistic" (Robinson 60). However, quite conversely, Truffaut himself pointed out that due to the fact that the film "takes place in the world as we know it," therefore it is to be seen as "a fable set in the digital age" (qtd. in Robinson 60). This choice then does not manifest itself less optimistically but indeed more so. The diversion here comes across not as more cheerful but simply as suggestively redemptive. In a 1974 interview about his film career Ray Bradbury lauded Truffaut's film, pronouncing, "It's haunting, it's touching, it's beautiful, and it does a remarkable thing" (qtd. in Atkins 99). The remarkable element of Truffaut's film for Bradbury is this updated ending; Bradbury sees what Truffaut has done as an injection of hope into the narrative. For Bradbury, "the great thing about *Fahrenheit 451* as a film is that it allows you choices; it allows you imagination. That ending is commensurate with the ending of *Citizen Kane*" (qtd. in Atkins 99).

While Bradbury's novel provides no deliverance from the evils of modern media the moral lesson to be taken from Truffaut's film is that salvation is to be found by those who heed warning. For Bradbury's city, there will be no redemption, but simply, execution. This cinematic vision, whose cinematography and score "are constant splendours" (P.J.S 3), of a future without destruction, where treasured acquaintances do not vanish but reappear, tells a much more optimistic story, but what is a parable without offer of redemption? Truffaut not only highlights society's road to destruction but in fact sheds light on a better path and offers direction.

As he had planned the production of *The Martian Chronicles* as early as the mid–1960s, Ray Bradbury compared its impending reception with that of Truffaut's film, hoping that "it's going to be quite something, possibly even as good as *Fahrenheit*" (qtd. in Strick 182). While *Fahrenheit 451* was largely celebrated, gaining a reputation much the superior of *The Martian Chronicles*, it was, however, ill-received by a small number of critics. Writing for *The Guardian*, Ian Wright — in an article suggestively titled "Too Hot for Truffaut?" — questions the choice of Truffaut as director, suggesting that "it is because it bears Truffaut's mark that it is disastrous as an entity" (8). Wright proposed that in the treatment of Bradbury's narrative, this "most delicate and sympathetic director" (8) possessed ill-suited sensibilities and as such "both Godard and Hitchcock would have been more at home" (8). Wright was largely displeased with Truffaut's ending, which for him was indeed *too* hopeful, because it too largely contravened Bradbury's, "in a characteristically kindly way" (8).

Far from "his bleakest film yet," *Fahrenheit 451* was received as one of Truffaut's best, as is attested by Phillip French commenting on "the commercial success of this remarkable film" (25). Clearly this unassailable and unequivocal master of cinema has "drawn on everything he knows about cinema to express unshakable loyalty to the written word" (Houston 42). As the *Monthly Film Bulletin* celebrated of the film at the time, "There may be other ways of putting Bradbury on film, but there can be none better than this' (P.J.S. 3).

Ray Bradbury's *The Martian Chronicles* explores the dangers of cultural desolation through an exploration of how new civilizations are established, and through necessity, how native cultures are deposed, offering some possible path for redemption. Bradbury's later novel, *Fahrenheit 451* extends these themes by examining them through the analytical framework of new media. While *The Martian Chronicles* miniseries' interplanetary focus considered less the state of the fallacious regime on Earth, François Truffaut's *Fahrenheit 451* took just that as its principle concern through which the idea of cultural edification was examined.

Works Cited

Atkins, Thomas. "The Illustrated Man." *Sight & Sound* 43. 2 (1974): 96–100. Print.
Banks-Smith, Nancy. "Carrot Flavour." *The Guardian* 11 Aug. 1980: 9. Print.
Bradbury, Ray. *Fahrenheit 451.* 1953. London: Flamingo, 1993. Print.
_____. *The Silver Locusts.* 1951. London: Corgi Books, 1972. Print.
Clive, James. "Donging the Gong." *The Observer* 17 Aug. 1980: 40. Print.
Durgnat, Raymond. "One Plus One." *The Films of Jean-Luc Godard.* Ed. Ian Cameron. London: Studio Vista Limited, 1969. 178–183. Print.
Fahrenheit 451. Dir. François Truffaut. Perf. Oskar Werner, Julie Christie, Cyril Cusack. J. Arthur Rank Film, 1966. DVD.
French, Phillip. "Book People Up in Flames." *The Guardian* 20 Nov. 1966: 25. Print.
Hewison, David. "Gold far surpassing Bradbury's sci-fi glitter." *The Times* 12 Mar. 1983: 5. Print.
Houston, Penelope. "Fahrenheit 451." *Sight & Sound* 36.1 (1966/1967): 42–43. Print.
Leeming, Jan. "Personal Choice." *The Times* 9 Aug.1980: 7. Print.
The Martian Chronicles. Dir. Michael Anderson. Perf. Rock Hudson. Stonehenge Productions, 1980. DVD.
McLuhan, Marshall. *Understanding Media.* London: Routledge, 1964. Print.
P.J.S. "Fahrenheit 451, Great Britain, 1966." *Monthly Film Bulletin* 34, 396/407, (1967): 3. Print.
Robinson, David. "Two for the Sci-Fi." *Sight & Sound* 35.2 (1966): 57–61. Print.
Strick, Phillip. "In the Picture." *Sight & Sound* 38.4 (1969): 181–183. Print.
Truffaut, François. "A Certain Tendency in the French Cinema." *Movies and Methods: An Anthology.* Ed. Bill Nichols. Berkeley: University of California Press, 1976. 224–237. Print.
Wetherby, W.J. "Mr. Sci-fi Hits Out, but What the Heck." *The Guardian* 20 Aug. 1980: 10. Print.
Wright, Ian. "Too Hot for Truffaut?" *The Guardian* 17 Nov. 1966: 8. Print.

Teaching Martians in Tucson
GLORIA MCMILLAN

Ray Bradbury's fiction resembles a giant Martian sand storm of themes and metaphors. He worked in an unusual way, spewing out word associations one day, using a bit of intellect the next day to clean them up, making further refinements each day until he had a finished story. At least that is the way Bradbury summarized his writing process to a variety of audiences over the years. So Bradbury's methods can open mental doors to engage college writing students, but there is a further dimension to Bradbury as a local writer that is not often explored. Yes, *local* writer. For although it is well-known that Ray Bradbury was born and grew up in Waukegan, Illinois, he spent a formative year over two stays in Tucson, Arizona: one visit of several months in 1927 and a second visit lasting of eleven months in 1933–34 when he was 12 to 13 years old. This is the age when the child turns into an adult in fits and starts, when many lifelong issues are being decided, as anyone who knows a pre-teen can attest. So how did Tucson imprint this boy named Bradbury and how can community college students in today's Tucson relate?

In the second semester of our first-year college composition class at Pima Community College in Tucson, Arizona, we close read *The Martian Chronicles* and compare it to the TV miniseries adaptation of the same episode, "And the Moon Be Still as Bright." This chapter of the novel encapsulates Bradbury's ambivalence about the project of space exploration and colonization. A focal point for the ambivalence in the text is where one character named Spender "goes Martian" and justifies his reasons for the killing of his fellow astronauts as his only method for preserving the worthy values of Martian culture that their colonization is rapidly destroying. Bradbury's parallels with the European invasion of the western United States and contacts with the Native American populations are obvious and intended. But there are many other starting points for students to connect the far-off with the here and now. We know

229

many cross-cultural disputes on our planet, but familiarity leads us to tune out the arguments of opposing sides simply because we hear them so often. We quickly become stuck in entrenched racial and class-based attitudes. But the science fiction genre has unique cognitive tools to offer. Students may feel safer in starting to explore other positions than their customary views with a story set on another planet. They can safely rehearse thinking outside of their accustomed boxes regarding cultural difference with Ray Bradbury, a writer who is a border-crosser, both local and extra-terrestrial in scope.

Studying a local writer stimulates creative energy in both the instructor and students in ways that are not possible with other writers. Yet, surprisingly, there is little in the professional literature about teaching the local writer, so we can begin with a brief tour of essays dealing with the motivating power that local writers display in the classroom. Then I will explore student responses to the challenges offered by a local writer such as Ray Bradbury. In particular, I will analyze student essays that tackle one of Bradbury's beloved metaphors: new frontier contact zones.

Lessons from Voices: Living and Dead

The idea of teaching a well-known local writer seems to fall into the cracks in our professional literature on the teaching of American writers. Without going into the possible reasons for this gap, I found little to guide me in teaching Bradbury in Tucson in the professional literature. Some similar topics might be the studies of the literature of place, literary landscapes, and literature allied with ecological concerns. Certainly, Bradbury was concerned about the places where he made his homes at various periods: Waukegan, Tucson, and Venice Beach, and greater Los Angeles, California. But to shift focus to place begs the question of teaching a local writer who has become well-known. Teaching a local writer who is famous is distinct from teaching any writer who is local simply *because* local. Teaching someone who, as Bradbury did, rose from Depression-era poverty to a prominent place in the literary field can be a kind of role modeling. On the other hand, this literary model can lead to the impossible dream of matching the success of a peak few nationally famous writers, so careful prep for class and a discussion of various meanings of "success" might well factor in teaching the local-writer-turned-famous. We need the likes of Shakespeare and Mozart, of course, because "they can speak to what is real and deep and lasting throughout the ages," the aesthetic critic Roger Scruton affirms in his televised debate with the literary theorist Terry Eagleton. But in addition, we need culture that is not just "high culture," because a rootless cosmopolitan culture doesn't appear "to speak to people where they are," according to Eagleton ("Terry"). Bradbury absorbed the traditional canon of literature that he encountered in the library, argued with its values, and created new metaphors from clichés. Indeed, he has often challenged the idea of one universal cultural "self" by setting up a myriad of contacts between high and low, western colonial culture and native culture.

In a circuitous way, John Blair Gambler's 2007 *PMLA* essay "Outcasts and Dreamers in the Cities: Urbanity and Pollution in *Dead Voices*" is a good place to begin our search for sign posts in teaching a famous local writer such as Ray Bradbury. Gambler covers many issues of the displacement of Native American culture and the indigenous voice that are handled metaphorically in *The Martian Chronicles*. Gambler reminds readers that the Native American novelist Gerald Vizenor uses defamiliarization as a tool of social critique in *Dead Voices*. And Gambler further defines defamiliarization as

> the condition of being psychologically lost that enables a person to experience something anew, without the preconceptions and preformed thought patterns that stifle cognition. [The novel *Dead Voices'* character] Bagese teaches that people must be ready and willing to shift their expectations as well as their personae to experience life fully [182].

Using science fiction tropes and metaphors, Bradbury is also trying to defamiliarize us from a process of global western expansion under the banner of progress. Instead, he asks his reader to take a slower pace and to reflect upon the costs and benefits of this global march to technological and commercial conquests. Beneath these fast-moving modern and post-modern trappings, ancient voices are never far from the minds of people in a place like Tucson, Arizona, where it is not uncommon to dig up thousand-year-old human remains and artifacts when digging a new stretch of buried power line. These silent voices remind some of us powerfully that we may put our stamp on the land but that others have done this before us and have gone partially or totally into oblivion. And the whispering voices ask who is in any position to judge those who lived in this place for far longer than the contemporary population has? Can we say that we and our culture will have a lasting power far surpassing those others?

Bradbury had to experience repeated departures and homecomings in his youth. His trek back and a forth the country as a child and teen between Waukegan and Tucson made him aware of the need to be inner-directed and not too bound to people and places. He returned to these themes of adapting to the new and homesickness for the old often in his stories, including parts of *The Martian Chronicles*. But how can these experiences of a local writer become moments to connect with students? When a writer is under the skin of a town as much as Ray Bradbury has burrowed deeply under Tucson's skin, there must be a way to use this inner knowledge to help students to spark their own imaginations. The challenge is to find that path to connect place and creativity as Bradbury did. Perhaps we can find such a meeting place in myths.

Biographer Jon Eller has described Bradbury's search for new myths to live by that he hoped would replace the traditional values that were quickly fading from society. In his *PMLA* essay, Gambler contrasts the cultures that enjoy a living mythos (storytelling cultures) with those who do not have such a mythos (mere "wordies") whose stories ring hollowly (180). Rather than the shadows of dead ancestors, the living "wordies" and their lack of connection with the land and the animals around them are the "dead voices" in Gerard Vizenor's novel of that name. The two contrasting cultures fit Bradbury's search for a system of belief that could create and sustain his metaphors, as if he knew that he were in danger, like most of the mainstream American culture, of becoming a mere "wordie." So Bradbury forged his own mythos that ran in many ways counter to the triumphal western "cowboy and Indian" myths that Anglo-Americans had been serving themselves since the nineteenth century.

The new mythos envisions a cosmic expansion because the direction of contact zones has gone aloft, according to Bradbury. Although the last frontier of the American West was long closed, Bradbury noted that the new frontier was "up" (Eller 206). Via *The Martian Chronicles*, students can explore with Bradbury the costs and benefits of moving out to colonize the latest new place. Like the Trickster figures in Native American lore, the Martians play many games with the initially unsuspecting colonists from the planet Earth. A two-point perspective with even further sub-groupings replaces the traditional Our Way Is Best approach to the enterprise of space exploration. Because of the varied subjective points-of-view in chapters of *The Martian Chronicles*, students find the Martians and the Earth astronauts to be at times, heroes, villains, anti-heroes, and anti-villains. Bradbury even shimmers between showing us a totally dead Mars and one that has pockets of Martians still living in their own culture. He revels in that ambiguity, which is the path of the Trickster.

Lessons from Lincoln — Illinois

Few writers of science fiction are as quintessentially American (yet critical of the country and its values) as Ray Bradbury. In his own cultural sphere,

Bradbury is iconic, like his fellow Illinois native Abraham Lincoln. However, it may be good to remind ourselves as teachers that students in today's college writing classes come from widely divergent global cultures and some of these international students may have to work a bit harder to digest the strong Midwestern accents and tropes that even surface upon Bradbury's fabled Mars. Considering the Illinois side of Bradbury caused me to turn to a web site about teaching the local place and writers. This website celebrated Route 66 and the little town of Lincoln, Illinois.

While this web site is not a scholarly essay, the creator of the site has documented many observations of Lincoln residents, both past and present. People are encouraged to write blog-style posts about what has made Lincoln, Illinois, memorable for them. Here is an example about the Logan County fair that sounds like a nugget of inspiration such as Bradbury would use:

> —When I was about 10 to 12, I could not get enough of those mechanical cranes. The trick was to crank them as fast as possible to get the cranes swinging wildly, banging the glass case, and then suddenly crash landing the bucket on the prize — a small piece of junk such as a cigarette lighter —, which I then traded for a few more dimes to play the machine again and again. More than once I went home to look under the sofa cushions for more change so I could return to the fair for more excitement [Henson "Lincoln"].

The trailing Route 66 descriptions meander past memorable grain elevators, the Caterpillar truck factory, The Tropics (a now-defunct South Seas cocktail lounge), and many other sights. Do these details add up to significance? This kind of a collection could be the day's inspiration for Bradbury.

We pull up on the side of the cyber-highway Route 66 at the mention of one Lincoln, Illinois, writer, Langston Hughes. Site creator Henson has collected a letter that Hughes wrote thanking his English teacher at Lincoln's Central Elementary School, Ethel F. Welch, congratulating her on getting him started in writing and congratulating the town of Lincoln's 100th anniversary.

Henson concludes his blog with a Hughes poem called "Dreams" that is on a bronze plaque in Lincoln, in which the poet exhorts his readers to hold onto their dreams. Ray Bradbury found that a constant struggle because of the prevailing economic conditions. Yet as is so often the case with a writer, what was a constraint turned into an inspiration. Often students who attend community colleges in particular are struggling with issues of being the first in their families to attend college with barely enough funds to do so. The Langston Hughes poem tells them to persevere because dreams that cannot fly turn into "a broken-winged bird" (1. 3). For many students then as now conditions of life are wintry with little to hope for in limited personal financial resources and small town settings. Both Bradbury and Hughes speak directly to such students growing up in hard times. As Hughes puts it, their young lives will be like "a barren field frozen with snow" if they give up their efforts to achieve a dream (11. 7–8). Ray Bradbury knew what Hughes meant and his talks to students over the years echo this poem's sentiments.

Lives in the Midwest often grew sour and embittered during the Depression when Ray Bradbury was growing up in Waukegan and when Langston Hughes was already a man in Cleveland. Hughes knew whereof he wrote. Little private tragedies that happened in the Bradbury family also found their echoes in Bradbury's stories and students can relate to these feelings across generations. For example, students today engage with the humor and pathos of the Bradbury family's Depression era trek from Waukegan to Tucson in their old Buick and the night they had to stay in a motel with a chicken coop in the crawl space under the rooms. Ray's father Leo Bradbury was in desperate need of work. The Bradburys were migrants crossing some borders and trying to hold onto tattered dreams. In his biography *The Bradbury Chronicles*, Sam Weller relates the attempt that Leo Bradbury made to market his invention, "the chili-brick," in Tucson. When he failed after some ten months, the family got in the old Buick and drove back to Waukegan. Bradbury called the farewell to his one true Tucson friend John Huff "gut wrenching" (66). These are conditions that many students face in hard economic times and they create moments for engaging students as writers. The alchemy of creation was never far from Bradbury's conscious mind, taking the worst that life could throw and turning that dross into metaphor. The short documentary film "Story of a Writer," directed by Terry Sanders, shows Bradbury at work on the story "Dial Double Zero," during which time, viewers get a rare glimpse of how this prolific writer used his everyday experiences in his fiction.

Along with the biographical details in Sam Weller's biography, I use the *YouTube* video lecture presented by Bradbury at Nazarene University in Point Loma, California. For those who have never heard and seen this excellent lecture, Bradbury was a highly charismatic speaker who polished and embellished his favorite anecdotes over the years — much to the confusion of his biographers. What comes across to students watching this video lecture is a man with very little he needs to prove, who is not full of his own importance, and who wants to reach across to them. Some events of Bradbury's life given in that talk move students in my classes surprisingly deeply. He never could afford college and he sold newspapers in street corners in Hollywood in the late 1930s, studying for years at the public library to educate himself. When asked what he planned to do after selling his newspapers, Bradbury would answer, "I am studying to be a writer."

Hecklers on the street corner would reply, "You sure don't *look* like a writer."

Bradbury would answer, "But I feel like one."

Essays from the Martian Contact Zone

After hearing Bradbury, my students feel like writers, too. They realize how much more Bradbury does with the issue of first contact between Earth's inhabitants and beings from another planet. One student explained how *The Martian Chronicles* differs from hack writing about space travel because the stories reverse the usual clichés about the good earthlings and the bad aliens. But students recognized more complexity than just that simple statement. They also gave a nod to Bradbury's uncanny ability to cause us to look through another's eyes, especially the eyes of the truly different.

Students often welcome the chance to rehearse new and different positions about large issues in history and current affairs when these can be examined obliquely via the lens of another place and time. One student observed that the story has aged well, noting that

> I feel the issues in the story are still the same. Society does not think about what we do before we do it. In our time we are trying to find ways to preserve the earth but we cannot take back what we have already done.

The same student showed an awareness that character development is an important part of making the shift to thinking outside the box. A major strength in Bradbury's fiction is his characterization. This student details a response to each major character, explaining,

> I sympathize with Cherokee, who talks about how "if there's Martians around, I'm all for him" (Bradbury 59), relating his story to his ancestors and how they lost their land. I also sympathize with Jeff Spender because he immersed himself in the Martian culture and saw what we had and could do to them. He even began to say "I've walked in their cities and I know these people and I'd be glad to call them my ancestors" (64) he also says "I'm the last Martian" (58). Instead of ignoring what he saw he took a stand and died for it. I feel Commander Wilder is sympathetic to Spender and you as a reader feel sympathy for him. Commander Wilder sees how Spender thinks and how the human race could ruin Mars, but he also has the knowledge that he came to Mars and has obligations to his job. I feel Bradbury's story was effective. It grabbed my attention and brought up the issues about the earth I would never have thought of. Do we think of the future, what are we doing to the earth, and do we value what we already have? Ray Bradbury's story was intriguing to think about and to read.

Students tend to notice that there are not the usual binary oppositions of good characters and bad characters in *The Martian Chronicles* that they may have experienced elsewhere in the science fiction genre. The characters grow, change, and embody points-of-view about large issues. The critic Christopher Isherwood summarized the theme of *The Martian Chronicles* as being that "there are no traditional homelands and values to save us anymore" (Eller 222).

Bradbury's characters Colonel Wilder and Major Spender circle around the issues of what we do and what we become when we colonize. The characters grow deeper as they change according to the demands that this contact of cultures make upon them. One student related to the complex characters and issues by deciding that the old Martian culture as Bradbury envisions it is a happy, but impossible world, arguing that

> it would be nice if there was a place where you could go and start over. Where there was no crime, no littering, no corruption just a place to live and enjoy all the things that was provided for you. Yes I sympathize with Spender; after he watched the men get drunk and Briggs take the empty bottles and drop them into the Martian canal (52). How it bothered him to watch them destroy this place like the one they came from. I also liked Captain Wilder; he came across as a caring man who respected the land. I think the values Ray Bradbury was trying to promote are the same values that we try to promote today, respect, honor, etc. It shows that Spender and Wilder have those values for this planet they have landed on. But the other men don't seem to show that same respect. The one thing I'm not sure about: was Spender acting alone or was he possessed by a Martian spirit?

However, when a text is translated to the film medium, some nuances may fail to be passed along and that is a problem for students who both read the print chapter "And the Moon Be Still as Bright" from *The Martian Chronicles* and view the TV miniseries episode. Several students have analyzed the directorial decisions in changes between the print chapter and the TV miniseries episode. We had discussed the ways that films can only approximate interior monologues, for instance.

Students often come to the TV miniseries with a preconceived idea that the print text must be stronger in all ways than the film. But I try to counsel them to "read with" the film first as an artifact in its own right where choices have been made with both costs and benefits. They change in their attitudes toward the film adaptation of *The Martian Chronicles* after they view the complete TV miniseries, in some cases. I give some background in the ways that screen writer Richard Matheson pulled together a very disparate group of stories into a more coherent form.

Students differed on whether having Bernie Casey, an African American actor in the televised episode, say many lines that were said by a character named Cherokee in the print version of "And the Moon Be Still as Bright" was a good or bad directorial choice. One revision made by screen writer Richard Matheson was to unify the often tenuous thread between the diverse Mars stories. And a prominent change was to build the character of Spender as an African American who was being passed over for the first Mars flights (perhaps) because of race. The "Martian equals Indian" theme that worked in print may have been too obvious on screen; at least, that seems to be what Matheson decided. But students frequently affirm that the character Cherokee was needed and that something important is lost from the dynamic among characters when that character is cut and combined with traits of Major Spender.

The characters of both Spender and Colonel Wilder in Bradbury's *The Martian Chronicles* are complex. Spender is someone defending a threatened culture but defending it in a way that is destructive. The empathic character Colonel Wilder is the nearest representative of Earth's authority and colonial power, but he wishes Mars no harm and wants to be as benevolent as possible. Adam Lawrence's essay elsewhere in this collection discusses the complex philosophical understanding of empathy as explored in the theory of Emmanuel Lévinas. In a similar vein, one student muses upon Colonel Wilder's mixed signals of both duty and empathy in response to Spender's actions. With the point and counterpoint between the two men, this student asserts that "Bradbury creates a unique theme to make the reader feel empathy and sympathy, and simultaneously feel anger toward his character, Spender, in the story "2001: And the Moon Be Still as Bright." Student writers in Tucson are able to see that these are no cardboard heroes nor cartoon villains but something far deeper, something that touches us here in the desert, in particular.

Tucson was the role model for a place of alien contact for Bradbury and Tucson forces writing students reading and viewing *The Martian Chronicles* chapter "And the Moon Be Still as Bright" to confront their own city's archeological past. Students take up the theme of renaming landmarks on Mars, saying that Bradbury understood the process of renaming and redesigning a place never takes away its old history and it makes those who would erase that history uncomfortable. A common theme among student essays is to examine Major Spender's motives and forebodings. A number of essays cite Spender's admonitions about the new trying to erase the old. They find the arguments in the story quite compelling, as where Spender argues that the colonists cannot erase

> all the things, which had uses. All the mountains, which had names. And we'll never be able to use them without feeling uncomfortable. And somehow the mountains will never sound right to us; we'll give them new names, but the old names are there, somewhere in time, and the mountains were shaped and seen

under those names.... No matter how we touch Mars, we'll never touch it. And then we'll get mad at it, and you know what we'll do? We'll rip it up, rip the skin off, and change it to fit ourselves [Bradbury 54].

Many students observe a bittersweet point in that, although Spender cannot convince the American leaders on Earth that what they are doing is wrong, he can, at least, convince Colonel Wilder to delay the flood of colonists and their destruction of Mars, perhaps by regulating what can and cannot be built on Mars. One student argues for the value of *The Martian Chronicles* as both eye-opening and a challenge to those in the dominant culture to change their subjective stance, saying,

Major Spender empathizes with a society experienced only second-hand, to the point of assuming the position of the "Last Martian." Radical 180 degree turns in allegiance leading to violence are still occurring. The tragic Ft. Hood shooting was the result of an American-born Muslim, who allegedly suffered psychological issues after hearing other soldier's accounts of the war in Afghanistan. While nobody has completely verified this as fact, it has (locally) been branded a brutal, indefensible act. I don't disagree with the brutality, but, as we say in "2001: The Moon Be Still as Bright," our emotions can sway us to cross the line morality/mortality if we empathize strongly enough with the beings who we feel are being oppressed/insulted/obliterated.

Students take away from Bradbury's text in accordance to what they bring to this text. For many of our students, the issue of racial justice is too obvious to be overlooked in reading "And the Moon Be Still as Bright" from *The Martian Chronicles* and viewing the televised miniseries episode. According to reader response theory, just how important the student feels that racial justice is as a theme in Bradbury's story depends upon that student's background *before* reading the text and seeing the miniseries episode. One student analyzed the racial context in which Bradbury matured and wrote, describing his milieu as being some kind of pressure cooker, due to unofficial racial barriers, noting that

[in 1945] Clair Drake and Horace Cayton founded a study of the Chicago framework entitled *Black Metropolis*. Their analysis of Black progress in employment, housing, and social integration, clearly revealed the existence of a color line that effectively blocked black occupational, residential, and social mobility (Cayton 2). Although the war boosted our economy, the issues of society were coming to a boil here on the home front. Poverty levels were rising, and racial segregation was more publicized and harsh.

The student concludes that *The Martian Chronicles'* publication in 1950 served as the harbinger of a new type of issue-oriented science fiction, arguing that the use of the subgenre of sociological science fiction was a fairly new concept at the time, and the remarkable lesson portrayed by the outcome that was *The Martian Chronicles*, will outlive us all. This novel was a lesson in one of the most profound studies of human common sense. Those who cannot remember the past are condemned to repeat it (Santayana). This was the first work of American science fiction to gain a truly broad reading public; thus, this book is of considerable historical importance in modern American literature.

Conclusions from Mars

What will students take away from Ray Bradbury's stunning meditation upon life in the desert, *The Martian Chronicles*? There are so many important themes that open fruitfully in discussion that it seems fit to note just a few:

Role modeling by Bradbury. What I mean by this is that Ray Bradbury can be viewed as a local writer and one whose voice takes up issues of race and cultural boundaries that remain current in Tucson and around the Southwest. When we read Bradbury, students connect with a writer as they may never have connected before, not only because he lived among Tucson's neighborhoods and walked our streets and deserts, unlike most writers whom we study in class, but because he took our surroundings and recast them into a Martian framework.

Race Issues and Bradbury. As outlined in the student essay above, Bradbury was thinking along lines ahead of his time. He was dealing with issues of racial boundaries, crossing international borders, and loss/betrayal in ways that mainstream fiction would not take up for years. His 1947 *New Yorker* story "I See You Never," among others, could have been written this year.

Remaking oneself on the Frontier. Tucson is a fluid and mobile community and many students come here from somewhere else. They have faced the packing choices when leaving and old home for a new home. They may also have to change in some ways to adapt to a new desert environment, just as Colonel Wilder's family have to adapt in *The Martian Chronicles*.

In "August 2002: Night Meeting," Tomás Gomez talks to an old gas station attendant about their adjustment to life on Mars in ways that must have been echoes of conversations that Leonard Bradbury and his son Ray had about coming to Tucson and adapting to its demands. Tomás asks,

How do you like life on Mars, Pop?
Fine. Always something new. I made up my mind when I came here last year I wouldn't expect nothing, nor ask nothing, nor be surprised at nothing. We've got to forget earth and how things were. We've got to look at what we're in here and how different it is. I get a hell of a lot of fun out of just the weather here. It's Martian weather [Bradbury 79].

Homesickness and separation anxiety. Along with moving in space and the emotional wrenches of saying good-bye come bouts of nostalgia. Bradbury's characters in some of the Martian stories such as "April 2000: The Third Expedition" find that they have not left home behind at all in a literal way. Other stories such as "November 2005: The Off-Season" make it clear that you cannot go home again.

There are many more themes and complexities in Bradbury's Martian stories because he is not doing just one thing in his fiction. He throws a pebble into the water of resonances with readers and develops further rippling implications as his stories roll on.

If forced to choose, I hope that students will recall that wonderful they-is-us moment of epiphany when Colonel Wilder solves the mystery of what happened to the planet's vanished ancient Martians by announcing to his children their own reflections.

> The Martians were there. Timothy began to shiver.
> The Martians were there — in the canal — reflected in the water. Timothy and Michael and Robert and Mom and Dad. The Martians stared back at them for a long, long silent time from the rippling water.... [182].

This last scene recalls Bradbury's memories of Tucson. Dried washes are "canals" and who has not found something very old in the pink, sandy soil here? Most students are transplants from "back East" and if not they, then their parents were. Tucson's students have heard of or experienced the agonies of what to take and what to leave behind. They may feel but lightly grafted onto a landscape that is challenging and can be almost otherworldly in its deadly and unforgiving nature. And who has not gasped at our blazing sky? The person from "back East" *must* gasp. In the Sonoran desert, the protective canopy of trees is gone and we are painfully open and vulnerable under the broadest horizon. Our eyes at first cannot adjust to the dryness and the heat. Our throats feel always parched. We ask ourselves if it was worth it, this move into the unknown, and, according to Bradbury, more than half unknowable, desert place. But the answer that comes through in *The Martian Chronicles* for student readers as for the rest of us is that change is inevitable and that we are far more adaptive and resilient than we ever believed. We do not conquer Mars and the Martians. We become one with them — at least the best of us do — by a bond of mutual respect.

Works Cited

Bradbury, Ray. *The Martian Chronicles*. New York: Bantam, 1970. Print.
"An Evening with Ray Bradbury." 2001. *YouTube*. 3 Dec. 2012. Web.

Gambler, John Blair. "Outcasts and Dreamers in the Cities: Urbanity and Pollution in *Dead Voices*." *PMLA* 122.1 (Jan. 2007): 179–193. Web.

Henson, D. Leigh. "Mr. Lincoln, Route 66, and Other Highlights of Lincoln, Illinois." 2004. 10 Aug. 2012. Web.

"Story of a Writer." Dir. Terry Sanders. American Film Foundation, 2004. DVD.

"Terry Eagleton in Conversation with Roger Scruton." 19 Sept. 2012. *YouTube*. 8 Jan. 2013. Web.

About the Contributors

David M. **Acklam** holds BSEE and MS degrees in engineering from the University of Arizona. He is a member of the Lunar and Planetary Society Kuiper Circle advisory board and is chairman of the Kuiper Circle Community Outreach committee. He volunteers in other astronomy-related organizations such as Project ASTRO at the National Optical Astronomy Observatory (NOAO) at the University of Arizona's Flandrau Science Center.

Howard **Allen** has worked for years as a professional actor, playwright, director, screenwriter, literary manager and dramaturg as well as a reporter, reviewer and editor. He holds an MFA in playwriting and screenwriting and teaches college-level courses in writing for film and television, film acting, art of cinema and theatre history.

Aaron **Barlow** is an associate professor of English at New York City College of Technology (CUNY) and faculty editor of *Academe*, the magazine of the American Association of University Professors. He earned his PhD from the University of Iowa with a dissertation on the science fiction writer Philip K. Dick. He is the author of *Beyond the Blogosphere: Information and Its Children* (with Robert Leston, Praeger, 2012) and *One Hand Does Not Catch a Buffalo* (Travelers' Tales, 2011).

Marleen S. **Barr** teaches English at the City University of New York and is known for her pioneering work in feminist science fiction. She has won the Science Fiction Research Association Pilgrim Award for lifetime achievement in science fiction criticism. Her published works include *Feminist Fabulation: Space/Postmodern Fiction* (University of Iowa Press, 1992), and *Genre Fission: A New Discourse Practice for Cultural Studies* (University of Iowa Press, 2000).

Christopher **Cokinos** is an associate professor of English at the University of Arizona, where he is affiliated with the Institute of the Environment. He is the author of two books of literary nonfiction, *Hope Is the Thing with Feathers: A Personal Chronicle of Vanished Birds* and *The Fallen Sky: An Intimate History of Shooting Stars* (both Jeremy P. Tarcher/Penguin, 2000 and 2009, respectively). He has published science fiction and essays on the genre in *Orion, Pank, ISLE* and *The New York Review of Science Fiction*.

Paul **Cote** is a PhD candidate in the English department at the University of Maryland, College Park, where he teaches film and American literature. His dissertation explores the connection between sound and childhood associations in Hollywood films. He is a member of the International Film Music Critics Association.

Grace L. **Dillon** (Anishinaabe) is an associate professor in the Indigenous Nations Studies Program at Portland State University in Portland, Oregon, where she teaches courses on a range of topics. She is the editor of two collections and has published in such journals as *The Journal of Science Fiction Film and Television*, *Extrapolation*, *The Historical Journal of Film, Radio and Television*, and *Renaissance Papers*.

Charles L. **Dugan**, Jr., began early in astronomy. During his senior year of high school he worked at Kitt Peak National Observatory in Tucson as part of the "Professional Internship Program." He attended the University of Arizona in Tucson and returned to the Kitt Peak National Observatory in 2002 as a program specialist working as a public speaker and coordinating Project ASTRO. He publishes the quarterly *Chuck's Astronomy Newsletter*.

Jonathan R. **Eller** is a professor of English, director of the Center for Ray Bradbury Studies, and senior textual editor of the Institute for American Thought, a research component of Indiana University's School of Liberal Arts. He has edited or co-edited a half-dozen limited press editions of Ray Bradbury's fiction. His book *Becoming Ray Bradbury* (University of Illinois Press, 2011) centers on Bradbury's early life and development as a writer through the 1953 publication of *Fahrenheit 451*.

Ari **Espinoza** earned both his BA and MA degrees from the University of Arizona. He is the media and public outreach spokesperson for HiRISE, the NASA-funded high resolution camera onboard the Mars Reconnaissance Orbiter. He is also the coordinator for the HiTranslate Project, a volunteer initiative that looks for people to help translate image captions from HiRISE into as many languages as possible.

Kimberly **Fain**, JD, is an adjunct professor at Texas Southern University. She has published on the socio-political intersection of race, gender, and class in classic literature and pop culture. A licensed attorney, she has won teaching and writing fellowships from various organizations such as the Houston Teachers Institute at the University of Houston's Honors College and is the associate editor of *World Literary Review*.

Wolf **Forrest** has been a freelance artist and writer for thirty years. He graduated with a BS in biology from St. Mary's College of Maryland, and studied architecture at the University of Arizona. His illustrations and articles have appeared in such publications as *Cinefantastique*, *Midnight Marquee*, *The Morning Herald*, *The Asheville Citizen*, and *Backyard Bugwatching*.

Martin R. **Hall** is a PhD candidate at the University of Hull, England, where he teaches British cinema. His research specialities are sixties British cinema, the French Nouvelle Vague, Italian cinema and the cinema of Woody Allen. His dissertation is on the emergence of the British art-cinema of the 1960s and includes the influence of European cinemas on the British cinema of the sixties, the British Free Cinema and the British New Wave, and émigré directors Joseph Losey and Richard Lester.

Francisco **Laguna-Correa** is a PhD candidate in Hispanic cultural studies at the University of North Carolina at Chapel Hill. He holds an MA in Spanish and Hispanic

American philosophy and an MA in social anthropology, both from the Autonomous University of Madrid. He is the author of two books of fiction and his essays on Mexican culture and literature from the 19th to the 21st century have appeared in academic journals and scholarly books in Spain, the U.S. and Mexico.

Adam **Lawrence** is an assistant professor of English at Cape Breton University, where he teaches introductory writing and literature courses. His specialties include late 19th-century British fiction, modern Irish fiction, science fiction, and literary theory. Lawrence has written on gender and myth in the fiction of Carlo Gebler and Julia O'Faolain, and folkloric elements in Robert Louis Stevenson's poetry and fiction.

Christopher P. **McKay** received his PhD in astrogeophysics from the University of Colorado. His research focuses on the evolution of the solar system and the origin of life. He is also actively involved in planning for future Mars missions including human exploration. He has won NASA's Exceptional Leadership Medal and the Urey Prize of the Division of Planetary Sciences among other awards.

Gloria **McMillan** received her PhD in English from the University of Arizona and an MA in literature from Indiana University. She is a research associate at the University of Arizona and teaches at Pima Community College in Tucson. She is a co-founder of the Arizona Theatre Company's Old Pueblo Playwrights and has developed science and science fiction–oriented curricula for the University of Arizona's first-year composition classes.

Carol **Stoker** received her PhD in astrogeophysics from the University of Colorado at Boulder. She is a staff planetary scientist at NASA Ames Research Center and is a co-investigator on the Mars Phoenix mission that recently performed sampling near the north pole of Mars to search for habitable environments. She has published in *Astrobiology*, *The Journal of Field Robotics*, and *The Journal of Geophysical Research*, among other venues.

Index

Numbers in *bold italics* indicate pages with photographs.